African American Holiday Celebrations and Traditions

African American Holiday Celebrations and Traditions

Celebrating With Passion, Style, and Grace

Antoinette Broussard

CITADEL PRESS
Kensington Publishing Corp.
www.kensingtonbooks.com

CITADEL PRESS books are published by

Kensington Publishing Corp.
850 Third Avenue
New York, NY 10022

All Kensington titles, imprints, and distributed lines are available at special quantity discounts for bulk purchases for sales promotions, premiums, fund raising, educational, or institutional use. Special book excerpts or customized printings can also be created to fit specific needs. For details, write or phone the office of the Kensington special sales manager: Kensington Publishing Corp., 850 Third Avenue, New York, NY 10022, attn: Special Sales Department; phone 1-800-221-2647.

CITADEL PRESS and the Citadel logo are Reg. U.S. Pat. & TM Off.

First printing: 2000
First paperback printing: October 2004

10 9 8 7 6 5 4 3 2 1

Printed in the United States of America

ISBN 0-8065-2654-8

Cataloging data for this title can be obtained from the Library of Congress.

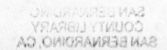

Contents

Dedication

To my mother, Maybelle Broussard, and my mother-in-law, Mallie Farmer, upon whose backs I've climbed. It has been a privilege to be a part of your lives. I will forever remember your generous spirit, unconditional love, wisdom, and guidance. I salute you!

Preface

As I approach the end of a year, I often begin an assessment of my life through the prism of what I have experienced over the past twelve months. Yet, sometimes before I really have had time to reflect, I find myself swept away by the demands of the holiday season: I'm getting my house ready for entertaining, sending out greeting cards, shopping for gifts, taking Christmas decorations out of storage, polishing up my holiday menus, and contemplating what to wear to all the seasonal festivities.

There's one thing for certain: this time of year ends up bringing me *home*—to my family and dearest friends, to my personal history and convictions, and to my deepest connections, which lie in my African, Native American, French, and English ancestry.

Ruminating on what the year-end holidays mean to me and my family inspired me to write this book. It also led me to think about how other African-American families and those influenced by our culture celebrate holidays, express their spirituality, charity, and warmth—and how they so often do it with grace, passion, and style.

This book presents not only my ideas for the holidays, but those of a cross-section of dynamic African-American women and a few men, including some participants from other regions of the world. I interviewed over fifty people about their family traditions, holiday memories, and favorite recipes, as well as the influences that touch and motivate them during the holiday seasons.

This book is my attempt to represent us all: African Americans of all colors, hues, and racial mixtures. We're up from slavery. We're survivors of discrimination. We've outlived apartheid. We're urban, suburban, and rural. We're keepers of tradition and seekers of new truths. We identify with southern foods, Texas barbecue, Caribbean cuisine, Louisiana Creole dishes, and West African cooking (to name a few).

Most of us want to be with family and friends over the holidays despite the complications this poses in our modern world. If we consider the vast distances in space and time, sometimes holidays are the only opportunity loved ones get to see each other at all during the year. The holidays are a time when, ideally, we can put our differences aside and join together to celebrate. It's a time to rejoice, celebrate Christ's birth, remember those who didn't make it through the year's journey, renew our values and principles, replenish our souls, forgive, bless one another, and express gratitude for the opportunity to enjoy the year ahead.

Dr. Gwendolyn Goldsby Grant—psychologist, wife, mother, and grandmother—summed it up beautifully when I asked when the holiday season began for her. "My contention is that the Christmas holidays start with Thanksgiving and last through Dr. Martin Luther King's birthday," she said. "Christmas holidays are like one big national family reunion. The thankfulness and blessings of the year start with Thanksgiving Day and extend through the celebration of the new year and beyond." This book celebrates precisely that season and more.

When I think about the December holidays I have these visions: a nativity scene with a black Jesus in the manger . . . an illuminated pathway leading to a front door where a eucalyptus-and-rosebud wreath hangs, tied with a red satin bow. Christmas carols sung in the melodious voices of the Boys Choir of Harlem . . . taking the family to the ballet to see *The Nutcracker* . . . the delicious gumbo my good friends the Andrew Jeanpiérres will serve Christmas Eve night. I remember all the Christmas season cotillions I've attended, including my daughter Zahrah's. I think about how my kids used to put out their favorite shoes on the eve of December 6, St. Nicholas's Day, awakening the next morning to find them filled with treats, and of the hilarious fun our family and friends had giving each other white elephant gifts at Amelia and Martin Austria's house on Christmas Eve. I hear the Temptations' rendition of "Silent Night" and Nat King Cole singing about "chestnuts roasting on an open fire" and think about making and buying Christmas ornaments that reflect my heritage. I see Kente cloth decorating my mantel, enlivening a shrine to my ancestors. I think about a Yoruba blessing of goodwill for the coming year and the West Indian Christmas dolls I bought at the flea market . . . about a Christmas table dressed with linens woven in Senegal . . . about singing Christmas carols at Ruth and Bobby Jemerson's dinner party to the accompaniment of a baby grand piano . . . about trying not to get caught up in holiday stress—then staying up most of Christmas Eve wrapping gifts and assembling toys . . . about looking for a church in Boston on my very first Christmas Eve away from home . . . about all the wonderful people I've met this year. My taste buds remember the savory flavors of Mrs. Watson's homemade gingerbread and banana nut bread. I think about making gifts of amaryllis and paperwhites, the pots painted with Caribbean colors. I'm thankful for my family and friends. I reminisce about cutting down our own Christmas tree and hauling it on the roof of my car, driving home with my mother on Highway 101 from Petaluma to San Francisco while my young sons wrestled in the backseat. I think about Mrs. Morgan's 7-Up cake and about those southern recipes for deep-fried turkey and Grandma Eugenia's greens and Aunt Simonetta's macaroni and cheese.

Did I really force my late husband to dress up in that hot Santa suit for my son's December birthday party all those years ago? He sure didn't fool anyone over six. I can taste that Creole pear and rum pudding made from a recipe in Eric V. Copage's *Kwanzaa*. I think about the Seven Days of Kwanzaa and the spiritual rejuvenation I feel when it comes to a close . . . about the Kwanzaa celebration at Sheila and Herb Fajor's house, the beautiful children lighting the kinara's candles, and the buffet table displaying an abundance of foods.

Am I not blessed to have made it through another year in good health? I'm grateful not to live an isolated, lonely existence. I think about my grandma Jeanie's prune cake and Sister Verda B's homemade bean pie . . . about the New Year's Eve party at Henry and Leilani Cotten's house where we performed lively karaoke numbers to Motown tunes and their musically gifted guests sang and played blues and jazz until the early morning hours . . . about Esther Higg's homemade eggnog, always served on New Year's Day, presented in a sterling silver punch bowl. I remember those beautiful pictures in Robert Farris Thompson's book *Face of the*

Gods of New Year's Eve altars on a Rio de Janeiro beach built by the locals and offered to the sea goddess Yemanjá asking for good fortune and her blessings for the new year. I think about the Muslim communities worldwide who are preparing to observe Ramadan and replenish their souls. It's also time to help the family clarify goals and set my own for the coming year—and before we know it the Mardi Gras celebrations begin, and then Lent, which brings spring and Easter!

Welcome to an African-American holiday adventure!

Acknowledgments

Many people were instrumental in getting this book published. First, I would like to extend a special thank-you to my mother, Maybelle Broussard, whose unwavering support assisted me in getting this project completed.

I am very grateful to my mother-in-law, Mallie Farmer, who has always gone the extra mile to help me.

Thank you to Lisa Carlson of Wordstream West, San Francisco, whose writing expertise, advice, and editorial support from start to finish were instrumental in making this book happen. I could not have done it without you. I look forward to our planned future collaborations.

A very special thanks to Linda Greenspan Regan, my *dream* editor, whose insightful editing, judgment, and caring helped me reach the finish line. A special thanks to Monica Harris, who was among the first to have faith in me, and also thank-you to Bruce Bender, Donald Davidson, Margaret Wolf, and the rest of the staff at my publisher who worked fervently to make this book a reality.

Thanks also to my wonderful agents, Andrée Abecassis and Letty Lee, at the Ann Elmo Agency, whose professional support, guidance, and belief in my ability have brought me this far.

A special thank-you to those whose rich contributions gave this book substance: Maryum Abdul-Shaheed, Duriya Ali, Amelia Austria, Ruth Beckford, Amy Billingsly, Sheila Bridges, Beverly-Anna Broussard, J. Garfield Broussard Jr., Pamela Herman Broussard, Alma Arrington Brown, Blanche Brown, Zora Kramer Brown, Marcia Carlson, Tisha Campbell Martin, Peggy Cooper Cafritz, Suzanne Costa-Castain, Norma Jean Darden, Margot Dashiell, Belva Davis, Quarana Davis, Joyce Burrows Dinkins, Zerita Dotson, Mary Dulan, Myrlie Evers-Williams, Sheila Hill-Fajors and Herb Fajors, Melanie Austria Farmer, Zahrah M. Farmer, Claudia Farmer-Perry, Vivica Fox, Sheila Frazier, Gwendolyn Goldsby Grant, Matthew Green, Irma P. Hall, Beverly Heath, Leola "Roscoe" Higgs-Dellums, Jacqueline Howell, Gloria Jean, Donna Katzl, Janet Langhart, Jesse Leonard-Corcia, Christel Albritton MacLean, Gale Madyun, Marijo, Father Jay Matthews, Joyce Matthews, Rahiema Muslem, Adwoa Afi Nyamekye, Kimberly Elise Oldham, Doris Peeler-Brown, Marcheta Q'McManus-Eneas, Jacqueline Mitchell Rice, Cheryl R. Riley, Mimi Rogers, Patricia Russell-McCloud, Synthia Saint James, Joan H. Sonn, Phyllis Yvonne Stickney, Pauletta Pearson Washington, Bernice Watson, Judge Horace Wheatley, Gwendolyn Williams, Aunt Marguerite Williams, Myrna Williams, Denise Wilson, Nancy Wilson, and Rhita J. Wilson.

I am forever appreciative of photographer Lewis Watts for his patience and professionalism in photographing my Christmas decorations.

Thanks also to my colleague, architectural interior designer Sandra B. Jimenez, who captured my visions through her illustrations, and to Brian Charron and Patrick Weibeler, whose decorating expertise always adds special charm to my home.

Thank you to Janine and Jacqueline Beachum of Bumbershoot, an interior and garden design studio, whose generous contributions of unusual ethnic Christmas decorations made my house come alive.

Thanks to Lloyd Perata of Perata Brothers Wholesale, San Francisco, for the Christmas wreath and garland that not only made my house beautiful but made it *smell* like Christmas.

I thank my brother, artist John Broussard, for his contributions of paintings and sculptures.

I'm grateful to Dr. Mona Lakes Jones and Joe C. Jones, president of Impact Communications, for giving me permission to reprint her wonderful poetic material from *The Color of Culture II*.

I'm grateful to my daughter-in-law, Melanie Austria Farmer (she started out on this project with me four years ago), for putting her research and writing ability to work in helping me develop my original material. Thank you to my daughter, Zahrah Mallie Farmer, a story contributor, who was instrumental in the development of the book's theme, traveled with me, and helped with some of the interviews. She used her writing skills to help me in the final weeks of the project. I appreciate the vision that Zahrah, Melanie, and I have shared since before the book's inception.

Thanks, too, to Cheryl D. Broussard. I so appreciate our inspiring brainstorming sessions and the vision you shared with me. It not only validated my ideas, it led me to this juncture. Thank you for your contribution to the book.

Thanks to Glenda Gutierrez, whose insight and direction will be eternally appreciated.

A special thank-you to Veronica Oliva, permissions editor, Brad Bunin, attorney, and Jill Fox, who helped as metric conversion editor, for their important advice.

Thanks to my sons Jule and Omar Farmer, my heroes at heart. I'm forever grateful for their constant support and belief in me.

Thanks to my brother Ernest Broussard for his many words of encouragement.

A special thank-you to friends and family: Clint Bolden, Charles Brown, Gerald Douglas, Larry Harrison, Aisha House, Joel Swisher, Elvin Tyler, Toni Wilson, Steve Wong, Mannie Lopes and Michelle Lopez, Zerita Dotson, Margaret Jones, and the Martin Austria, Charles Guyton, Bobby Broussard, George Craig, Harry Willliams, Shirley Jackson, Scott Farmer, Nowling, Valmassy, and Singleton families for their unwavering support.

African-American
Holiday Traditions

1

The Lure of the Season

Part of our tradition, as people of African descent, is celebration.
We celebrate life, the harvest, our blessings, children, our elders,
and the fact that we have our daily bread on our table. We
brought the model of celebration with us, and we have celebrated
the most meager existence. The fact that people can still celebrate
life under oppressive conditions, in the midst of low socioeconomic
standing, is a model for America. The holidays have a double
meaning for us: I survived, I breathe, I live—I have my being.

Gwendolyn Goldsby Grant

In San Francisco, where I live, the air smells different as summer turns to autumn. The coolness holds the scent of dry leaves and wood-burning fireplaces, and the misty mornings signal October's arrival. That's when my family and I inaugurate three months of gaiety as we prepare for our birthday celebrations, Halloween, Thanksgiving, and the December holidays.

Of course, fall also signals the beginning of a time for cooking that sends memorable aromas wafting through the house. Not that I don't cook year 'round for my grown children, who visit frequently. However, this time of year I cook and entertain more lavishly, preparing hearty foods and traditional dishes. As I wait in line at the checkout counter and peek at my neighbors' purchases, which include yams, cranberries, bread stuffing, twenty-pound turkeys, serious-looking hams, baking ingredients, and wines, I know I'm not alone.

The Passage of Tradition

When I first inherited the role of Thanksgiving hostess, a tradition passed on to me by my mother, I tried to re-create the atmosphere of my god-mother's house, where I often spent the holidays as a child. My god-mother was Mrs. Eva Jones, but we affectionately called her Aunt Eva. (She first became a friend of my family after being a student of my maternal grandmother, Mabel Bohannon Craig, a teacher of domestic sciences at Prairie View College in Texas at the turn of the century.) A seamstress for wealthy local women, she made many of my clothes when I was a girl. Her husband had retired from Southern Pacific Railroad, where he worked as a waiter on the trains. Aunt Eva was an elegant woman, and she served an elegant meal. They lived in a grand Queen Anne house in West Oakland, California, from the 1930s through most of the 1960s.

As soon as we walked in, our hosts took our coats, escorted us into the parlor, and offered us something to drink, like Mr. Jones's rich home-made eggnog, his holiday specialty. After updating each other on our lives, we made our way into the dining room. There we sat at a mahogany table draped in damask, set with heirloom china, fine silver, and crystal stemware. I felt so grown up drinking from Aunt Eva's water goblets.

Seated at the head of the table with my father to his right, Mr. Jones always carved and served the turkey, carefully draping a white cloth napkin over his sleeve. With an accommodating smile he asked what kind of meat we wanted: light or dark, drumstick or wing. The meal was scrumptious, of course, and always followed by buttery ice cream and homemade pie served on delicate French glass dishes. What an unforget-table sensual experience that was—over forty-five years ago. I try to emu-late Aunt Eva's sophisticated entertaining style to this day.

Two years ago my eldest son Jule got married, so our newly blended families celebrate Thanksgiving together. At one of these celebrations my now six-year-old granddaughter-in-law, Annalyn, came into the kitchen to tell me she, too, wanted to drink out of a long-stemmed glass. I remembered how proud I had felt drinking from Aunt Eva's exquisite stemware. So I filled a sherry glass with punch and set it at Annalyn's place. She was delighted.

My family and I think of Thanksgiving as a day filled with reflection, gratitude, and appreciation for our bounty and good fortune. We offer a prayer to our ancestors, remembering their struggles. We recall that Native Americans—who showed settlers how to live off the land and helped runaway slaves—are part of our heritage, too. For example, on my paternal grandmother's side there is Cherokee, and on my paternal grandfather's side there is Creole from the mixture of the Africans, French, and indigenous Americans in Louisiana. Thanksgiving Day is a special time to celebrate the bonds of family and friendship. I am grateful that I have a family and for the progress our people have made. I thank God that my people are together now, that we no longer have to suffer the imposed separation of loved ones that my ancestors did, and that we no longer live in isolation and fear.

A Family Prayer Given by My Daughter, Zahrah

Dear Lord: Thank you for this food which we are about to eat. We pray for those who are not as fortunate as us and send them strength, love, happiness, and all blessings. Lord, we thank you for bringing us together; we thank you for our strength and for each other. We pray that those who have passed on are at peace and thank them for being our angels. Lord, thank you for the incredible love you have blessed us with and for the beauty of this family. Amen.

For our Thanksgiving dinner, with our busy modern lives, every guest brings a favorite dish. The menu is traditional and starts out with cocktails and hors d'oeuvres. The main course includes roast turkey and cornbread dressing, some type of fish, biscuits and French rolls, sweet potatoes, fresh green beans, tomato salad, macaroni and cheese, rice, and giblet gravy. Dessert is as sumptuous as in the old days, with an assortment of pies and ice cream.

We always make a holiday punch and serve wine and champagne. Before we eat we gather around the kitchen table, now laid out buffet style, and hold hands. My daughter, Zahrah, rarely at a loss for words or inspiration, is the designated leader of the family prayer. By then we're famished. It's time to eat.

Setting the Scene

Thanksgiving is a time of harvest and celebration. For me, setting the season's mood begins with my home's entrance décor. I first got the idea of a wheat wreath with sunflowers from a Sunset book, *Wreaths* (1995), and have added my own touches. On my front door, I hang a wreath woven from wheat and decorated with Indian corn, sunflowers, and dried pomegranates, all tied together with an autumn-hued cloth bow made of a cranberry cotton Senegalese weave. Along my entrance stairway, I set out clay flowerpots and pottery urns overflowing with flowers I have planted, including chrysanthemums, French lavender, and the less exotic mums in maroon and gold, easily found at this time of year.

This year I used autumn leaves and foliage to create garlands. Draped from my mantels, chandeliers, and staircase, they bring the colors of fall inside. My vases are filled with the hydrangeas I grow in my yard. Whether fresh or dried, these shrubs of the saxifrage family make lovely, rich arrangements with their large clusters of white, red, pink, or blue flowers. For the dining tables, I cut sunflowers into short bouquets and arrange them with local greenery, then position the stems among colored marbles inside melon-colored antique glasses I found at a flea market.

At one garage sale (something San Francisco has plenty of most weekends), I bought several candleholders in a variety of sizes. My friend Brian Charron, an interior decorator, spray-painted them gold, dressed them up with gold organza ribbons, and placed them between the smiling sunflowers. We also bought forest-green fabric lining at a bargain ninety cents a yard. Brian made tablecloths from it and draped and pinned a pale orange tulle along the table's edges. This setting was inspired by Brian's decorations for my eldest son's wedding rehearsal dinner. At that time we used a cream-colored muslin fabric as the base, washed it so that it would crinkle slightly, and pinned the tulle to it. This idea can be used for your dining table or buffet table as displayed in the photograph to the right.

Small pots of fragrant lavender and paperwhite narcissus, found at the local flower mart, also decorate my rooms. To dress them up, I cover the flowerpots with some of the same Senegalese cloth I use to tie my wreath. I also drape a swag of it over a gold velvet chair in my living room.

How Others Celebrate

Restaurateurs Mary and Adolf Dulan have owned Aunt Kizzy's Back Porch in Marina del Rey, California, for over twenty-five years. Holidays are a busy time, with patrons coming in to dine or pick up catering orders of fresh, home-style southern food served with good old-fashioned southern hospitality. Along with the traditional foods, one special dish that Mary learned from an aunt—an award-winning Liberian collard greens with shrimp, ham, chicken, and sausage—is popular among their clientele.

Mary decorates her Thanksgiving table at home in traditional American style, using autumn leaves, straw, turkey figurines, and Pilgrim dolls set in miniature historical scenes on various buffet tables. She's also a miniature train collector, and amidst these table decorations she puts her hobby to practical use. Creating an original, entertaining, literally movable feast, Mary places candies and delicate desserts on her trains. As the tempting treats go 'round and 'round the tables, guests can serve themselves from the boxcars and cabooses. She keeps the trains assembled all year and changes the decorations with the seasons; for example, at Christmastime the trains sport miniature wreaths. The children love it.

Actress Tisha Campbell-Martin, costar of the television series *Martin*, is the designated cook for Thanksgiving and Christmas in her family. "You know no one is going to eat if I don't cook," she told me. "Sometimes my friends help out, but most of the time I just hate people to be in my kitchen. Every year I say I'm not going to cook this year, but then the holidays roll around and I pass by the Williams-Sonoma Gourmet Cooking Store, and I start getting that bug as soon as I walk in there."

Tisha, who calls herself "really visual and a Miss Susie Homemaker," also loves to create table settings. "When I was younger," she says, "I'd tear out the pages from Sears or Spiegel catalogs and put them in a photo album. It was my dream book. I still do that to this date. As a matter of fact, that's how I furnished my house, through my dream book. That's how I keep in touch with my goals and my dreams."

Tisha's dream-into-reality for Thanksgiving includes a turkey decorated with flowers, lettuce, and carrots: "My turkeys are the *bomb*! They are some bad wenches!! They are always brown and gorgeous." Her Thanksgiving table is set with an orange tablecloth, green placemats, white china, and crystal. Decorations include potpourri and two kinds of candleholders: crystal, and ones she makes herself out of little pumpkins. (She uses an apple corer to carve small holes in the tops that tall tapered candles fit into.)

Beverly Heath, a cultural therapist, constructs altars in celebration of people's lives and identities. She celebrates Thanksgiving as a time of harvest—the time before death (winter). "During the fall the rhythms slow down. This is the time to nourish oneself and to celebrate because it is going to be a long sleep," she says. It's her favorite time of year. Her celebration is something like a blues festival, in part because her husband, "Tootie" Heath, is a professional jazz drummer. Their guests participate in the musical performances that follow the harvest feast.

Vivica A. Fox, who starred in the film *Why Do Fools Fall in Love?* and the Fox sitcom *Getting Personal*, often spends Thanksgiving with the family of her manager, lawyer, and good friend Lita Richardson. Vivica and her husband, R&B singer Sixx-Nine, bring macaroni and cheese and greens for the feast. Thanksgiving Day with Lita's relatives and friends is like being with her own family, full of laughter and love, Vivica says.

Amy Billingsley—community activist, political organizer, special assistant to Secretary of Labor Alexis Herman, and mother of two grown daughters, Angela and Bonita—says Thanksgiving sets the stage for the holidays, including her own birthday. Amy and her family and friends like to get together for a potluck, and after eating, they take turns saying what they're thankful for.

Amy Billingsley
JAMES JOHNSON PHOTOGRAPHERS

Paying Tribute

Blanche Brown, wife of San Francisco mayor Willie Brown, calls Thanksgiving the most enjoyable holiday of the year. "The entire family gets together and shares the food and cooks together," she says. "We all bring the same things every time, so we know what to make. I always make the turkey and the stuffing just like my grandmother Pearl Brown did. As I was growing up, I used to get up with my grandmother at four or five in the morning to prepare the turkey for Thanksgiving dinner. I would toast the bread and cut it up for her. Her recipes have been an inspiration for my cooking."

Blanche has taught dance, including jazz and Haitian, for over twenty-five years and is artistic director of her own dance company, Group Petit La Croix. Her family heritage includes African, Caucasian, Filipino, and Native American bloodlines. "It's a really ancestral thing when we do Thanksgiving," she says. Her spiritual nature is reflected throughout her gracious home, which is filled with African art, shrines, and masks.

In many parts of Africa, the people revere their ancestors and pray to them for protection and guidance. Yoruba (African people who inhabit the west coast, especially Nigeria) priests honor them with shrines. Blanche—a respected elder of the Yoruba religion as an ordained priest of Oshun—long ago decided to use dolls to represent her own ancestors. Among them, she includes a Caribbean doll in a shrine along with a photo of a Haitian woman—reflecting her feeling that someone in her lineage must have been from Haiti. For the Thanksgiving table decorations, Blanche sets out the doll collection among pumpkins and flowers. "I've always felt they were helping me to cook," she said.

Blanche recalls the especially fun-filled Thanksgiving when she got everyone to come home because her mother would be turning eighty. "We took snapshots of the whole day—cooking, family arriving, when my mother came in—and right then and there, we put together an album in a special book. My daughter, an artist, and my sister, a calligrapher, designed it as the day progressed. Now my mother has that great album."

Sweet Potato Casserole

Contributed by Blanche Brown

NOTE: Bake potatoes instead of boiling them. They will come out sweeter and maintain their color. This is a recipe that is measured by taste. Gradually add the sugar to get the amount of sweetness you desire. You may not need the entire cup.

5 large sweet potatoes, baked and cooled	1 cup sugar
Juice from 2 oranges	1/2 teaspoon cinnamon
1/2 cup butter	1/2 teaspoon nutmeg
	1/2 teaspoon ground allspice

Preheat oven to 350°F. Peel the baked potatoes and mash them, using orange juice to moisten. Add remaining ingredients and mix well. Bake in a greased casserole until it is thoroughly hot, 20 to 25 minutes. Serves 6 to 8.

Another memorable Thanksgiving for Blanche was when her husband's family came to California from Texas. "His mother, Minnie Boyd, called and said that we never got all the families together. She said, 'Let's do it this time.' And then, sadly, the day before she wasn't feeling well and couldn't come. But in the meantime she sent all of his siblings and some of their children out here to San Francisco. There were about thirty-five people. This whole house was packed! We had to move the furniture!"

Synthia Saint James is a busy writer and artist whose illustrations can be seen on over fifty book jackets. She is also the designer of the first Kwanzaa stamp for the U.S. Post Office (see photo insert). Over the Thanksgiving holiday, she works on her art, something that gives her enormous pleasure, and lists the things she's thankful for. She loves to whip things up for friends in her kitchen and has begun cooking for all the older mothers she knows who have spent a lifetime preparing meals for others. "To cook is to share love," she says.

Synthia Saint James
LEROY HAMILTON

Creole Shrimp Pilaf

Contributed by Synthia Saint James

This recipe is reprinted with permission from Synthia's book, *Creative Fixings From the Kitchen: Favorite Multicultural Recipes,* edited by Jerald Stone (Port Chester, NY: Persnickety Press), p. 60.

1 pound large shrimp, shelled, deveined, and rinsed
Juice of 2 limes or 1 large lemon
1 tablespoon Creole or Cajun seasoning, or to taste
1 teaspoon ground turmeric
Garlic salt and freshly ground black pepper to taste
1 8-pounce package frozen petite green peas, defrosted
4 garlic cloves, finely chopped
1/2 medium yellow onion, finely chopped

1/2 green bell pepper, finely chopped
1 large stalk celery, coarsely chopped
1/4 cup fresh parsley, coarsely chopped
1/4 cup fresh cilantro, coarsely chopped
4 tablespoons extra-virgin olive oil
1 cup long-grain white rice
1 6-ounce can minced clams
Spring water as needed
2 medium tomatoes, coarsely chopped

Place shrimp in a medium bowl. Mix in the lime or lemon juice, Creole or Cajun seasoning, turmeric, garlic salt, and freshly ground black pepper. Cover and refrigerate 15 to 20 minutes, until needed.

Remove the peas from the freezer. Clean and prepare the rest of the vegetables, parsley, and cilantro; set aside.

When ready to cook, heat 2 tablespoons of the extra-virgin olive oil in a medium casserole or heavy pot and add the marinated shrimp. Cook 3 to 4 minutes over medium heat. Remove shrimp from pan with a slotted spoon, leaving all the juices in the pan. Set the shrimp aside, covered.

Add 1 to 2 tablespoons more olive oil to the pan, then add the garlic. Sauté on low to medium heat 2 minutes, then add the chopped onion, green pepper, celery, parsley, and cilantro. Cook 2 or 3 minutes more, stirring frequently. Add the rice and cook, stirring, for 2 more minutes.

Pour the minced clams into a large measuring cup and add enough water to make 2½ cups. Add this mixture to pan and heat on medium to high until it begins to boil. Cover and simmer on low heat until rice is almost tender, about 13 to 15 minutes.

Gently stir in the defrosted peas, half of the chopped tomatoes, and reserved shrimp. Cover and cook on low heat for 5 to 10 minutes, or until rice is tender and liquid is absorbed. Garnish with remaining chopped tomatoes before serving. Serves 4.

James Vernon Matthews II, fondly known as "Father Jay" to his parishioners, and a childhood friend of mine, was ordained on May 3, 1974, as the first black Catholic priest in Northern California. He serves as chaplain of the Black Catholics of the Diocese of Oakland and pastor of St. Benedict's Church in Oakland. Recently he returned from spending a year-long sabbatical at the Vatican in Rome. Since A.D. 1300, every twenty-five years, the Roman Catholic church has celebrated a jubilee: a time that emphasizes personal reconciliation and renewal, an experience that is spiritually and emotionally moving. As the new millennium approached, the Vatican prepared for the great jubilee in Rome. So far, over 32 million people made the pilgrimage. Father Jay was among them.

Father Jay

Father Jay's perspective as a parish priest is that major holidays bring relatives together and show the true essence of family. He contends that as human beings we go in cycles and cycles enable us to start over again. Likewise, the yearly cycle of the holidays gives us the opportunity to put aside our differences and start over again each year.

Father Jay celebrates an early Thanksgiving mass at 9:00 A.M. and holds an open house afterward, serving coffee, juices, pastries, and gin fizzes. This opportunity for people to relax and visit before they return home to finish preparing for their Thanksgiving celebrations has turned into a wonderful church tradition, where Father Jay hosts about 150 people.

Leola "Roscoe" Higgs-Dellums, a mother, grandmother, attorney, and writer, has devoted much of her life to helping other people. The wife of Congressman Ronald V. Dellums for thirty-seven years (they divorced in 1999), she was a founder of the Congressional Black Caucus Spouses

Leola "Roscoe" Higgs-Dellums
POINT OF VIEW PHOTOGRAPHY

Education Scholarship Fund, which has raised millions in tuition aid for minority students. Roscoe and I are cousins through our mothers, who were also the best of friends.

Roscoe says that holiday memories are like "the library of your life." Her own fondest memories go back to her childhood in a musical family. Her mother, Esther Higgs, was educated at the University of California at Berkeley and at the Juilliard School and loved the arts. In their living room stood a white baby grand piano, a wedding gift to Esther from her groom. To complement their academic education, she had all six of her girls study dance, theater, the piano, and a string instrument. Their responsibility for each holiday was to produce a program and entertain the adults, while the elders honed their recipes for fabulous holiday foods.

"You could see and smell Thanksgiving coming because of what was being purchased at the grocery store and being prepared in the kitchen," says Roscoe. Her mother, who was born in Oakland, California, and her maternal grandmother, Mrs. Lee, from Ann Arbor, Michigan, did all the traditional cooking for Thanksgiving and the December holidays. "Even though we were girls, we were never allowed in the kitchen, so the holidays were filled with great expectations and a longing for our favorites." While Roscoe is a traditionalist, her husband's southern background—early in her marriage, she vowed to become as good a cook as his grandmother—influenced her, too, and she makes a savory cornbread dressing.

Roscoe is known as "the sugar plum fairy" for her dessert specialties. Her candied nuts are popular holiday gifts. So are her oatmeal cookies, called "mistakes" because she made a mistake the first time she used the recipe. Now that "mistake" is her secret ingredient.

Roscoe's mother believed that part of the holiday ritual is to display flowers and natural decorations. Their Thanksgiving centerpiece was a basket filled with fruit and nuts. Roscoe places different-size pumpkins on her front porch and uses dried corn and fall leaves as decoration.

"The Higgs family was a family of a lot of laughter, and holidays were important," says Roscoe. "No matter what your differences were, on the holidays there was a covenant to be happy. My father, a prominent businessman and the first black realtor in Berkeley, California, made sure the needy had food. It was a time to be thankful and to share."

The family entertained themselves on Thanksgiving cracking walnuts and playing nut games. The one sitting on Daddy's lap and learning how to crack those walnuts was special, and "it was a rite of passage when you were a bigger girl and you helped others crack their walnuts," Roscoe recalls.

"Never sit down to Thanksgiving not knowing what you are thankful for," says Roscoe. "In my

Emma, Roscoe, Elizabeth, Mary, and Rosa at Elizabeth's debut party

family, everyone has to give a blessing and tell what they are thankful for. Thanksgiving is not about gluttony, but truly a time to reflect."

Roscoe's mother, like my Aunt Eva, delighted in displaying an elegant table for formal dinners. Esther Higgs was a gracious, accommodating hostess, and every year she entertained my mother, Maybelle Broussard, for her birthday. When Esther was diagnosed with breast cancer at age forty-three, the family realized that March 31, 1961, might be their last birthday celebration together. Esther's daughter Elizabeth was to debut in the Links, Inc. cotillion that year, so Esther gave a grand coming-out party for Elizabeth earlier in the year. Esther died in the fall, close to Thanksgiving, and the Higgs family didn't know what to do. The holidays seemed devoid of meaning. Roscoe felt that a light had been extinguished. As she mourned, she eventually found a way to turn that light back on through her spiritual growth. Roscoe no longer considered death a loss. She understood her relationship to God and the lesson of the resurrection and how nature operates. "Life is a continuum," says Roscoe. "I understand who I am as a spiritual being and not just a human being. Everything is in God's time," she says. Roscoe is now the mother of three grown children (Brandy Dellums, Erik Dellums, and Piper Dellums Ross) and the grandmother of three. The family rekindles that essential joy each holiday, remembering the past and creating fond memories for the future.

Something Different

Actor Denzel Washington's wife, Pauletta, says that for their family, "Thanksgiving is the eleventh hour, a lead-in to Christmas. My mother made Thanksgiving special. We were taught that it was a time to set aside for thanks, rather than for asking for anything." To wake up on Thanksgiving morning in Pauletta's mother's house was to experience the magic redolence of turkey roasting in the oven.

Starting her own family, Pauletta passed down her mother's traditions. But one year she and Denzel decided to do something a little bit different: they leased a beach house and celebrated the holiday there. Pauletta told her children that she would prepare the turkey at the main house and bring it over. The kids protested. "Oh no," they said, "we want to smell that turkey!"

Washington family   BILL JONES, PHOTOGRAPHER

My friend Marcheta Q'McManus-Eneas, originally from South Carolina, is of Gullah ancestry. (A Creole language is spoken by the Gullah, a black community living on the coast of South Carolina or the nearby Sea Islands.) Now that she lives in Nassau with her Bahamian husband, Dr. Judson Eneas, she puts together a Thanksgiving dinner for American-born wives married to Bahamians, and their families. While Thanksgiving as we know it is not celebrated there, Marcheta and the other American wives want their children to learn about that part of their heritage. She remembers fondly how important the holidays were for her as a child—a time for family to come together. She has passed along her strong sense of self and family to her daughter, Kemba, and two sons, Judson and Kashta, now all grown up and graduates of black colleges.

Marcheta and Judson Eneas

Patricia Russell-McCloud, professional orator and author of *A Is for Attitude: An Alphabet for Living,* says she and her husband, who is from Alabama, return there to attend a family celebration centered around the football game between Alabama State and the Tuskegee Institute on Thanksgiving Day. Her husband, the Rev. Dr. E. Earl McCloud Jr., and others in his family are Tuskegee grads. The "big game," like the reunion of family and friends, is always very spirited.

Jessie Leonard-Corcia, chef and former owner of Jessie's Restaurant in San Francisco, was born in Haiti and moved to the United States as a young child. Though Thanksgiving isn't celebrated in Haiti, Jessie makes up for it here. As a one-time owner of a Cajun-Caribbean-style restaurant, she plays with that combination during the holidays. For example, she might make a Caribbean-style or Cajun-style turkey instead of the traditional one. For Thanksgiving she prepares a special: marinated turkey with collard greens, red beans, and rice. You can find her turkey recipe on page 110.

For many years, Myrna Williams, owner of the London restaurant Sweet Georgia Brown, has cooked for Americans who come to town during the holiday, as many as 300 at a time. Since Thanksgiving isn't celebrated in

England (for obvious reasons), Myrna, a former music executive and manager, often finds herself at the epicenter of a coterie of American recording artists missing home. (She has managed, among others, Deniece Williams, Roy Ayers and Thelma Houston, and the Jones girls.) When she launched her restaurant, Myrna found that the British equated soul food with Cajun cooking and white southerners, so she decided to educate them with a taste of the real thing—African-American soul food. Now her restaurant is known for its authentic American cuisine.

"Not all the foods we have in the States are found in England," she says, so some of the edibles—like sweet relish, ranch dressing, grits, cranberry sauce, maple syrup, cornmeal, and frozen pie shells—have to cross the ocean as well. For starters, she serves oysters Rockefeller, breaded mussels cooked in wine, or stuffed mushrooms. This is followed by the American classics, including roast turkey, ham, stuffed trout, creamed corn, potato salad, and macaroni and cheese. Myrna also offers a vegetable gumbo and a vegetarian loaf with a Creole sauce. And, of course, corn muffins. Desserts include Sweet Georgia Brown's pecan pie—imported, since pecans can be extraordinarily expensive in England.

Whether we celebrate Thanksgiving on the East Coast or the West, up North or down South, at the beach or in jolly old England—we African Americans do it with our own sense of style, and with the grace and spirit of gratitude that comes from our racial memory of hardship, our mother wit, and our endurance. Our spirits soar.

2

'Tis the Season

The true spirit of the holiday is captured by remembering the purpose of the celebration it is, not to receive, but to give and forgive. It is true, giving is its own reward. Be reminded, "Love is not what makes the world go 'round, love is what makes the ride worthwhile!"

Patricia Russell-McCloud

October launches a season of celebrations for me that goes right through Easter. I just love giving parties, and this is the time for a lot of them. Ever since my days as a flight attendant for American Airlines, I've enjoyed making sure my guests are happy, relaxed, and enjoying themselves. I want my family and friends to have the best of what I can give.

My mother and father were always very kind to everyone, and they raised their children to treat people right. While not much was verbalized on the subject of hospitality, my brothers and I just naturally followed their example, as was expected. My mother, Maybelle, is a gracious hostess and influenced me greatly about how to do things the right way. She always tried to make the house comfortable for visitors, and I do the same thing. I want to enjoy myself, too, and that takes preparation. My guests also have a responsibility—to contribute and participate when they visit, and to try to have a good time.

When you're inviting people over, everyone in the family should know what is expected of them. The children can be appointed junior hosts and hostesses. Decide who should greet and take the coats of guests, who will serve the drinks, and who is *definitely* cleaning up before and after the gathering.

The tasks can be made into fun. Even though my family sometimes growls or balks at doing them, they usually feel good (and tired) when it's all over. And the kids learn about responsibility, too. (When my younger son, Omar, was a child, one of his holiday jobs was polishing the silver. When I gave this task to someone else one year, Omar complained that I had taken away his job; that's when I realized that he had derived some pleasure from the responsibility.) Also, if young people are treated as an integral part of the process, their confidence is boosted, and they will feel at ease with entertaining.

Once you decide to entertain, all you need is faith in your own abilities, good planning, and preparation. If you don't have lots of experience, start small and focus on providing a warm, positive atmosphere. Invite only a few people to your first get-together to establish your comfort level. Don't get caught up in trying to impress them, but think of ways you and your guests can have fun.

Planning and Preparing

The key to entertaining and enjoying the holidays is to always be prepared. I make sure to think out all the details and write them down. No matter how roughly sketched out my list, it proves helpful. I want to avoid getting overwhelmed. My strategic planning for the season overall includes creating a budget, a schedule of events, and lists for everything I have to do, including the following:

- ◉ To-do list
- ◉ Family chores list

- Gift and greeting card lists
- Holiday must-call lists
- Supplies shopping lists
- Grocery lists

Keep a file of your holiday events and chores lists so that you don't have to re-create them year after year. Post the events calendar for this year in the kitchen or another good place where all can see it. Get out that list and start your preparations weeks in advance.

Many of the same basic rules apply to planning a family gathering for Christmas, a New Year's Eve party for a large group of friends, or any festive event. The scale may differ, but many of the same needs exist. Plan every detail: budget, menu, liquor, guest list, invitations, decorations, entertainment, food preparation, serving, and cleanup. Visualize every aspect of the event you're preparing. Remember that entertaining is like planning a film or theater production. The host's house is like a set, and it must be decorated and ready before the first actor (your first guest) arrives. And the crew (if you have one) must be ready to start work.

Don't be afraid to delegate. It's always helpful, too, if your significant other is involved and understands precisely what you need in the way of support. Whether this person becomes your *aide-de-camp* as chopper, shopper, knife sharpener, bartender, or eggnog expert, you'll be a lot more relaxed having that extra hand around. When I was a girl, my father did all of the cooking on the holidays and my mother was in charge of the house preparations. My brothers and I had designated chores.

My friend Gwendolyn Williams, who knows a good party when she sees one, says today's best parties are given by people who are down-to-earth, "not pretentious, not 'Miss Thang' or full of themselves, just people who are fun-loving, nice, and cordial to everybody." Her advice for successful entertaining includes doing things as simply as possible and not taking yourself too seriously. "Just do the best you can. Be yourself," she suggests.

Some thoughtful tips from furniture designer Cheryl R. Riley: "Stay elegant and simple. Think about the logistics and the flow of traffic in a room—how you lay the room out so that the party flows and you are

Gwendolyn Williams
SOLOMON BEKKELE, PHOTOGRAPHER

Cheryl Riley
DAVID DUNCAN LIVINGSTON

free to entertain. If you keep it simple, you can set up before everyone arrives so that you can be with your guests. Use logic and common sense. Remember what you liked or disliked at other parties that you have gone to."

Budget

Budgeting may not be a problem for you, but you'd be amazed at how many people don't think it through before launching into shopping—then find that they have over-spent on one aspect of their event, so they have to scrimp on another or dig deeper into their wallet. To avoid this, establish your budget by figuring out your guest list and determining the costs: location, invitations, food, drink, entertainment, and decorations. Then decide if these expenses reconcile with your "pocketbook" and fine-tune accordingly. Set aside an extra 15 percent of your budget for unexpected costs.

The Guest List

For family celebrations on Christmas Day at my house, the guests are usu-ally the same every year, but I still maintain a list to ensure that I don't forget anyone! This compatible group mixes well, so we have a great time together.

For your holiday parties, of course, you'll want to put people together who will enjoy one another. Invite congenial guests who can contribute to the atmosphere and conversation. Not everyone on your list has to be an extrovert, but finding a good balance between personality types will add substance and interest to your event. Not everyone has to be of the same age group, either. A mix of ages can add sparkle and zest to any gathering.

Draft a list of people you feel you would like to invite, then trim your list according to space and budget. You can create a substitute list to go to if people decline an invitation early. Make a copy of your guest list for

R.S.V.P.'s, a record of gifts received when applicable, and to use for a seating plan, should you need one.

Invitations

Invitations for a party should tell your guests who, what, where, and when, and indicate the attire. They may also include directions and a map, which will keep you from having to field all those phone calls for directions. A request to R.S.V.P. by a certain date (at *least* one week before the event) should also be on the invitations. (People sometimes forget what most of us learned in school, that R.S.V.P. is the abbreviation for the French *respondez s'il vous plait*—please respond.) Give a telephone number with voicemail and an e-mail address; otherwise you'll spend a lot of time answering calls. It's the guest's obligation to accept or decline by telephone or in writing. Unfortunately, as manners in general continue to decline in our culture, this responsibility is sometimes overlooked.

Try to mail the invitations in time for your guests to receive them three to four weeks before the event. For formal occasions, or during a busy social season like the year-end holidays, five to six weeks is even better. You may also want to send out reminder cards ten days before the event.

Of course, not every party requires formal printed invitations. You may invite your guests by telephone or with a note written on your own stationery. Those with computers can design very personal, imaginative invitations. An unusual or inspired invitation can build anticipation for an event.

When actress Phyllis Yvonne Stickney sponsored a party in New York to exhibit black art and memorabilia, she used her talent to put together an original, funny voice invitation. Sounding like a machine, she left messages on her guests' answering machines or voicemails. They were timed to lead the recipient of the call through the message with a sequence of prompts like, "I'll hold while you get a pencil." She also made it clear that the party would be informal, saying, "Bare feet and your presence are all that are required."

Holiday Menus

For the holidays you may want to have a set menu every year and expand on it. But do keep a list of what everybody usually brings if you're having a potluck.

I try to make food preparation as easy as possible while serving a nutritious, balanced menu and ensuring that the foods compliment one another. Also, I would rather err on the side of preparing too much food than not enough. After all, leftovers can always be frozen or sent home with your guests as a reminder of what a great party you gave.

Belva Davis, a well-known social-political reporter and anchor on San Francisco Bay Area radio and television for over thirty years, has always done her own holiday cooking, which includes preparing fourteen dishes for Thanksgiving. Influenced by the years she spent living in Hawaii, her favorite recipes include a slow-baked ham swimming in rum or brandy with bing cherries, orange juice, orange rind, and lemon juice; sweet potato with coconut milk; potato salad; cornbread dressing; and, of course, turkey. Now that her son, Steven, is a chef and graduate of the San Francisco Culinary Academy, they go crazy creating her favorite dishes together. He is documenting some of Belva's recipes, which she had never written down before, so that the family will always have them.

Belva is lucky to have a second cook, too. Her husband, William Moore, is retired now. (He was the first African-American television cameraman in the Bay Area.) Bill helps Belva in every way, including cleaning up the kitchen as she cooks. She says she couldn't manage all the food preparation without him.

Every Christmas season Belva cooks a holiday dinner for her women's club and the members' husbands. An example of her gourmet menu includes sizzling rice soup, greens with a mint dressing, a crusted roast beef, breast of chicken, a pasta dish with homegrown fresh garden herbs, and a homemade herb sauce, a sweet potato soufflé, and snow peas with red bell peppers, which all together guarantees a classic red-and-green Christmas theme. To accommodate all her guests she sets two tables of equal status. Belva likes sit-down dinners and the conversation that goes along with them. She says she works very hard to make her guests feel comfortable and puts a lot of thought into arranging the seating to generate stimulating conversation. She suggests that if you are going to spend extra money on anything, by all means spend it on someone who can help you clear the tables between courses and wash the dishes. This allows you to enjoy your own party more. By preparing attractive but budget-conscious dishes, you may be able to save some money to put into cleanup assistance.

If guests ask if they can bring something, "one good idea is to have newcomers bring the hors d'oeuvres," Belva says. "This guarantees they will arrive early, and it gives the host an opportunity to get to know the newcomers and introduce them to regulars. It's also a nice starter to conversation and an icebreaker."

Janet Langhart and her husband, Secretary of Defense William Cohen, frequently entertain international guests, including dignitaries. They are considered to be wonderful hosts. (Of course, they can call on a full staff overseen by the U.S. Department of Protocol!) Some of her tips for successful entertaining: "A good hostess considers less her own tradition than the traditions of the people she is entertaining. She has to consider her guests' dietary needs and their food preferences." She generally keeps the menu American/continental unless she knows the caterer can do a real ethnic dish that her guests would enjoy. Janet notes that many international people love to hear jazz, a true American original.

Liquor

The idea that a fully stocked bar is needed at every party is losing its hold on Americans as we become more health-conscious. Naturally, you won't be pushing alcohol on the designated drivers! Select an assortment of beverages according to your guests' tastes. Also, don't be afraid to ask your friends to bring a bottle to the party. You'll want to have lots of sodas and juices on hand if there will be children or nondrinkers in the crowd. It's also smart to have lots of good bottled water around.

Choose what to have on hand for your guests from the basic liquor list: dry sherry, cream sherry, vodka, gin, scotch, tequila, light and dark rum, bourbon, dry vermouth, sweet vermouth, Dubonnet, port, light and dark beer, wine coolers, Cognac, Grand Marnier, Amaretto, Kahlúa, Cointreau.

Select one or two kinds of wine to complement your food. For example, a light white wine goes well with fish, and a hearty burgundy is a good accompaniment to red meat—but don't be afraid to break the rules! Provide enough for every wine-drinker to have at least two to three glasses with the meal. My favorite types of white wine are blanc de blancs and chardonnay; for red, I choose zinfandel, cabernet sauvignon, merlot, or pinot noir. It's always great to have a few bottles of decent champagne or one of the less expensive California sparkling wines on hand.

You'll also need mixers: club soda, cola, diet cola, sparkling water or seltzer, tonic, ginger ale, tomato juice, orange juice, grapefruit juice, and cranberry juice—and slices of lemon, lime, and orange. Don't forget the green olives, bitters, maraschino cherries, Tabasco sauce, and Worcestershire sauce.

The Bar

One pound of ice per person is a rule of thumb. You'll also need an ice bucket, tongs, a water pitcher, a bar spoon and a blender; for champagne, a champagne stopper; for wine, a corkscrew and a wine stopper; and for juices, a can opener. Also useful are a jigger, a cocktail shaker, a shot glass, a bottle opener, a zester, a strainer and a paring knife for the fruit.

For serving, you'll need cocktail napkins, highball glasses, wine and champagne glasses, and juice and water glasses. Restaurant supply stores offer an assortment of bar glasses at bulk price, or you can rent them from party rental companies. I prefer the glass ones because they add a touch of class to your party, but I am a realist, and sometimes I use better-quality plastic cups for *very* large parties. I have collected many bar glasses, beautiful decanters (which add a nice touch to a party), and bar supplies from secondhand stores, flea markets, and estate sales. They do not all have to match—a little variety makes it interesting.

In the center of my kitchen, I have a bar from which I can serve food or drinks. If you don't have a built-in place like that, create a bar for the occasion in a spot that lets you set everything up in a convenient, attractive way. You can set it up so guests can serve themselves, but if you're expecting more than twenty guests, it's a good idea to have someone there to fix drinks and replenish bar supplies, especially if you are the only host. Remember to take your traffic flow into account, as people tend to crowd around a bar.

Festive Holiday Drinks

Ask people what they remember about Christmas and New Year's and someone will inevitably fondly recall a sinfully rich homemade eggnog. Fruit punch made with cranberry juice and other berries and fruits, spiked with brandy or rum (or plain), tastes great and complements the season's colors. Spicy hot apple cider garnished with cloves, allspice, and cinnamon adds that wonderful nostalgic aroma to your house and creates a welcoming atmosphere for your guests.

Location

Make sure the location you choose is appropriate to the affair. The setting is a big part of the ambience, and you don't want your guests to feel crowded. If you decide your home is not the best place in which to entertain, investigate other spaces. Museums, art galleries, historic houses, landmarks, showrooms, and botanical gardens can be interesting and comfortable party sites. (Rented places usually have to be reserved well in advance of the date, so plan ahead.)

I enjoyed a recent book-signing party at a gallery exhibiting African and African-American art and jewelry, as well as clothing made from traditional African fabrics. We were served chicken-and-seafood gumbo, traditional jambalaya, red beans and rice, cornbread, and bread pudding with whiskey—which we ate to the sounds of steel drums and African music.

Another possibility was suggested by Patricia Russell-McCloud, listed by *Ebony* magazine for four consecutive years as one of the 100 most influential persons in America. She does a "round robin" with her friends, which gives everyone a chance to play host without having to do all the work. For example, five neighbors get together and share the event: cocktails at one house, hors d' oeuvres at the next, dinner at the third, dessert at the next, and dancing at the last house. Patricia says, "What takes your event up a notch is not necessarily money, but maximizing your creative thinking."

For four years, Patricia was president of the Links, Inc., an organization of women linked in friendship to improve the quality of life in their African-American communities throughout the United States. One year she gave a high tea in a "botanical garden" for her board members: she arranged for a hotel to put park benches, streetlights, and flowers in two large banquet rooms. Patricia said, "You would have thought you were in a beautiful botanical garden." She held another board dinner at a Boston hotel overlooking the harbor. For that one, she had the invitations painted in watercolors on 8½″ by 11″ paper and written in calligraphy, all done by a fellow Link, who is a fabulous artist. Each board member received an invitation packaged in a large envelope that said ESPECIALLY FOR YOU.

Entertainment

Music can set a celebration's mood or convey its theme. (It also can fill conversational voids!) Mary and Adolf Dulan love having live entertainment. For example, if they are having a party with a Caribbean theme, they might hire a musician to play steel drums, and it's not uncommon for some of their guests to sing or bring their own instruments to play. Think ahead, keeping your location in mind. Is the room large enough to accommodate musicians? Can their electrical equipment be plugged in without disruption? If you're hiring a piano player, make sure the piano is tuned. Live entertainment is a luxury for most of us, of course, and wonderful music can just as well come from records, CDs, or tapes.

You might consider getting the guests to entertain, as many people do. Everyone has something to offer. For example, for over a dozen years, Amy Billingsley has invited her guests to "give the gift of their talent." An eighty-six-year-old friend may show off her famous ragtime steps, a child will sing, another gives a poetry reading—whatever the people want to give as a gift of themselves. Her sister, Dr. Eileen Tate Cline, Dean Emeritus of Peabody Conservatory of Music and Amy's niece, Dr. Joy Michele Cline-Phinney, a concert pianist, entertained family and friends in their music room by playing classical music on the two grand pianos.

Sometimes in my family we have heartfelt conversations by the fire or play traditional card games, dominoes, Scrabble, Monopoly, and so on. Irma P. Hall, who played Mother Joe in *Soul Food*, Ella in *Beloved*, and Minerva in *Midnight in the Garden of Good and Evil*, said that when she was a child she played the piano, twirled the baton, and sang, because children were expected to entertain people: "You got up and performed your little stuff like my grandchildren do now." Being an actress limits the time Irma is home, even during the holidays. On the road she and her fellow performers entertain each other by reading their own poetry and stories, singing, or playing an instrument.

Setting the Scene

Whether it means designing a few flower arrangements or decorating an entire room, every celebration and party is enhanced by a theme. What better theme can you have than the December holidays? My stage-setting begins outside, and I work my way in. I decorate for the Thanksgiving Day celebration, then make a few obvious changes—Christmas tree, ornaments, fresh flowers, wreath, etc.—for the transition to Christmas décor. Your "scenery" does not have to be costly or extensive just to be inviting and hospitable, part of an atmosphere that puts your guests at ease. You want your guests to feel: The entrance is beckoning, and I feel welcome here. The path to the door, the front lawn, the entrance hall, all tell me I will be embraced by those who live here. The healthy flowers in the yard, the potted plants on the front porch, look like someone tends to them with loving care. A wreath made of magnolia leaves and berries tied with a rich gold-and-black bow hangs on the front door. A welcome mat reflecting nature's colors rests at my feet. When the door opens, the smell of a soothing, absorbing fragrance from incense or fresh-cut flowers wafts over me, making me feel a genuine sense of warmth and comfort. Throughout the home, things that are loved and valued by the residents are honored and displayed. The dining tables are set with extraordinary care. The sound of smooth music and the smell of food cooking make me feel as though I am home. As my host greets me with a smile, I relax to enjoy my stay!

Table Settings

When Christmas arrives I begin by laying out a crisp, freshly ironed table-cloth on my dining table, maybe damask or lace, or a simple solid-color cloth that will accent the other table accessories. For variety I sometimes use a colorful runner stitched in seasonal colors or made of an African print to accent the center of the table, or I lay a beautiful piece of fabric that captures the season's theme over a plain tablecloth (which serves as a table skirt). For the centerpiece, I arrange flowers into short-stemmed bouquets with local greenery. Try to avoid centerpieces that hide your view of the person seated opposite you, and while it's nice to have a few small ornaments or other decorations on the table, remember you need as much space on it for eating as possible (see photos in insert).

One Christmas I placed gold candleholders between my brother John's sculptures. The African print fabric in black, gold, and silver was purchased from a fabric store and used as a tablecloth. Decorative gourds and bouquets on a champagne satin runner completed the decorations for this Christmas table setting. The place setting's napkin ring was made from a gold organza ribbon.

At garage sales (something San Francisco has plenty of most week-ends) and flea markets I have bought candleholders in a variety of styles and sizes. I picked up a stylish set of antique china to complement my dining room colors for about a third of its value at an antique sale, and

The author's Christmas mantel LEWIS WATTS

my crystal goblets came from an estate sale. I don't buy sets of seasonal china, because it's too limiting. It's more practical to buy seasonal accessories—a set of Christmas salad or dessert plates, or glasses—that coordinate with your table settings. The china I like to use at Christmas is gold and white and mixes well with the season and with other china I own, so I can use it year 'round.

Cloth napkins are my preference. I always want my guests to have the best. I may use elegantly designed paper napkins for a very large party, however.

If someone among your friends or family has a fine handwriting or calligraphy skills, you can create charming menu cards or place cards. My good friend Denise Wilson suggests an entertaining way to tell people where to sit: make photocopies of childhood pictures of your guests, frame them, and set them out as place cards.

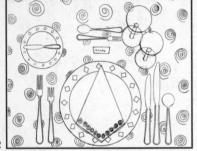

ILLUSTRATION 1. A CASUAL ENTERTAINING SETTING

This is an informal place setting that includes (l. to r.) salad fork, dinner fork, dinner plate with napkin in place, dinner knife, and a teaspoon. The water glass is placed directly over the knife. My table settings are placed a thumb's length from the edge of the table and they are always symmetrically spaced. Remember to give your guests enough space to eat comfortably.

ILLUSTRATION 2. A MORE FORMAL DINNER SETTING

This is a more formal place setting. It begins (l. to r.) with a dinner fork, a salad fork, a dinner plate with napkin in place, salad knife, dinner knife, and soup spoon. Above this (l. to r.) are the butter plate, with butter knife, the dessert fork and spoon with place card beneath, a water goblet, and a wineglass.

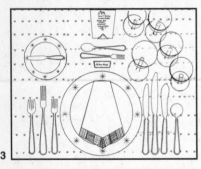

ILLUSTRATION 3. A FORMAL TABLE SETTING

This place setting is for a five-course meal that includes soup, fish, entrée, salad, and dessert. From left to right, the fish fork, dinner fork, salad fork, place plate with napkin centered, salad knife, dinner knife, fish knife, and a soup spoon. Above the main setting (l. to r.), are the butter plate, with butter knife, dessert fork and spoon with place card beneath, and water goblet. Behind the water goblet are the champagne glass, red-wine glass, white-wine glass, and the sherry glass (to be used for the soup course). A menu card is placed above the dessert utensils. Remember that silverware is placed in the order it is to be used, working from the outside in. The use of a butter plate is becoming more common in formal table settings. If there is no finger bowl used, the dessert silver will be set as shown.

ILLUSTRATION 4. THE BUFFET TABLE

There are two ways to set up for serving buffet style. The dining tables can be set using the necessary utensils or the guests will pick up their eating utensils and napkins at the end of the buffet table after they have served themselves. The plates should always be laid out at the head end of the buffet table, and a menu card (as shown) is a nice addition to inform your guests what they will be served.

ILLUSTRATION 5. THE BEVERAGE TABLE OR BAR

The nonalcoholic drinks (including bottled water), the ice bucket, punchbowl, eggnog, or cider can all be set up on a separate table in a way that makes it convenient for guests to serve themselves. The wines, champagne, and a variety of glasses are also placed on the beverage table.

ILLUSTRATION 6. THE DESSERT BUFFET TABLE

This table is set up like a regular buffet table. The menu card (optional) and serving plates are at the head of the table and the napkins and eating utensils are placed at the far end (for when the guests have finished serving themselves). Dessert candies can also be placed on this table or left on the dining tables for your guests. My guests have the coffee service in conjunction with dessert. I also offer champagne for those guests who prefer it with their dessert.

ILLUSTRATION 7. THE AFTER-DINNER COFFEE TABLE

If you are having a large party this is one way to serve coffee after dinner. Include a pot of regular brewed coffee and a pot of decaf, tea, a sugar bowl with white or brown sugar cubes, creamer, sugar substitute, fresh lemon, and honey (for the tea). Champagne, glasses, cups, saucers, and spoons are also placed on this table.

NOTE: For a small dinner party, I prefer to serve the dessert from the dining-room table. The after-dinner coffee service is brought in on a silver tray and the host or hostess serves both. A variation would be to serve dessert and coffee in another room. This gives your guests a chance to get up from the table and mingle. After-dinner liqueurs, drinks, and water can be offered after the dessert and coffee service have concluded.

SANDRA B. JIMINEZ, ILLUSTRATOR

Once my guests have served themselves from the buffet tables, everyone sits down to eat at a set table. An extra bottle of red and white wine and or champagne is always on the table, and I ensure that white wines and champagnes remain chilled. I also provide each guest with a cool glass of water, leaving a pitcher filled with ice water on the dining table(s).

Seating Arrangements

At family dinners, the parents might sit at opposite ends of the table, with the grandparents or elders seated in places of honor, or the elders may prefer to sit together. Song stylist Nancy Wilson, who sometimes has over seventy people for Thanksgiving dinner, sets aside one dining table for the elders in the family. Sometimes kids like to have their own table for holiday dinners. On the other hand, my own kids always enjoyed eating with the adults; otherwise they felt excluded. It is all a matter of preference and style.

For more formal occasions, there is always a designated host for each dining table. This ensures that everyone at the table is introduced to each other and seated comfortably and that the conversation flows. A prominent guest in your home—for example, your minister—should have a seat of honor at the table. The spouse of this person is given equal rank at the table. For example, the most important man is seated to the right of the hostess, and the second most important man is seated to her left. The most important woman is seated to the male host's right, and the second most important woman is seated to his left. Seat people in alternating sexes around the table—unless you are short one or two of either sex. Let common sense prevail, and have people who would enjoy one another sit together.

Special Toasts

It keeps the joy and focus of the season alive to offer a toast before sitting down to dinner, or at an appropriate time during the course of the meal. You can toast your ancestors, the new year, your host, a special guest, or family elders.

Bargain Hunting

Sheila Bridges
PHOTOGRAPHER CARL POSEY

You don't have to fly to Paris or Rome or scour Bloomingdale's or high-end antique stores to find decorating elegance. One Sunday morning I surprised myself by actually getting to San Francisco's Alemany Flea Market around 6:30 A.M., early enough to find a bargain hunter's dream: for fifteen dollars I picked up two complete sets of banquet-sized chafing dishes. On another visit I got a steal on punch bowls and matching cups, along with several antique linen tablecloths and elegant French plant containers.

Scouring the flea market makes it easy to find all sorts of unusual housewares, including vases and glassware. I have also found bargains on sterling silver candlesticks, chandeliers, furniture and all kinds of useful items for entertaining.

My partner in crime when it comes to shopping for bargains is Gwendolyn Williams. We have both furnished our homes through visits to estate sales, antique auctions, garage sales, and the like. For us, shopping is like a treasure hunt, and we find the whole experience therapeutic and fun. Some beautiful pieces can be found at great prices.

New York interior designer Sheila Bridges also uses the past to enrich the present. She works out of her apartment in a landmark 1901 building in Harlem, a neighborhood she finds important to her as an African American. "There's such rich cultural history here," she says. Sheila buys a lot of her entertaining accessories from auctions, flea markets, estate sales, and specialty stores, which she says are "great resources that people should tap into to buy beautiful glassware, porcelain, glass crystal, and china. Even if there are a few missing pieces, you can buy largely intact sets. I have a few sets and they coordinate well. I also mix and match the glassware." She uses her wonderful collection of Depression-era glass as part of her stylish table settings. "It looks elegant by candlelight, and people appreciate something a little out of the ordinary. It is a free-spirited way of decorating your table," says Sheila. At a recent holiday party, she used place cards to encourage people to meet new friends, mixing people up so that those who were already comfortable together didn't necessarily get to sit together.

Outside Help

If you don't have fun at your party, why have a party in the first place? Be a participatory host. The key to enjoying your party is to not overwhelm yourself with too much work. Know when to ask for outside help from friends, family, or professionals.

Be sure not to disappear into the kitchen for long periods of time. Also, try to clean up as you go along, keeping your kitchen organized as you cook. That way, by the time you serve, you won't have a daunting mess to deal with later. I'm constantly washing pots and utensils as I work and putting away excess kitchen implements before guests arrive. Once your guests have settled in, don't start cleaning up while you should be entertaining them. Clean up after they leave.

For a catered event, look for a reputable caterer, with referrals from satisfied customers. Get feedback from people you know, if you can, and interview each caterer personally. Obviously, you won't want a caterer who arrives late or is poorly prepared. Make sure you understand how each caterer works and what the cost will be before you decide on which one to hire.

Rental companies can provide everything a person needs to put on a successful event. I like Alma Arrington Brown's idea of renting gold bamboo hotel-style dining chairs to replace her heavier, larger chairs for Christmas dinner so she can comfortably accommodate more people at her dining room table.

Oh Dear, What to Wear?

Guests may ask you what you are going to wear to your dinner or party. I try to choose something sophisticated, yet comfortable enough so I can enjoy freedom of movement. Sometimes it's fun to ask guests to dress in a certain color, or even in period costumes. Blanche Brown, in the tradition of black-and-white balls, gave a birthday party and asked her guests to wear black and white—then surprised them all by turning up in a hot red number. It was certainly easy to spot the hostess that night.

It is important for couples and families to be on the same page when dressing for an event. Talk over what you are wearing so that you will compliment each other.

Tips for Guests

The guest's responsibility is to have a good time. Your host invited you anticipating that you would contribute to the party. Don't arrive empty-handed. Guests who bring something, no matter how small, are appreciated for the gesture.

Some of my pet peeves include the following:

- People who don't R.S.V.P. when asked to on the invitation
- People who "wolf down" their food
- People who use toothpicks at the table to clean their teeth
- People who don't give their host a chance to say grace before eating
- People who don't help the elders at the table
- People who monopolize the conversation
- People who don't thank their hosts
- People who gossip about the hosts or other guests at a party

Christmas Pleasures, Christmas Treasures

The giver is always superior to the gift; it's the spirit of the giver that makes the gift what it is or is not.

Gwendolyn Goldsby Grant

When Marcheta Q'McManus-Eneas was seven years old, her family moved from South Carolina to an African-American community along the Chesapeake River. Started by Frederick Douglass, Arundel on the Bay was a community of seventeen middle-class families who hailed from West Virginia, Tennessee, the Carolinas, and other points south. There were also summer homes owned by professionals who would come down from New York, Baltimore, Washington, and Philadelphia for vacations and holiday gatherings. "Christmas was a time for cousins and our immediate family," she says. It was also a time for regaining a sense of community and strengthening family ties.

Every house had something going on. Once the kids were out of school for the holidays, Marcheta's house became a neighborhood focal point. Her mother, a church music director, would play the piano and all the neighborhood kids would rehearse singing Christmas carols together.

After drinking hot apple cider and eating cookies, they would bundle up and go caroling from house to house, performing four or five songs at each. Their neighbors would then invite them in and offer them something to eat. "We'd sure be well fed after a night like that," she says. Even though Marcheta now lives in the balmy Bahamas, she continues this enchanting tradition today.

Marcheta also remembers Arundel's snow-covered hills in winter, and that every child had a sled. "The kids would tie their sleds together in a straight line—there could be as many as twenty sleds—and the lead sled would be tied to their neighbor Dr. Theodore Johnson's Thunderbird. He would then drive slowly around the neighborhood, pulling all these sleds with kids in them. We had hours of fun, sometimes falling off and having to run to catch up to the others, then diving back onto our sleds. One year we did it in a blinding snowstorm."

There were also snowmen and snowball fights, and another Maryland tradition, the snow cream. "We would always go outside when the snow was fresh and remove the top layer to get really clean snow and put it in a pitcher and pour cream and sugar in it and stir it up and drink it—this must have been the first slushie!"

Blessings Bestowed—The Art of Gift Giving

What does Christmas mean to you? Do you also celebrate Kwanzaa? Is the end of the year a time for you to reflect on the past months and gather strength for the year to come?

Is it a time to rejoice in your friends, count your blessings, and cheer on those you love? Is it a time to give back to your community? To reconnect with your forebears? A time to worship, to celebrate tradition, to keep joy alive, to accentuate the positive? For me it's all of these things.

One of my most profound Christmas experiences came about many years ago on a trip to Cost Plus, an imported food and home accessories store, with my dear friend Gale Madyun, a single parent of three children, the same age as mine. Gale and I had a good time shopping for the kids that day. She was overcoming some financial challenges, and I saw how excited and appreciative she became at being able to purchase Christmas gifts. There were Christmases when she couldn't afford to buy gifts. Sometimes when you think you have it hard, something happens to make you aware of the sacrifices others make during the holidays. I came to appreciate how fortunate my family was, and I admired Gale's strength and endurance.

It's not the gift that counts, but the thought. I've now lived long enough to understand what "simple abundance" means, and how much pleasure we can have during the holiday season, no matter what our financial circumstances. In the end, it's the spirit with which the gift is given that resonates.

"People think they have nothing to give if they have no money, and they get the blues," said Gwendolyn Goldsby Grant, a specialist in relationships and author of *The Best Kind of Loving: A Black Woman's Guide to Finding Intimacy.* "But you can give words and stroke people with your beautiful words. The problem is that we often don't think we have anything valuable inside of us worth giving."

There are all kinds of ways to give gifts and all kinds of gifts to bestow. I begin the process by thinking about who needs what and what I can give. The worst thing you can do, I think, is to give someone a gift that has no relationship to the recipient's values or style. Think about others' needs and wants, and the great idea will surely come to you.

I don't want to buy into the raw commercialism the retailers barrage us with. And I dislike going into stores before the fall school season starts, only to find the shelves full of Christmas items. The marketing of Christmas has distracted many in our society from its true spiritual meaning. I doubt the Wise Men bringing incense and myrrh to baby Jesus had to max out on their credit cards to pull it off.

Some people judge the joy of the holiday on what they get materially. Gift giving should be pleasurable and done with a sense of freedom. So give what you can and give how you want to. Don't lose the true meaning of the Christmas season, which is about the spirit of giving of ourselves.

My spirituality is reflected in my nature, in my soul, and in the way I walk and talk and treat those around me. That's the part of me that will know what to give a friend at Christmas, or for Kwanzaa, or for a birthday, and year 'round. When I give love it comes from my soul.

We can teach our kids about charity—that's one aspect of giving. They also must appreciate the value of giving itself. The act means, "I thought of you and gave you what I could. I gave you something of myself, or I made you something with my own hands, which cost that precious commodity, time."

Zora Kramer Brown, a public relations professional and founder and chairperson of Cancer Awareness Program Services and the Breast Cancer Resource Committee, agrees that Christmas is a holiday for giving of oneself. As a holiday present, she might cook a friend's favorite meal or take care of her niece's children for a weekend.

Peggy Cooper Cafritz, founder of the Duke Ellington School of the Arts in Washington, D.C., is guided by the spirit of the person to whom she is giving her gift. She has traditionally given her children works of art for Christmas and their birthdays in order to ensure they have an art collection as they grow older. "It's also a good time of the year to contribute to the African-American economy," she suggests.

Toys From Christmas Past

Myrlie Evers-Williams, chairman emeritus of the National Board of Directors of the National Association for the Advancement of Colored People (NAACP), told me the following story to illustrate what giving means to her: "I wanted a scooter, a red scooter. I craved a scooter. One Christmas, I had wanted it so bad, but I didn't get it, so that desire carried on to the next Christmas. My parents couldn't afford to buy that metal red scooter for me. So my dad, who was not necessarily handy with tools, made a scooter for me from extra wood he had. He found some old, discarded roller skates. Back then, roller skates had two wheels in the front and two wheels in the back. He pried off the four wheels and put them on the wood plank and painted it red. I cherished that scooter until I was a teenager. Because one, it was done out of love, and two, it was a lesson to

Myrlie Evers-Williams
JAMES V. PHOTOGRAPHY

me—one that my grandmother brought to my young attention—that you don't always get what you want when you want it, but eventually, you will if you work toward it. It's a lesson I've never forgotten. It was one of patience, one of perseverance, and I think, without preaching to our children, we need to be able to impart the lesson to them that Christmas is a time of rejoicing. It's a time of giving. I think it's also a time of professing one's life and where you'll be going, leading into the next year."

Medgar and Myrlie Evers were married on Christmas Eve 1951. As most people know, Medgar Evers, field secretary for the Mississippi NAACP, was assassinated outside his home in Jackson, on June 12, 1963, for his work in the civil rights movement. "So I'll always have that little twinge of something on Christmas Eve," she says. "It was something my second husband understood. I didn't burden him with it, but he knew it would be on my mind."

Myrlie's husband Walter E. Williams, himself a civil rights activist, died in 1995. "In 1994, that Christmas was an extremely special one because we both knew that would be the last Christmas we had together," she told me. "So we enjoyed each other. We laughed, we cried, we remembered. We had the tree and the festivities; we had people in, and we made the most of the situation."

Myrlie's schedule no longer permits her involvement in all the Christmas preparation these days. Her work keeps her traveling, but she makes sure she spends the holidays with family and friends.

Myrlie's children, Darrell Kenyatta, Reena Denise, and James Van Dyke, all adults now, always reminisce about what Christmas was like for them growing up. Her four grandchildren may request, "Grandmama, tell us what it was like in your day." The Christmas after their grandfather, Medgar Evers, was killed, the family declared a "black Christmas"—not in the sense of "black is beautiful," but in terms of buying no gifts. Although they did have a tree that year, the lights were all green or red, which to Myrlie represented the pain that they were all in.

"Now I'm at a point in my life where I want to simplify instead of complicate," she says. "I want to be thankful for what I have and put that to use and not be the kind of consumer I have been in the past. This thing keeps coming back to me: *simplify, simplify, simplify*. When I get carried away over the thrill of an expensive Christmas, I remind myself of what I have and remember those who have less. I try to reach out and help others—that's something I've tried to impart to my children."

"Images tell us about ourselves," says Gwendolyn Goldsby Grant, who grew up in Canton, Ohio, where no colored dolls were to be found. "Mother believed I should have a colored doll. So she looked in a lot of catalogs and the black newspapers and finally found some in Memphis, Tennessee. The dolls she got me were cute ones with cherubic faces and brown skin, not those more-common ugly black dolls that were caricatures of blackness, with that hideous, wide-eyed look like they are in a constant state of surprise or fear, with red lips, and hair sticking straight up. My mother rejected those. I could even give my dolls a bath. No one else in my community had a black rubber doll. If someone gave me a white doll, Mother would say I had to have a black doll, too, because this is not just a white or black world, but a world with all kinds of people."

Dr. Gwendolyn Goldsby Grant

Gifts From the Heart

One year when my youngest son Omar was in elementary school, he gave me "love coupons"—a coupon book he made in school in which he promised to do different things to help me. The coupons entitled me to a night out, a Sunday off, breakfast in bed, and hugs and kisses.

Though he's now twenty-five years old and an ensign in the U.S. Navy, I think there may still be a coupon left in that book—and I don't think there was a time limit on his future good deeds. (Wouldn't this make a great gift idea for a grandparent? A child could include a coupon for washing the car or mowing the lawn.)

Another year my son Jule presented me with a scroll he made during his elementary school days regarding a covenant he made with God: He promised not to fight with his brother and sister so much! Jule, a strong young man, has given me many gifts from the heart during his twenty-seven years, including painting the exterior and interior of our house, rebuilding a part of my deck, and landscaping our yard.

Following Jule and Melanie's wedding, I made photo albums using color photocopies of some of their wedding pictures and presented one each to my mother and mother-in-law.

A card given to someone we are fond of takes thought and effort, and that's a gift in itself. Melanie and my daughter Zahrah will send you a card out of the blue, just to surprise you and make you feel good about yourself. They always choose meaningful cards and write sentimental messages to me and the rest of the family. Why not? The holidays aren't the only time for telling a person exactly why she's special to you, recalling things she's helped you with or fond memories you've shared.

When Zahrah was a financially challenged graduate student, she used to spend hours at Christmastime searching for beautiful frames and decorating them with flowers. Inside, she'd put a poem she'd written or the recipient's name, drawn in calligraphy.

As a special gift, you may want to write a letter of appreciation to someone who has been particularly kind to you this year, or send your friends a framed photo of them that you took during the year.

Or you might consider lending someone a hand, using your own skills to get something done they can't handle themselves. For instance, you might surf the Internet for someone who doesn't know how to use a computer, string holiday lights for a senior citizen who can't get up on a ladder, or run errands for a neighbor who doesn't drive. Ask your friends and neighbors what you can do for them. You might be surprised at how easy and rewarding it is to be of service.

Actress Irma P. Hall grew up in Beaumont, Texas. She loves to make her own Christmas gifts. Using paint and other handicrafts, she creates small treasures for her dearest friends, always giving something of herself. If she's working during a holiday season, she likes to surprise everyone in the cast and crew with a homemade inspiration; she may make something for the actors based on the characters they're portraying. She also designs Christmas cards and decorates dolls as gifts. Irma believes the meaning in a gift comes directly from making it as personal and heartfelt as possible.

Phyllis Yvonne Stickney, who made her television debut in *The Women of Brewster Place*, is "proud to have been nurtured above 110th Street in Harlem." This time of the year the principles of Kwanzaa have special meaning for her; she reflects on the fact that she as a real *nia* (purpose) and that her *imani* (faith) has been working all year to bring her to this time and place. Giving back to the community is important to Phyllis, and so is giving back to her mother, who has always been so understanding. But Phyllis does not get caught up in "you have two more shopping days left 'til Christmas." When it comes to gifts, she searches for "objects made by black artisans, a weaver, a worker of wonderful patterns." She likes her mother to wear these fabulous textile designs: "Mom used to dress me, now I want to dress her." If her mother admires something Phyllis wore, Phyllis tries to buy that for her—that's the African way, she says.

The Stickney family

Artist and furniture designer Cheryl R. Riley says, "The Christmas season allows us to expose our higher nature." What bothers her, though, is that

Christmases Past

- Sheila Frazier will never forget the burgundy "Mary Jane" shoes with little holes on top she received as a girl and how wonderful it felt to put them on. She also remembers how she and her sisters saved their pennies to buy her mother blue and orange plastic earrings (they had little fans on them), which they proudly watched her put on and wear to walk down the street. "Mom treated the gift so special," says Sheila. "They were gaudy, and now I think she looked absurd, but at the time, we thought they looked like diamonds," she said.

- Amy Billingsley wanted a dog when she was little. "Look at that toy dog, he's so pretty!" she exclaimed one Christmas morning. "Then the little dog moved, and I jumped sky high, I was so excited," she recalls.

- Pauletta Pearson Washington remembers her greatest gifts, which she likes to give in turn: "a chance, life, love, and the gift of forgiveness."

- Ruth Beckford recalls her father insisting that each child start his or her own Christmas bank account to make sure they had money to buy their gifts at year's end. Ruth still maintains this practice today.

- Gwendolyn Williams was moved by this gesture her family made one year when she was having kind of a rough time: They switched from the tradition of each picking a name to buy one gift for, and instead each bought something thoughtful just for her.

- Janet Langhart remembers how her mother used to number the family's gifts according to which one she wanted them to open first, beginning with the least valuable.

- Growing up in Leola "Roscoe" Higgs-Dellums's family, the older siblings had the responsibility of keeping the Santa Claus fantasy alive for the younger ones. As an adult, she once gave the gift of gab: She was able to surprise her sisters, who were scattered all over the map, by arranging a Christmas-day conference call.

- Joan Sonn is married to the former South African ambassador to the United States. On her first Christmas visit from her native South Africa in the 1970s, she was amazed by the number of gifts children received: "In my country, children don't get that many presents. They may get one or two, and are satisfied with that." Her Christmases were very simple, but being with family and the happiness they shared was very special. They were always mindful of Christmas's true meaning.

some people feel this is the only time of the year to do so. "I like to see that holiday spirit carried throughout the year." Not comfortable with spending a lot of money on presents, she often makes her own gifts. An admitted pack rat, she accumulates unusual things all year long, and these eventually become gifts.

Cheryl starts making her presents in November: bottles of homemade salad dressing embellished with her own hand-printed labels and adorned with ribbons; fans bought from an art supply store, then decorated with paints and varnishes; and gift boxes, which she buys plain and decoupages using paper printed with Chinese scenes, then fills with Chinese candies and decorative crystals. Her boxes also make terrific jewelry boxes or desk organizers.

Remembering how sick she was in May 1996, after the delivery of their third child—complications of childbirth left her paralyzed and in a wheelchair for a year—Jacqueline Mitchell Rice told me how wonderful it was when her husband, San Francisco 49er Jerry Rice, asked her what the one thing she really wanted for Christmas that year would be. She asked him to send for her family; most of them hadn't seen her since she had become ill. So Jerry sent for her relatives, and that year there were thirty-five of them under one roof for a week and a half.

The Rice family

On Christmas morning, her daughter Jaquí played the piano, and they sang Christmas carols. They then prayed together and exchanged personal thoughts about the meaning of Christmas. "Their blessings and responses were so heartwarming," says Jacqueline, who is now recovered from the illness she says "was the hardest struggle of my life."

The Gift of Charity

Sheila Frazier
JAMES FEE, PHOTOGRAPHER

Sheila Frazier grew up in the housing projects on New York's Lower East Side. She began her career as an actress and is now producer and associate director of Black Entertainment Television's west coast network operations. Her motto for the holidays is simply, "Send me someone that I can be a blessing to." That's exactly what happened in 1997 when a mother and grandmother who was caring for nine children and going through tough times faxed her a letter asking for help. Sheila was not only glad to help, she also enlisted her son, Derek, and others to chip in, with contributions of toys and money for the troubled family. She truly enjoys helping people who can't help themselves. "It's the most wonderful feeling to know you've been able to affect someone's life. I thank God for putting me together with people at the right time," she says.

For Pauletta and Denzel Washington, Christmas is a time to be grateful for the wonderful lives they share with their four children. It's also a time to give back to the community. For the past several years they have participated in a toy drive. The Washington family goes to impoverished areas of South Central Los Angeles and distributes new clothing and toys donated by friends and associates. "To see some of these children's faces light up just to receive a gift as simple as a ball just makes it all worthwhile," Pauletta says. "This also keeps things in perspective for our children, who don't demand a lot of presents."

Gifts to Yourself

Don't forget to soothe holiday stress and renew your own spirit over the holidays by giving yourself a gift or two, as well. My childhood friend Joel Swisher gave me a gift certificate to Nordstrom's spa for my birthday present one year. A manicure and a pedicure, a bubble bath, a facial—all are great ways to treat yourself.

Memorable Wraps

Belva Davis's family has fun wrapping small gifts as though they are big ones. They pile all the gifts high in front of each recipient, then open them in round-robin style. There are so many ways to wrap a present and so many places to find beautiful gift wrap, fabrics, boxes, bags, tags, and bows today, whether you shop for them at an estate sale, stationery store, discount emporium, specialty boutique, art store, or flower mart. The Christmas Tree Shops in the New England area are great places to buy quality wrappings at discount, too. Buying cloth at fabric stores can be less costly than traditional wrapping paper and prettier, too. You can also use seam binding instead of ribbons. Patricia Russell-McCloud used yards of white tulle to wrap a gift basket, and it looked like a cloud. For her, "the gift and presentation are of equal importance."

I find it's also fun to make my own gift wrapping, using unusual printed paper or ethnic fabric. African prints can be used to tie gift packages or to wrap your gifts. You can contrast colorful ribbons with plain brown paper. A picture or map of Africa (or any geographical area favored by the recipient) can be blown up to a larger size and used to wrap a gift.

Tissue comes in all sorts of varieties today; there's metallic paper in silver and gold; you can also find rice paper and colorful cellophane. Raffia (long, thin, neutral-colored fibers used to make hats and baskets and tie plants), rickrack (silk rolled into a cord), or grosgrain ribbon with decorative elements can be used to dress up any paper or cloth.

I always include a gift card with the gift.

I remember all the times I stayed up late wrapping gifts. This is certainly the moment of truth if you forgot to buy enough wrapping paper and all the stores have closed. That's when it's time to improvise. Once when my friend Denise Wilson found herself out of wrapping paper, she remembered that the fellow the gift was for liked to read the comics. So she wrapped the present in the comics section and tied it decoratively. He was delighted.

Still, better to be prepared. Have plenty of tissue, boxes, tape, ribbon, and wrapping paper around during December.

4

Holiday Decorating, Our Way

As a child there was the wonder of waking up and knowing that Christmas was a special day. I was not quite sure what was in store for me. It was just having that childlike wonder of the day, knowing that the spirit in the air was different. It was a child's time in our household. My mother really tried to make it festive for me. I deeply loved it. She decorated the house with a dramatic flair, transforming what we had to something that was really magical!

Christel Albritton MacLean

The smell of pinecones in the air takes me back. I remember how much fun my family had together decorating the house and tree and creating a warm and inviting atmosphere when I was a child. We also felt so proud once my father finished stringing the lights outside, which would signal the excitement I felt anticipating Christmas. On weekend evenings my family, friends, and I would drive around Oakland and the East Bay hills to see the neighbors' houses in all their glory, aglow with colorful Christmas lights.

O Christmas Tree

Sometimes grown kids need a bit of coaxing when it comes to helping decorate for the holidays. But overall, my kids feel that decorating our house should be a family event.

The tree is definitely my family's Christmas focal point, but it's getting expensive to keep up this tradition. One year I must have spent eighty dollars on a tall, graceful tree that only lasted two weeks. We certainly did enjoy it; I wouldn't spend that much again, though. The kids always had fun helping to choose the tree, though we wouldn't always agree on which one to pick. Then there were those years we'd drive up to Petaluma in Sonoma County to cut down a less expensive Christmas tree in majestic farm country. The kids just loved seeing the farm animals, something they had missed out on, growing up in the city. Once we came back with a crooked tree, but we shimmed the base, hoping to straighten it out. Our efforts were unsuccessful, and that was the year we decorated a somewhat tilted but beautiful tree.

Another year, my brother John's family came along with us to cut down our tree. This time we made a family outing of it, ordering pizza and socializing before we unloaded our trees at our respective homes. Then there was the year I said we just couldn't afford a tree. But driving home the day before Christmas I passed a lot with only three trees left. The owner was closing down, and he practically gave me a lovely, tall tree for free.

Recently my son Omar went with me to select a tree. At one lot, we looked around and started to walk out; the owner came after us and asked what was wrong. I said it was all just too expensive. He asked me what I had expected to pay. I answered, "Around twenty-five dollars." He told me to point out the one I'd like, and off we went with a lovely seven-foot tree.

This year I remind myself to do a better job of packing away my ornaments and to stow them away in the same place so I'll find them easily next year. Every year I feel I must be missing one or two boxes of decorations somewhere.

When my children were young, I used to have Christmas decorations enthusiastically scattered in each of our four bedrooms and an Advent calendar hung for each child. We had some type of decoration or ornament hanging from somewhere in each room, as well as stuffed animals dressed up in their Christmas finery, or garlands with Christmas greetings. As my children have gotten older I've decided to decorate only the main rooms of the house. I also give myself more than one day to arrange my decorations. Otherwise, I feel rushed and it's no fun. And why is it inevitable that every year, some of my lights don't work?

Hearth and Home

These days, there are great outdoor light displays, even sophisticated moving ones. During the holiday season the home section of most newspapers offers lots of advice and ideas on holiday decorating, including tips on installing outdoor lights. Safety is my biggest concern. For example, I've learned you have to use the proper lights and extension cords for outdoors and, of course, *never* staple or nail lights, since this can damage the wiring, creating a fire hazard. My best advice? If you're not sure how to put up outdoor lights, get knowledgeable help.

A dramatic front door intrigues the visitor about what's inside. Ruth Beckford, dancer, choreographer, teacher, actress, and author of *Still Groovin': Affirmations for Women in the Second Half of Life*, used to lavishly embellish the front door of her apartment (in an interior hallway) by making it look like a big Christmas package covered with aluminum foil and a big bow, or she would cover the door with Christmas wrapping paper and hang all of her holiday cards on it. One year she managed to mount branches with cones on the front door so it looked like the entire tree was growing right there.

Traditional wreaths on the front door are always charming. My son Jule made a wreath hook so I wouldn't damage my front door. The hook hangs over the top of the door so nails aren't needed to hold the wreath. It's easily made using part of a wire clothes hanger, or you can buy one at the hardware or crafts store.

I love to buy a fresh wreath from the flower mart, then add a gold-and-silver bow or one made from an African fabric. A hydrangea wreath or a wreath made of magnolia leaves with dried fruits and berries makes a lush and unusual decoration. Since I got to the flower mart a little late this year, I found a fresh wreath and garland at half price. Prices were being reduced as we got closer to the Big Day. I also bought three iris bouquets and a spray of eucalyptus and holly berries, all for twenty-five dollars. Although most people like to complete their decorations a little earlier than that, my timing was right this time.

SANDRA B. JIMINEZ, ILLUSTRATOR

Aromatic eucalyptus wreaths can be displayed year 'round and last for several years. You can change the decorative accessories to reflect the season. For example, for Thanksgiving, add ears of dried corn or miniature pumpkins and an orange bow. For Christmas, use ornaments or imitation apples and pears, and tie it with a rich red taffeta bow.

An entryway can be decorated with seasonal plants such as topiaries, poinsettias, and cymbidiums. Topiaries in turn can be decorated with tiny Christmas lights or small ornaments. Urns, garden statues, Christmas lights, and garland make an inviting entryway. This illustration includes window decorations with red, green, and gold ribbons (some of the colors found in Kente cloth or Kente cloth could be used), hung with miniature holly berry wreaths. The fresh pine wreath on the front door is accented with holly berries.

Alma Arrington Brown, senior vice president of Chevy Chase Bank Corporation and widow of the late United States Secretary of Commerce Ronald H. Brown, selects a huge fresh wreath from the same florist every year for her front door. It comes decorated with pinecones and imitation apples and is tied off-center with a wonderful oversize red bow.

You can drape swags of garland anywhere—over mirrors, doorways, mantels, around urns, down staircases, over outdoor fences, around pillars, gates, or mailboxes. Christmas tree lights and ornaments can be intertwined with the garland, as seen in the insert photo. The garland was provided by Perata Brothers Wholesale of San Francisco. It has small red lights and imitation fruit. I used heavy green florist's twine to connect the garland to my banister, so that I wouldn't damage the paint or finish.

By the way, certain types of fresh garland are very fragile. They become dry and the needles fall out, making a real mess. A professionally preserved garland is best for indoor use, as it won't drop a lot of needles all over your carpets and floors. It can be found at nursery wholesalers, florists, and other plant specialists. It's a little more expensive to buy these, but cost-effective in the long run. These preserved garlands should last for many years.

Nutcrackers sit in front of a pedestal in the entranceway photo. I used a Kente cloth with red as the dominant color, accenting the gold chair for Christmas. Miniature cherubic black angels hang on the background wall of the staircase, all accented by gold frames.

Mantels can be decorated with candles in various sizes and scents. Decorate the mantel garland with bows or ornaments for a rich, classic feel. African cloths can be draped from the mantel, too. I buy red and pink amaryllis (indigenous to Africa) and scented paperwhite (narcissus) bulbs and plant them in urns or decorative pots in time for the bulbs to be blooming at Christmas and Kwanzaa. They are a nice addition to a mantel, entranceway stand, or coffee table. Christmas tree clippings are also great for accessorizing your mantels or Christmas table.

You might want to place decorative bowls on the mantel filled with pecans, macadamia nuts, walnuts, and a variety of dried fruits, including pineapples, apricots, apples, pears, persimmons, raisins, cranberries, and plantain chips. Boughs of holly hung over the fireplace or placed in vases around the living and dining rooms can also add a classic touch to holiday décor.

Friends Brian Charron, owner of a business that specializes in creative furniture and interior decoration, and Patrick Weibeler decorated my mantel with gold mesh fabric and bows they made out of red and gold paper. They also pinned bows around the fireplace screen and windows. We used a collection of black angels, a regal Black-a-Moor (African prince), and Father Christmas, to decorate the fireplace mantel. The angels

The author's buffet/mantel with black angels
LEWIS WATTS

include a Kwanzaa angel, choir angels, colorful tree toppers, mantel top-pers, and tree ornaments, as well as ceramic stocking holders that hold needlepoint Christmas stockings. The angels are interspersed with my African statues, including an elder tribesman from Nigeria, a Somali war-rior, a carved fertility statue from Ghana, and a bust of an African woman my mother brought from Zimbabwe. There's also a Somali mask I picked up at a flea market.

Most of the ornaments, candles, and angels pictured in these pho-tographs were provided by Bumbershoot, an interior and garden design studio Janine Beachum owns in collaboration with her mother, Jacque-line Beachum. It specializes in African-American collectibles. Decorations that reflect my culture are sometimes difficult to find. When I saw Bum-bershoot's collection I was ecstatic.

Perata Brothers provided the dried herb strings that adorn the sides of the mantel mirror; they come in a variety of choices from bay leaves, garlic, dried apples, cinnamon, pomegranates, quince, chilies, beans, corn, and gourds. A collection of candles hand-sculpted with black angels and choir children, a cherub playing a horn, and decorative Christmas boxes adorn the cocktail table.

When my front door opens to greet family and friends they are surrounded by the pleasant fragrance of fresh pine from the garland and Christmas tree. This is the primary scent, but sometimes I also burn incense (nag or classic champa) or essential oils, which are fragrance essences that come from flowers, leaves, barks, roots, and berries. Pour a few drops of the oil mixed with water into the top of a tea-candle container and light the candle at the base. As the liquid heats up, it releases a wonderful fragrance. These oils are therapeutic and have been used to treat many ailments, from insomnia to the common cold. They are used in massage oils, baths, room sprays and perfumes and to refresh potpourri.

The ancient Egyptians used incense and fragrant oils for their religious ceremonies, as well as for medicinal and cosmetic purposes. Erik Holte and Lloyd Sanner, owners of Plain Jane's, a gift emporium in my San Francisco neighborhood, carry Christmas holiday scents, including pine and juniper, evergreen blend, cedar, sandalwood, cinnamon and clove, frankincense, and myrrh. I sometimes burn potpourri during the holidays, too (it's one of the oldest forms of natural fragrance), using cinnamon, orange, or apple aromas. I keep the potpourri in a variety of small urns, decorative dishes, or antique glass bowls on pedestals. Fresh flowers like tuberoses also add a sweet, distinctive scent to my house.

Make sure your scents are compatible with each other; they shouldn't compete. One Christmas scent will always remain in my memory: the smell of a turkey roasting. On Christmas morning my house is redolent with the combined aromas of roasting turkey and that morning's breakfast, which delights everyone as they wake up. I try not to compete with the turkey, as it's the best aroma going.

I avoid overpowering my dinner guests at the table with strong scented candles. A candle with a soft fruit or herb fragrance gives a light, soothing scent and is compatible with the food. For example, Q Limited makes Essence of Nature candles that are blends of such natural fragrant oils as essences of lemon, grapefruit, lavender, tangerine, vanilla, or ylang ylang. Beeswax candles with their attractive honeycomb texture are also popular because they burn slowly and emit a clean honey scent.

Uncommon Scents

- The ancient Egyptians used frankincense for skin preparations. Frankincense trees grow wild in North Africa. It's a popular incense in China, India, and the West.
- Cedarwood was also used by the Egyptians in cosmetics and perfumes—and in the mummification process.
- Myrrh, a resin found in trees in East Africa, is also used in perfumes, incense, and medicines. In China it's a medicine for skin infections and arthritis.
- Eucalyptus is used as a medicine by the Australian aborigines.

The fifty-year-old baby grand piano that belonged to my husband, Jule Edward Farmer, since childhood, has become sort of an altar to his memory. (Though we were divorced when he passed away in 1990, we still remained close as a family.) The piano is pictured in the photo insert. On it I've placed a statue of Selket, one of four goddesses who guarded King Tutankhamen's mummified remains. Selket symbolically protects this shrine, too, with her arms outstretched. The shrine includes a candelabra with candles and a flexible Christmas angel wrap, framed photographs of him with our children, and a bronze head sculpted by my brother John. There are a few Egyptian figurines bought at a garage sale and exquisite hand-blown glass ornaments provided by Bumbershoot depicting an Egyptian scene, including a mask of King Tutankhamen.

My piano bench is draped with a West African print runner in black, red, and peacock blue, given to me by my friend Patrick Wiebeler. On the walls behind the piano are a painting of praying Muslim women called *Mother of Civilization* and a charcoal drawing of James Baldwin, both done by John.

The Tree

As I live in a house with high ceilings, my cut tree is usually between seven and eight feet tall, and quite dramatic. Brian Charron and Patrick Weibeler have kept a potted Monterey pine on their deck for seventeen years. The pot restricts its growth, so it stays a reasonable size, and they keep it fertilized and watered and they bring it inside to use as a Christmas tree each year. They use a quilted tree skirt that belonged to Patrick's mother, something that brings back fond memories of childhood for him. You may decide, particularly if you live in a small space, to buy a small living tree from your nursery, for example, a blue-green spruce or Alberta spruce. You'll need to have a place to plant this in your yard afterward, or you can keep it as a potted plant outside, as Patrick and Brian do.

A cut tree must be kept in water so it won't dry out too fast, causing pine needles to invade your floor space and creating a fire hazard. When you bring the tree inside, it's also a good idea to wrap it in plastic or in a sheet so those pesky pinecones and needles don't scatter all over. It's an even better idea to leave the wrap at the base of the tree, under a skirt of African fabric in seasonal colors or a beautiful fabric with Christmas scenes. Then, when it's time to take the tree down, all you have to do after you denude it of ornaments is pull the plastic or sheet up to rewrap the tree and take it away.

Cheryl R. Riley, owner of Right Angle Designs, whose furniture designs have been exhibited nationally, finds it hard to see all those trees cut down for decorative use. "Trees are living things, and they contribute to our environment," she reminded me. Cheryl decorates her mantel, pictured in the photo insert, instead of a tree. It incorporates family icons—including a photo of her mother and one of Cheryl dressed up in a cowgirl outfit she received for Christmas at age five—African objets d'art, gold, green, and red velvet apples, and a fallen branch from a tree in the backyard, now adorned with gold stars.

Tree Ornaments, Past and Present

String the lights on your tree first, arranging them as evenly as possible around the tree, then put up the ornaments, beginning with spacing the largest ones first. Then weave in the next size, and so on. This way, when your tree is finished it will look balanced.

My dear elderly neighbors of twenty years, Mr. and Mrs. Edgar Kolm, recently passed away. Many years ago, Mrs. Kolm, who said she had passed the stage of wanting to put up a tree, gave me several boxes of delightful ornaments she handcrafted, some going back to the 1950s. My favorite ornament from the Kolms' collection is decorated with pink pearl hatpins, felt ribbon, gold braiding, and sequins; another is made of silver and red sequins trimmed with red felt ribbons; another is white satin with white pearl hatpins intertwined with strands of pearls. Arranged with a group of brown angels with cherubic faces and an assortment of craft fruit and squash (as pictured in the insert) they're quite impressive.

I've also found old ornaments at my favorite treasure-hunting haunts—estate and garage sales. You may have to rummage through boxes of junk at these sales, but you'll eventually find some great items like sparkling crystal chandelier drops to hang on your tree.

My favorite ornaments have always been the ones my family and I related to personally. When my kids were younger, we had fun making some very simple ornaments. We'd cut circles out of colored cardboard, spread a little glue on them, and scatter glitter in simple designs like stylized trees, ovals, circles, or stars. We also made ornaments out of walnuts or pinecones sprayed gold, and one year we made pomanders (oranges with cloves in them) to scent the house. Another year we made Christmas cookies and hung them on the tree. Anything my kids made in school for the tree would hang on it, and I still display their old Christmas artwork and homemade cards.

I began my ornament collection at a Macy's half-off sale right after Christmas. Working in retail as a teenager, I was put to work in the card and ornament department the day after Christmas. Here I used to think those people were insane to be standing outside bright and early the day after Christmas waiting for the store to open. What a madhouse! I swore to myself I'd never do that. But somehow, after our first Christmas as a family, I found myself trotting downtown to Macy's Christmas decorations department. There I found many of the ornaments, decorations, and lights I had so admired before Christmas but had felt were overly expensive, and now they were half off. I got the bug.

Stuffed animals are fun to pose near the tree. The popular ones during my children's youth were Snoopy, Garfield, and Woodstock. Today's equivalents must be those retro teddy bears and Beanie Babies. We always had stuffed animals dressed for the occasion, having tea at a small table by the tree.

Ruth Beckford always reached for the stars. She remembers the year she hung a Christmas tree from the ceiling in the place of a chandelier, during a time when homes were making the transitions from chandeliers to lamps. Before she hung the tree she sprayed it black. The mobile tree didn't touch the floor. She decorated white Styrofoam balls with sequins and beads, tied with white satin, then decorated the tree with them. Like a proud teenage girl showing off her first prom dress, the tree kept spinning around and around on its own. It was a beautiful sight.

Creating the Mood

Cover Styrofoam balls with African cloth (maybe in gold, silver, and pearl), use pearl hatpins, ribbons, and sequins as accents, then hang them on a stark white artificial tree. Dangle black cherubs, tiny African sculptures, and black Santas along with them. Add a string of white lights, a few garlands of crystal beads, and place a black angel on top of the tree. Cover the base of the tree with gold satin lining and wrap gifts in metallic paper tied with the same African cloth used for the ornaments.

Bring the holidays home by displaying your Christmas cards, perhaps on a wall hanging made of Kuba cloth. This sets off the cards' designs and makes them easy for you and your friends to read.

Over twenty years ago I made Christmas stockings for the whole family (we even had one for our cat) and each Christmas we put up those same stockings and filled them with treats. The stockings were easy to make from a simple pattern of red and white cotton bought at a local fabric store. On the mantel over the stockings were large beautiful Christmas boxes decorated with bears. They were once used to hide special gifts for my children.

You can also make slip covers for your dining room chairs in seasonal fabrics or African fabrics that reflect the season's colors.

Gwendolyn Williams's Dickens scene

Scene Stealers

My lifelong friend Gwendolyn Williams has always been successful in melding cultures in the decoration of her home. Her rule of thumb? She buys what she likes, and it can come from any ethnicity. Visiting Gwendolyn's house is an adventure. Funky antique shops, garage sales, estate sales, yard sales, flea markets, swap meets—all have a place in Gwen's travels for treasures in search of new and old things for her home. An astute negotiator, she knows how to bargain for good deals.

Entering Gwendolyn's house, I am greeted by the gently mesmerizing sound of a waterfall. She has two indoor fountains in her house, eleven inches high and six inches wide. A black cherub holds a vase pouring the water, and two other black angels hold a big bowl into which the water falls. Gwendolyn leaves the fountains on all day and night because she finds the white noise of water running so soothing.

She has been collecting black Christmas ornaments and memorabilia for over a decade. Her colorful miniatures depicting jazz bands, ballerinas, clowns, choir ladies, and calypso dancers are all made by black artists. Her sources include crafts fairs in the East Bay near San Francisco.

"Several years ago, I decided to get into the Dickens scene," she recalls. Seeing a classic display of an English village reminiscent of a Charles Dickens tale in a hardware store, she decided to create one of her own—that demonstrated a diverse ethnicity. She now has over 800 pieces. "It was entertaining. It was part of Christmasizing my house, something I thought everyone would enjoy. I painted the porcelain faces in a range of colors from dark brown to light, to demonstrate that all nationalities celebrate Christmas. The guys with the shovels and the drivers and mailmen are white, but I made the gentry riding in the stagecoach and some of the other figurines black. I wanted to reflect a Victorian era of equality; the way I feel it should have been," she says. Gwen used Styrofoam, cotton, and artificial snow to create the witty winter scenes, all in a built-in hutch in her dining room. The landscape features a skating scene, a gazebo, an electric train (she has another train around her Christmas tree), and its own decorated miniature Christmas tree. While many of these tiny pieces are expensive to buy in a department store (the miniature church alone retails for about $600), Gwen, a woman after my own heart, always picks up hers on sale.

Dolls and Commemorative Spirits

The nativity scenes I use to decorate my house always include representations of people of color, including those from South American and African countries and people indigenous to the Middle Eastern region where Jesus lived.

Patricia Russell-McCloud, who appreciates "the sanity, purity, cleanliness, and holistic approach the holidays bring," uses theme colors such as burgundy and gold throughout her house. Patricia's artifacts and vignettes, made of small figurines and statuettes, are illuminated by a spotlight. She frequently displays a collection called "All of God's Children," and a collection of black life-size porcelain dolls made by her sister. Often, the theme is Africa. She may even include a collection of black Santas.

Zora Kramer Brown, an outspoken advocate for minority and women's health issues, has replaced the traditional tree with a four-foot black doll dressed in a long red satin gown and gold jewelry. The Red Diva, pictured in the photo insert, looks toward Zora's holiday guests from her perch on a credenza covered with a gold tablecloth and stacked with presents and pinecones.

"I never imagined that when I wanted a black Christmas-tree angel for my Christmas tree, I would be embarking on a new career," says Quarana Davis. A self-taught sculptor and dollmaker, she uses authentic African fabrics and beads, weaving together her family's southern heritage with her African roots. Her dolls (some can be seen in the insert), used as tree toppers or mantel decorations, have names like Abota, Alexandria, Arielle, Aunt Mattie, Bona, Grace, Isaiah, KaKa, Miss Pearl, and Ukhwini, also include characters from daily life, such as a woman soaking her feet. They depict the African-American experience.

Blanche Brown says, "My Christmas is made up of ornaments that I have purchased over thirty years. Some of the older ornaments that my kids like, I've given to them for their trees." Her tree includes objects picked up during her travels, as well as fond mementos her children won't let her part with and decorations symbolic of each child's birth, with their names on them.

Many of Blanche's ornaments reflect her African religious beliefs. For example, she always hangs up something to represent Oshun—the priest of the god of love, creativity, and wealth, who loves pumpkins, bells, and beadwork. There'll also be something to represent family members who have passed away: a fishing boat in memory of her father, a Filipino fisherman; a cooking pot to commemorate an aunt who was a good cook. "I have teddy bears on the tree," Blanche said, "because I had a godfather who loved teddy bears." She also has lots of dancing ladies, reflecting her love of dance and her own life as a dancer.

"Think about those ancestors who really are not that far away from you—grandparents or great-grandparents, for example—and pay homage to them during the holidays. I do this through the decorations on my trees and the tables. When my children ask me about them, I have a good excuse to give them stories about the people I knew and they didn't have the chance to. It's a way to keep our ancestors alive," says Blanche.

Gwendolyn Goldsby Grant, known as "the Energizer" on the lecture circuit, has been decorating her home with Christmas and Kwanzaa cards for twenty-five years. She hangs them from one wall to another over a thread and displays them over the doorway. In addition to a traditional wreath on her front door, she always has a light in the window. "A light is a way of saying, 'You are welcome; come in.' Christmas reignites the welcome in all of us," she says.

She once told her children she had always wanted a silver Christmas tree. Amazingly, her wish was granted one day when her daughter's ninety-year-old landlady gave her a forty-year-old silver tree along with a box of ornaments tagged 25 CENTS. Dr. Grant had put her wish for that tree out into the universe.

In addition to the traditional garland running down her staircase, Belva Davis decorates her fireplace with garlands and poinsettias. Her farmhouse, which is surrounded by a fence, has decorative lights running along the entire length, some fifty feet.

Marcheta Q'McManus-Eneas remembers when she was a child in Arundel-on-the-Bay, December 15 was a magical date. School was out, and fathers, sons, and some of the daughters, herself included, would go out into the nearby forest and look for a tree. "You could hear the echoing of people using hatchets cutting down their trees," she recalls. "Then they would drag the trees home through the snow."

Marcheta's mother had a tradition from North Carolina: Before the Christmas tree could come into the house, the place had to be spic and span. Only after all the cleaning would her father be allowed to put up the tree, which was then decorated with unusual heirlooms, ornaments handed down by her great-grandmother, and strung popcorn. "The tree reflected who we were," she said.

The big tree in her living room is a replica of the one she grew up with, and everything on her tree has significance. Like me, she loves to use anything her children made over the years as ornaments—they all hold special meaning, and just seeing them there always brings back memories. Marcheta also has strong feelings about her ancestors, so she hangs special ornaments representing deceased relatives; for example, white doves represent her father. She also hangs miniature pictures with homemade frames on the tree.

The year Denzel Washington played an angel in the movie *The Preacher's Wife,* his wife, Pauletta, decided to use the angel motif throughout the house. Now they own a huge collection of black angels. They also have black Santas and Shona queens, their tribute to the enormous strength of black women.

Balancing Acts

Marcia Carlson

Marcia Carlson was born on the isle of Manhattan, grew up in all its boroughs, and came of age in Greenwich Village as a young poet. The daughter of Jamaican immigrants, she married Eric Carlson, the son of Swedish immigrants, who became a city planner and international housing expert. They spent a decade in Latin America, where their two sons were born. Raising three children abroad during the 1950s gave the family an unusual perspective on Christmas. She wanted to maintain her British-influenced American traditions and also wanted the children to absorb her husband's Swedish customs. The Latin influences of Colombia, Costa Rica, Mexico, and Venezuela, where they lived and traveled extensively, provided another dimension.

Marcia remembers: "At Christmas, while I explained the basics of 'fruit kéké,' 'plom pudín,' and 'papercorker' cookies [Swedish gingersnaps] in Spanish to a baffled cook in the kitchen, Eric would make his annual foray into this mysterious realm to compose his *glögg*—a hot, spicy Swedish fruit-and-alcohol 'punché.' No matter where we lived, he always managed to stock the larder with Scandinavian delicacies: hardtack in various shapes and degrees of thickness, lingonberries, sweet goat cheese, pickled herring. Some of the Scandinavian foods were remarkably similar to Jamaican foods: the round, sweet bread studded with raisins and called 'bun' in Jamaica; the saltcod in white cream sauce called 'saltfish and ackee' in Jamaica, but lethally soaked in lye in the Swedish version known as 'lutefisk,' at which we both drew the line! And the lingonberries were reminiscent of cranberries in North America. Then he'd turn on the record player with his collection of Swedish Christmas folk music and really get into the spirit. Before too long, however, the strains of sambas, mambos, and merengues were wafting through the house!"

Two of the children spoke Spanish before they spoke English. Marcia's daughter learned her third language, French, at the Lyçée Français in Colombia, as well as how to make a *pesebre* (nativity scene) using the classic figurines handcrafted of wood and clay by local artisans, and fragrant moss (a Colombian custom) to cover the manger floor. And always, there were the golden Santa Lucias, spinning in circles, candles gleaming on their angelic heads—a Swedish tradition.

"Eric and I always lived in interesting houses—from a simple adobe in Costa Rica, overlooking a river with rocks for basking iguanas, to a Frank Lloyd Wright–inspired villa in Venezuela—and I learned to decorate with whatever was available as I pursued the dramatic and unusual with pure joy," says Marcia, who also studied at the New York School of Interior Design.

"One year we dressed a lush tree all in white and silver, another year in cobalt blue velvet with gold and silver glitter. Another year, pure gold with tiny Italian white lights. In the seventies when we returned to New Jersey, we always had a live tree, which we planted out back after the holidays. As the years passed and the children grew up to live in their own places and spaces, we moved to Rancho Santa Fe, California. We eventually abandoned the tree. For some time now I have transmuted the spirit of the tree to a manmade garland of thick green pine needles as a mantelpiece—it lasts forever!"

Mary and Adolf Dulan's southern-style restaurant, Aunt Kizzy's Back Porch, is decorated with two trees, garlands throughout the room and on the back porch, and twinkling Christmas lights everywhere. Red pointsettias, along with cheerful black Mr. and Mrs. Santa Claus statues, give the place the warmth of a cheerful home. She uses red tablecloths and fills bowls with bright Christmas ornaments.

The restaurant walls are covered with photographs of famous people and moments in black history, and there is also a mural of a window into yet another dining room, depicting lifesize luminaries from the arts, sports, and politics, including Martin Luther King Jr., Whoopi Goldberg, Magic Johnson, and Satchmo, being served dinner by the Dulans.

In contrast, Mary's home is modern. There she places a couple of trees surrounded by miniature Christmas scenes featuring her trains, garland around the doors, and twinkling lights, which also illuminate a glass-enclosed atrium. Her trees are hung with all sorts of beautiful decorations, including wooden sculptures of African men and treasures her daughters have given her over the years, as well as figures of African musicians and dancers, violins, small hearts, and traditional balls.

An eighteen- by twenty-foot room reminiscent of an African art gallery has high ceilings and four skylights. It features antique masks from Ghana and Zimbabwe, Shona sculpture on pedestals, and other objets d'art, such as African stick figures and carved wooden pieces bought from a friend who once lived in Nigeria. In the center of the room, on a round sixty-inch glass table, she places nag champa–scented candles and a tropical floral arrangement of orchids, red ginger, star lilies, and anthurium. Green decorative boxes and potted plants indigenous to Africa add to the charm. Two big white reading chairs make it a great place to relax and soak in the morning sun.

Every year Mary picks a color scheme to feature for the holidays, a different one for every room in the house. Last year the entry-hall tree featured homemade silver balls and bows. Decorative boxes under the tree were wrapped in silver and hunter green, with silver ribbons. Sometimes Mary throws a tree-decorating party to pull it all together with ease and efficiency.

Mary also collects American silver antiques, and her dining room table features a centerpiece of antique silver teapots and cream and sugar containers—some used as vases, others holding sugar and cream—butter dishes, gravy bowls, and a silver water pitcher. She loved designing this display so that her flowers could be arranged in a variety of heights.

Christel Albritton MacLean, owner of Hattie's Restaurant in Saratoga Springs, New York, features authentic Louisiana home cooking at its best. Her home is lavishly decorated with unusual antique furnishings, including an eighteenth-century settee, and a variety of paintings. She has textured walls in persimmon, deep apricot, and golden yellow ochre and loves to display flowers and candles throughout. She remembers walking by the windows of B. Altman's (the department store that used to be on Fifth Avenue at 34th Street in New York City) as a girl with her mother and admiring the festive Christmas windows, depicting a winter wonderland. "I think that's what I have taken from Christmas—the wonder and the transformation. And when I entertain and decorate, that's what I try to do," she says.

Today she loves simplicity, but she also revels in miniature white lights and candles, both in the restaurant and at home. She even lines both sides of her forty-foot-long walkway with candles. Inside, there are yet more. The traditional tree is decorated with white lights and homemade ivory satin bows.

A Word From the Next Generation

When I asked my daughter-in-law, who is a staff writer for CNET.com, a technology news Website, to give me her thoughts about Christmas, she replied with the following:

Hi, Mom!

I've always loved the holidays. And, although I'm classified as an "adult" at the age of 27, I still act like a kid with a capital *K* when it comes to the holidays. Ask anyone you know (I'm sure you've experienced this already). On Christmas Eve, I can barely sleep. On Christmas morning, I'm always one of the first in the family to get up, and I get up with *energy*. I run to the tree and literally stare at my presents— and I shake a few. As a result, my mother has adopted a secret coding system on presents, so now I don't even know which gifts are mine! Regardless, I snoop and I snoop just to snoop; I don't really do it to find out what I'm getting. As you can see, presents are a *big* thing for me. But most of all, I enjoy being with family and giving gifts. I really and truly enjoy watching people open the gifts I've chosen for them. That's the funnest part. (And the food of course.) It's just an all-around special time—the air is different, people are nicer, and it gives me time to reflect on all the good things in life. It's one of my favorite holidays, next to Valentine's Day and Halloween.

Love,
Your "crazed for Christmas" daughter-in-law,
Melanie.

Keeping in Touch via Year-End Correspondence

Five days before Christmas and we have one box of Kwanzaa cards left, out of the hundred of boxes we got.

Blanche Richardson, Marcus Books, Oakland, California

'll never forget the pleasure I felt when a friend from childhood sent me a card out of the blue. Although this wasn't during the Christmas season, the content of the unexpected note touched me deeply. He had taken the time to write something in his exquisite handwriting that made me feel special.

Gwendolyn Goldsby Grant sends out both Christmas and Kwanzaa cards—one religious, the other cultural—according to what she feels the recipient would appreciate. To her, a card says, "I didn't keep in touch during the year, but I'm not going to let the entire year slip by without getting in touch." In a way, cards are our way of extending that apology or simply making a connection by saying, "You are still in my heart."

Write Right

Here are a few tips for your year-end correspondence, whether you traditionally celebrate Christmas or Kwanzaa, or some of both.

Update your card lists annually to keep up with moves, name changes, and births and deaths. Be sure to always address people properly, using their correct names and titles, and be *very* sure to spell everyone's name correctly.

All year long, I keep a drawer full of stationery and cards, which I rummage through in selecting the right card for a particular friend or family member. The same principle applies to boxes of seasonal cards. Take the time to choose an attractive card with an appropriate greeting that shows you put some thought and care into its selection. If you're sending cards across several religions or cultures, it's best to choose greetings that say something general: *Season's Greetings; Our Best Wishes for This Joyous Season; Happy Holidays; Peace on Earth.*

Instead of boxed cards, you can send out formal white or cream-colored stock cards with holiday motifs printed at the top. These sometimes come trimmed in seasonal colors. If you prefer something with a more Afrocentric look, you may want to order from an African-American card designer. Include a printed message or write your own.

Some of my friends send out a fact-filled, one-page holiday newsletter that gives us an opportunity to catch up on their family's progress, and that's appreciated. But I hate those letters that are filled with far more information than you'll ever want to know!

Card by artist Brenda Joysmith, Frederick Douglass Designs

Recent years have also brought us the inevitable: e-mail greeting cards. Some of these are simply an illustration with a simple text greeting. Others go all the way, with music and clever animation. Warning: They can drive you crazy as you wait forever to download them onto your computer.

Sometimes I write a personal message such as "I hope you have a wonderful holiday" or "I would like to see you soon," or provide an update on my family and mutual friends.

A sincere note heightens the significance of the card in the eyes of the recipient. Only when I'm relaxed can I concentrate on what to say. If it will be a long note, first I write it out on scratch paper, then edit it before writing my message in the card with a good black or blue pen.

The timing is important. Christmas cards should go out early enough to be received by Christmas. If this means mailing them two months early to your friends who live abroad, make it a point to do so. Send out Kwanzaa cards so they will be received between December 26 and January 1. I write my Kwanzaa cards the week after Thanksgiving and get the envelopes ready, using the Kwanzaa postage stamp designed by Synthia Saint James.

Favorite Greetings

Mary Braxton-Joseph did a lot of decorating when she was growing up, and one of the things she remembers well is putting up a paper Christmas tree on the wall to display the family Christmas cards. "When I buy cards I look for something colorful, unusual, or something people would want to save," she says.

My grandmother Eugenia Guyton—Grandma Jeanie—would always send me a Christmas card. One year she wrote, "I am a little short on the Do, Re, Mi, [money] but I want you to know that I was thinking about you." She enclosed a dollar bill, which I still have some twenty-five years later. These are the things I keep—things that a loved one's hands touched.

Years ago Leola "Roscoe" Higgs-Dellums sent me a Christmas holiday card with a picture of the Dellums family on the front. It gave me a chance to catch up on how the family had grown and what everyone looked like; it also made a lovely framed picture. Roscoe wrote the text: "Ours is a vision of a world at peace with good will toward all humankind. May we continue to work toward the kind of world we should leave our children. The Dellums Family wishes you Good Health, a Safe Environment, and Prosperity During This Most Joyous of All Seasons."

The author's mother's homemade card for her grandson Omar.

The year my son Jule got married, my friends Ronald and Rosemarie Clark sent a wonderful Christmas card and surprised me by including the photographs they had taken at his wedding.

Every holiday season, I still display a black Santa Claus card my mother made for my son Omar when he was a young boy. We love the fact she took the time to make it.

Margot Dashiell
MICHAEL JONES

Margot Dashiell, president of Frederick Douglass Designs in Oakland, California, is in her eighteenth year of creating cards for all occasions including a wonderful line of Christmas and Kwanzaa cards, as well as gift items, wrapping paper, and calendars with African-American themes. As an African-American studies professor at Laney Community College, she felt there was a void in cards expressing African-American culture and values and decided to do something about it. Her brother, Joseph, who has a business background, combined his skills with hers to create the successful enterprise.

The cards and other items are designed by local artists under Margot's supervision. They use vivid images and meaningful messages. Bonds between people and spiritual suggestions are accentuated. Popular visuals include the classic Madonna and child, angels, and people embracing. Margot's aunt Vera Griffin, always an inspiration to her niece, was very adamant that the business keep to the true meaning of Christmas—to them, the belief in a higher being. They also work hard to capture the spiritual principles of the Kwanzaa celebration in their Kwanzaa cards, said Margot.

Patricia McCloud sends out Christmas cards expressing a sense of serenity. Among her favorites are cards using photos taken by a photographer friend of children as angels, complete with wings.

Mary Braxton-Joseph and her husband, U.S. ambassador to South Africa, James Joseph, send an eagle-ornamented card with a diplomatic emblem and official language. Every year the card is issued in different colors—always a nice treat to receive as a sort of collector's item.

Restaurateur Christel Albritton MacLean says her favorite cards always give you the feeling they took time to prepare, just like her own good food. The year she was moving to a new house two days before New Year's, she made her own cards so she could integrate her change-of-address cards with her Christmas greetings. They featured a tree drawn in gold ink on ivory paper with a gold border.

Gwendolyn Williams admits she doesn't send out cards. Yet she has kept all the cards and invitations she's received over the years from and by black artists.

Amy Billingsley, a proponent of the family newsletter, sends out one page a year along with a family photo. She has begun saving the newsletters for her children so they can later see their own changes over time.

Zora Kramer Brown, founder and chair of Cancer Awareness Program Services and the Breast Cancer Resource Committee, recently sent Christmas cards that were created using a painting donated to the latter organization. Called *Women of Color*, it symbolizes the organization and its goal—"to institute a comprehensive cancer prevention program focusing on awareness and education programs targeting women."

6

Spiritual Renewal and Religious Observance

It's been a marvelous journey, so far!
We've had to kick some fairly large stones from the road and
*   often maneuver a sharp turn*
And even back way up to start again when the pathway has
*   been hard to discern.*
Sometimes we've been forced from the road to let some others
*   pass by*
And had to sit on the side with our heads hung down so folks
*   wouldn't see us cry.*
It's been a marvelous journey, so far!
Because since we started this life God has been traveling with
*   us each day*
So we've been able to explore and venture to the edge, yet still
*   find our way.*
When we've fallen, we've gotten up again, because God has
*   been right above.*
Yes, we've had joy in our travels and even found folks we
*   could love.*
It's been a marvelous journey, so far!

Now we've gotten rid of some baggage so we're traveling light
And we've learned to read directions to find the path that is
right.
Our journey ahead is still considerable, we know,
But if we keep God as our compass, we'll know which way to go.
It's been a marvelous journey, so far!

Dr. Mona Lake Jones

In October 1995 I went to Paris with my mother. She had traveled extensively, though she had never been to France. I had never been to Europe, and I had this deep yearning to go. We stayed in Paris for a week and, as my then eighty-two-year-old mother said, "We didn't let any grass grow under our feet." I had been around my mom for forty-nine years by then, but this was the first time in my adult life we had spent seven entire days together, just the two of us. That trip to Paris enabled me to get closer to my mother—a sweet lady who is just as real, sincere, and true as you would want your mother to be. So during the year and at each year's end, I reflect upon how blessed I am to have spent that valuable time with her.

Spiritual renewal is an important part of the holiday season for me, as it is every day. I advise anyone who truly wants to grow and achieve peace of mind to take an inventory of how you did this year and where you want to go in the coming year. It is prayer, reflection, meditation, gratitude, and "moving those feet" are key to bringing forth the accomplishments you desire. Above all, we must thank God for bringing us here and giving our spirit another opportunity to evolve.

I'm grateful for what I have and thankful for the loving people around me and the strength and encouragement they give me. The December holidays make me constantly aware of this amid all the whirlwind of socializing among family and friends.

*"Journey, So Far," by Dr. Mona Lake Jones is from *The Color of Culture II,* published by IMPACT Communications, copyright 1996 (reprinted with permission).

Honoring Our Spirit

By the grace of God we have been blessed to be here one more year.

When I prayed to God a thankful prayer affirming the strength that I needed to achieve my goals, I was blessed with it. When I thanked God for something ahead of time, it was there. That is called affirmative prayer, knowing that God is my source.

In order to evolve and reach a higher self, I have to be willing to stretch myself mentally. Every time I have had to step out of my own comfort zone, sometimes forced out by the universe to meet the next challenge, it has always worked out in the end. I maintained my faith and God helped me through it. Once, the San Francisco Chamber of Commerce asked me to speak on a panel on international protocol. I was frightened and nervous, especially after I saw the list of prominent panelists, all experts in their field. But after I gave my presentation, a Japanese panelist with expertise in the business protocol of his country told me he had never heard a foreigner speak so knowledgeably about Japan.

In times of despair, of trouble, when things just aren't right, I may want to give up, but a spiritual force always keeps me from going down. To just throw my hands up and quit never seems like an option to me, but rather a death wish. I know challenges are not meant to defeat us. They're meant to force us to evolve and find our higher level. Difficulties eventually pass, and good times do lie ahead if we keep telling the universe by our word and deeds that we want to do better.

You can't expect the universe to treat you any differently than you treat yourself. Show the Almighty that you're serious and willing to grow. Stop rushing and be still. If we don't take care of ourselves, our families may eventually resent us for letting ourselves go, even though we were busy taking care of them. It is the positive, healthy role model they need to see, and for their sakes and for our own, that's what we must be. I believe we were given life to evolve as much as we can. It would be a sin against ourselves and the universe not to grow.

When my son got married, the mothers stood before the guests during the ceremony and offered words of encouragement and guidance to the newlyweds. My advice was to cut each other some slack if one of them made a mistake. Well, I need to do that for myself and not be as hard on myself as I sometimes can be. I need to treat myself the way I would treat my own child or best friend—with love and compassion. Meditation and visualization have made me realize that I need to take better care of myself spiritually and physically, to be kinder to myself. No negative inner monologues and destructive self-criticism allowed.

I need to pull the weeds and inner conflicts out of my mind, to work through those mental blocks that need deep searching and breaking down so I can maintain focus and reach new horizons. Nourishing my mind gives me confidence. I need to maintain a daily journal of things to be grateful for, so at day's end I can appreciate simple gifts like that parking space I got or a friend who lifted my spirits . . . my good fortune in having a happy, functional family, a healthy mother and mother-in-law . . . the brisk touch of the air on my cheek . . . that my daughter called me to tell me she loved me . . . that I raised two sons who will give something good back to society . . . Thank You, almighty God.

The author's mother, Maybelle

I am here by the grace of God. It's important for me to count my blessings. I know it sounds like a cliché, but it works. When I think of all the older people I have known who have made it through lives of struggle, poverty, or misfortune, the one thing they've all had in common is that they seemed to be able to do just that—count their blessings.

When we bestow good wishes upon our friends, there's an exchange of energy at work. Just as a smile to a stranger often yields a smile in return, the grace we give eventually comes back to us.

To me, prayer, meditation, reflection, and gratitude are the keys to happiness and peace of mind, in addition to taking action and staying true to what I believe in. I find that my prayers are answered as long as I take the time to pray, and that creative visualization helps to make my dreams come true. Reflection centers me and puts things into perspective. Gratitude generates positivism and additional blessings. All of these things solidify my mind.

Cheryl Riley uses the year-end holiday season to reflect on herself and get herself centered. She fasts for a couple of days and makes an effort to stay away from alcohol. She looks back and gives herself credit for the good things she has achieved over the past twelve months, and also thinks about areas she wants to improve in her life. She clarifies her objectives and regains focus on her goals.

Leola "Roscoe" Higgs-Dellums tells me her spirituality is fed by self-awareness and growth, as well as an appreciation for the true essence of life in all its simplicity—she stops to listen to a bird's song or to smell a rose. Over the holidays, she tries to remember how important these spiritual lifelines are to her.

She believes in celebrating life, for when you have to deal with death early, as she did when her youngest sister died at four years old, you realize that nothing is promised. "Poems such as 'I'll Lend You a Child' by Edgar Guest attempt to help those who are mourning the loss of a child through the protracted period of agonizing grief. I continuously seek to be exposed to these loving messages to gain more insight as to why our Mother or Father God calls little children to His or Her side. I have found comfort in the realization that my little sister Penny has become one of my blessed guardian angels. She remains protectively vigilant over my life. Therefore, I believe her spirit has never departed." The lesson that she learned from attending Unity Church is that Penny's premature death is that of the Resurrection: "There is only life after life; we are really spiritual beings having a human experience. Therefore, only the human is vulnerable to death, the spiritual is eternal. Penny lives!"

Roscoe believes we should appreciate the spiritual and not become distracted by the physical. "Christ lived to only be thirty years old. It's not the length of years; whatever Christ came to do, he did it in his given time. The Christ example is what we should live by. He was born and died simply with nothing. He is the one who talked about the richness of the kingdom, the value of our gifts such as offering a smile," she told me.

Life artist Beverly Heath calls herself a root woman and a cultural therapist. She helps people get in touch with their own spirit through a process she calls Reclaiming, Redefining, and Reaffirming. She says she "gathers and keeps the history and celebrates life's unfolding events." She has always been aware of her "third eye," having been taught by her grandmother how to use the "gift of seeing."

"My grandmother gathered plants and herbs from the neighborhood gardens or weeds growing wild along the curb or road and mixed plants and spirits together to evoke healing. Granny would search for the perfect container, cloth, metal, or glass. She would assemble all the needed ingredients and objects and make an offering to the Spirit of Divine Life. This was done by placing the objects on an altar, using candles to light the way, water to purify, and the ether to transport spirit," she said.

Beverly Heath   DONALD GURLEY

Beverly works with clients through art therapy. Her art is not intended merely to entertain or please the viewer; it is "created for the sake of inner peace and is designed to increase the individual's awareness of his or her relatedness to the world."

Her art, often in the form of altars, is infused with the meanings her clients provide. "Altars celebrate our being and create a sacred space of worship. They occur where worlds start and end. The altar is a school of being, designed to attract and deepen the powers of inspiration," she says. The art can also work as a balm to soothe weary spirits and can transport the person for whom it is created on a journey.

About fifteen years ago, Beverly gave up the practice of formalized Christianity, letting go of her traditional CME Methodist upbringing. Believing that religion "lends itself to our highest aspirations," she wanted to find out how others saw God, in particular from the African worldview. Her readings led her to the writings of scholars like Robert Farris Thompson, a professor of art history and the African Diaspora at Yale University. He had been studying African-Atlantic altars for over twenty-five years and is the author of *Face of the Gods: Art and Altars of Africa*

Painting of the Candomblé deity Oshum, goddess of sweet water and love, by Synthia Saint James

and the African Americas. She read books about voodoo in Haiti and about the Yoruba tribe of West Africa and learned how Africans throughout the world took their religion with them, often concealing it within Christianity. In Brazil, this evolved into a blended religion, Candomblé; in the Caribbean, into Santéria. Beverly found that Africans in general were expansive and inclusive in their beliefs.

The altar is a vehicle Beverly uses to commune with God. She began this work during her own evolution and process. The altar became a metaphor—a sacred space around which people could collect all the pieces God dispersed around the globe through the middle passage. (The middle passage is the navigational route taken from the West Coast of Africa by those who would enslave her children. This three-hundred-year journey carried its human cargo across the waters to the Americas and laid claim to the suffering and death of over 100 thousand souls. The middle passage is our most sacred altar.) She also feels people also get dispersed in their daily lives, and thinks of her altars as "a promise to restore the integrity of wholeness."

Beverly recalls working with a dozen women who were HIV positive in preparation for a conference of the National Council of Women With HIV and AIDS, helping them to construct altars in celebration of their own lives. "These women brought their total selves to the project, both their positive selves and their shadow selves," she said. "It meant each woman could say, 'This is who I am in reference to God, and I have created this space and made myself whole and I'm in the process of healing myself. I'm a child of God.'"

After Beverly's twenty-six-year-old stepson, Mtume Patrick Heath, a rap artist known as Half Black, died as a result of a tragic accident, she created an altar to celebtrate his life and spirit. Pictured in the photo insert, the altar has four compartments. In one is a doll with a peacock feather, symbolic of the all-seeing eye. One arm holds a music staff. The doll sits on a jar with a spoon attached to it, to feed the spirit. There's a

P for Patrick, and an acupuncture needle holding a crucifix piercing the doll's heart. The needle is meant to energize the spirit of the piece.

Another compartment holds a see-through glass doll surrounded by beads. This doll invokes the *orisha* (deity) Yemoja, the guardian of creativity and of the ocean and what emerges from it. Yemoja, considered to be the most creative force in the Yoruba pantheon of gods, resembles a mermaid. Her colors are blue and white. "Half Black at twenty-six was a rapper who traveled the road of the ancestors before his time. Yemoja sings sweetly of his rite of passage and holds him close to her breasts so she can feel the rhythm of opposites [his parents] making love in his name," Beverly has written.

Patrick was the youngest son of an African-American father and a mother from Sweden. In recognition of his Scandinavian side, the altar holds a Swedish sterling silver cup as an offering to spirit, and a miniature bottle of spirits—Black and White whiskey. In another compartment, there's a carving of an old African with pins in his ear—he who hears all. He holds a lock and a key, which opens and closes the door to the other side. An old bicycle is symbolic of Patrick's journey.

New Traditions

New traditions and ways of reaching back to honor our roots and history are being invented, perhaps inspired by the success of Kwanzaa. For example, Adwoa Nyameke, a practitioner of Religious Science and a counselor in spiritual and personal development, works with people to connect to their spirituality in an attempt to bring "the human self into balance and divine order." Adwoa, who is president of the Black Employees Association in Los Angeles, also facilitates a women's circle called the Higher Learning Healing Circle of Sisters. This group focuses on women's issues and healing and comes together periodically with their brother group to focus on higher learning (spiritual evolution).

"Celebrations are holy days. They're special. They remind us who we are and help unify us," she says. On the last Sunday of November she celebrates a "holy day" called Umoja Karamu or Unity Feast. It celebrates the solidarity of the black family and looks at the black family not only in terms of individual nuclear families, but in the context of black families throughout the Diaspora. Five periods are celebrated:

- Black family and the motherland
- Slavery in North America
- The emancipation fight
- Liberation
- Future creation

Families and friends gather together to discuss these time periods, each of which is represented by a different color and a different food. Black represents the first period, and the food is black-eyed peas. The color white and bleached white rice represent the slave period. Red symbolizes emancipation, and the representative foods are beets or red juices. Liberation is the color green, and greens are the food. The fifth period uses gold and candied yams or cornbread to represent the future and the ancestors' striving toward freedom. Following a group discussion about each period, the group eats a serving of the related food, using their hands. No utensils are used during the ceremony because they are recalling their ancestors; they are going back to the earth.

After all five periods have been honored, everyone talks about where they are and where they are going in their own life. Then the group commits to move forward, to remember who they are, to stand for integrity, and to adhere to the values passed down by their ancestors. They vow to advance themselves as a people, to remember God, to remember love—our most valuable tool—and to honor how we feel about one another and how we treat each other. "If we treat each other the way we want to be treated, we can find harmony and peace in this world, because we attract to ourselves others similar to what we are," says Adwoa.

This is followed by a big feast, which is always a potluck to reinforce the idea of everyone contributing to a greater whole, and a party. The group realizes it's creating traditions for its children to carry on, just as

A Christmas place setting. The antique china mixes well with the seasonal place setting, spiced with an African print tablecloth and decorated with ornaments and my brother John's sculptures for an especially festive look.

PHOTOGRAPHS BY
LEWIS WATTS

Author's entranceway decorated for Christmas with fresh pine swags intertwined with holiday lights and ornaments. Draped on the chair is a predominantly red Kente cloth, a nice intracultural touch. Miniature cherubic black angels, accented by gold frames, hang on the wall behind the stairs.

A holiday mantel. Besides the traditional stockings hung by the chimney with care, the mantel boasts a collection of angels and African sculptures accented by seasonal ribbons and garlands, some scented with essential oils of cedar, sandalwood, and pine.

The fifty-year-old piano that belonged to the author's husband is used in part as an altar to celebrate his memory. A statue of the Egyptian goddess Selket protects the altar year-round. During the year-end holidays, it is decorated with candles wound with flexible Christmas angel wrap.

SCULPTURE AND PAINTINGS BY ARTIST JOHN BROUSSARD

The author's Christmas dining table. The table was set the day before, and dinner would be served buffet style—so that all family members and friends can enjoy the festivities together. Serving dishes would be arrayed along the sideboard just before suppertime.

PHOTOGRAPHS BY
LEWIS WATTS

A festive collection of ornaments, many of them handmade by a beloved neighbor, make a handsome table display combined with a group of brown angels and craft fruit and vegetables. By changing the Christmas elements, this display could easily be adapted to suit any year-end harvest holiday.

Cheryl Riley's mantel. As a committed environmentalist, Cheryl opposes using cut trees as Christmas decorations. Instead she ornaments her mantel every year with family icons, African objets d'art, velvet apples and, here, a fallen tree branch adorned with gold stars. PHOTOGRAPH BY DAVID DUNCAN LIVINGSTON

This four-foot black doll, the imposing Red Diva, has replaced the traditional Christmas tree in the home of Zora Kramer Brown. The Diva stands atop a credenza stacked with presents and pinecones.

Sheila and Herb Fajor's Kwanzaa table with African objects and candles representing the principles of each day of the holiday. Kwanzaa is the Swahili word for "first fruits of the harvest," and the table holds an abundance of these, representative of the bounty we are meant to share.

Holiday dolls made by Quarana Davis, self-taught sculptor and dollmaker. These colorful figures, used as tree toppers, dramatic ornaments, or mantel and table decorations, are inspired by characters and experiences in the daily life of African Americans.

A household altar created by Beverly Heath to honor her stepson. The various elements are an homage to the young man's spirit and help keep it close to his home and family, enabling them to celebrate with him even though he is not physically present.

Myrna Williams (right), owner of the London restaurant Sweet Georgia Brown, and Jaime Foster Brown (second from left) get together with employees to do some serious Thanksgiving cooking overseas. PHOTOGRAPH BY SISTER 2 SISTER MAGAZINE

A guest at a holiday party carries plates laden with luscious buffet treats

Synthia Saint James, artist, author, and illustrator, designed the Kwanzaa stamp for the United States Post Office. Here she stands beside a giant version of the stamp.
PHOTOGRAPH BY LEROY HAMILTON

Margot Dashiell, president of Frederick Douglass Designs in Oakland, California, shown here with her lively collection of Christmas and Kwanzaa cards.
PHOTOGRAPH BY MICHAEL JONES

Mardi Gras offers the opportunity to have a ball before the solemn season of Lent begins. Here Garfield and Pamela Broussard are formally costumed for a Carnival celebration in New Orleans.

The author and part of her family, Jule, Zahrah, and Omar, just before a traditional holiday celebration; our joy in being together is plain to see.
PHOTOGRAPH BY J. K. PHOTOGRAPHY

our ancestors have always done. "We modify those traditions and create new traditions that suit the needs of this day and this time. Holy day celebrations help make us strong," she said.

For those who find the holidays depressing, Adwoa has this advice. "This is a time for reaching out. Throughout the year we practice unity and outreach, so we work to remember that we are truly connected. Those who are feeling blue also have a responsibility to reach out to others. When you reach out, there's always someone who will reach back. But the most important place to reach is deep inside yourself—because if you could answer why you are feeling the way you are, you may also find the solution inside of you.

"We use this slogan in the sister circle when someone is having a problem," she said: '*What is happening to you is happening to me and what is happening to me is happening to you.*' And if we can stand in divine consciousness based on the principle that when two or more come together and agree upon a thing, it is done, then we can stand in the truth of who we really are, and you can stand in the truth of your joy, because it is your choice to be happy. Choose that. Choose what you want as opposed to what you do not want. Take hold of what you want and let go of what you do not want, so you create the space for what you want to unfold."

Personal Reflections

For professional orator Patricia Russell-McCloud, named one of the top five business motivators by *Black Enterprise* magazine, the very concept of the holy day is beautiful. As a Christian, the birth of Jesus Christ is crucial to her belief system. She loves the season—not only because it's His birthday, but because it's such a serene yet festive time. She enjoys the celebration inherent in people emerging from their daily routines and doing something different for themselves and their families. She is humbled by the fact that someone gave birth to a baby that came to save the world.

Jacqueline Mitchell Rice, who comes from a long line of churchgoing women, says, "Sometimes the holidays get to be known as a time for getting gifts, but you can't forget that Christmas is about God and the birth of Jesus Christ." She and husband Jerry believe it's "not all about Santa, but about God's love for his people and about how he gave us his son, the main reason we celebrate Christmas."

Christel Albritton MacLean, owner of Hattie's Restaurant in the renowned resort town of Saratoga Springs, New York, believes that during the Christmas season, with so many people thinking and giving in a spiritual way at the same time, "something transformational" takes place. "A special unity comes to the forefront more than at any other time of the year. And that's a very calming and elevating thing that comes into the air."

Ambassador and Mrs. James A. Joseph

Mary Braxton-Joseph, wife of the former U.S. ambassador to South Africa, was raised a Baptist. Although she now practices Buddhism, she says, "I love the holidays and I love the spirit. I think the spirit of Christmas is universal regardless of your religion. And if we could capture that spirit and spread it out year 'round, then I think there'd be a lot more peace on earth and good will toward man. I like the fact that, once a year, we get to really stop and reflect. I think that's healthy, particularly for Americans. Seeing Christmas through the Christian viewpoint can also help us appreciate other religions because they, too, celebrate important holidays and different times of the year. If you find out which holiday from another country is the most like Christmas, then I think it will help you to appreciate another religion."

Song stylist Nancy Wilson says that the holidays are about Christ more than anything else. She sees Christmas as spiritual and a way to reconfirm faith. Her husband, a minister, counsels prisoners and teenagers. On Christmas morning he contributes his time to helping feed people who have no food. Nancy says there are many preachers in her family, and they all have a great time together celebrating the holidays.

Zora Kramer Brown, an activist who has spent a lifetime in community service, feels it's important to bring African-American culture into daily life. One of the reasons she attends church for Christmas, she says, is to maintain tradition. "Culturally, that is what we have always done," she said.

"Black women need to realize who they are and to carry themselves with dignity, pride, and modesty," said Pauletta Washington, who considers her greatest accomplishment to be giving birth to four beautiful children. Over the holidays, Pauletta and Denzel make sure their four children feel the sense of security that comes from having lots of family around. "The black woman is probably the strongest of any female, of any species," she says. "We had to be mother to everybody and everything. We need to support each other more and celebrate ourselves as women."

Phyllis Yvonne Stickney, whose film credits include *How Stella Got Her Groove Back, Malcolm X,* and *What's Love Got to Do With It,* feels herself to be a collection of all peoples, a fusion of all cultures. When it's time to celebrate Christmas, she tries to recall all the places she has visited during the year and incorporates them in her gratitude. She recalls each place she touched, each child she met, "remembering that this year will never be again." Then, she tries to learn from the lessons life has offered as the new year approaches.

"Happy Birthday, Jesus," says television executive Sheila Frazier on Christmas morning. She reflects on the powerful image of a Jesus who died for her. "All that we are is because of him," she says. It's a quiet time for her, a time to give thanks for being black and for remembering.

Sheila also feels there's a positive spirit in the air at this time of year. It's important to her to incorporate the African-American culture into the Christmas celebration and to be reminded "of where we have come from and of the incredible power of our people. We have struggled and we still struggle, but we are a gifted people. We are going to make it through. We excel at anything we put our hands on," she said.

Living in the Bahamas, Marcheta Q'Manus-Eneas often remembers that her grandmother, a minister's daughter of Gullah ancestry, "did a job on her family," imbuing them all with the importance of the Holy Scriptures. Marcheta attended Sunday school and went to church. Her mother was the church music director, so little Marcheta was always in the choir and would inevitably participate in the Christmas pageant. She regrets that these are no longer popular, as they used to provide a grounding in public speaking for children. "That's where you learn to speak in front of an audience, do recitations and Bible readings, read poetry, and act in plays," she said.

Her grandmother made certain they understood what they were celebrating, even down to the meaning of the tree. On Christmas, after saying grace and before eating, each child read verses from the Bible—a tradition Marcheta has maintained with her own family.

Finding Africans to be a very spiritual people, London restaurant owner Myrna Williams attends a Nigerian church. Her church has sent people and money to help her and other members of the church through tough times and the congregation even encourages people to start their own business. "We project community values, and we're united," she says.

Myrlie Evers-Williams recently published her autobiography, *Watch Me Fly*. Her grandparents and aunts instilled in her a belief in God and taught her to give thanks for the birth of Jesus. Today she calls those beliefs "unshakable." They have helped carry her through a sometimes difficult life. She values "the whole aspect and appreciation of one's own people where we celebrate that and also take the time—as a responsibility—to learn about our own culture."

Joan Sonn, whose husband was the first black ambassador from South Africa to the United States, comes from a family of religious people who believe in and celebrate the birth of Christ and try to live by the Bible's rules. Joan believes "in a higher authority and that there is somebody that designs your life."

She also believes in the power of prayer. "You have got to have this anchor in your life, otherwise you're lost and trying to find your way, like a little boat in a storm," she says. "Your prayers are answered in God's way and his own time."

To bring a sense of spirituality into Christmas Day, after the presents have been given to each family member, the Sonn family has everyone sit around in a circle. Everyone contributes a few words—even the small children. "After saying a prayer of thanksgiving, they may want to thank Mom and Dad, or the Lord, for the blessings bestowed upon them."

Actress Irma P. Hall mixes together Judeo-Christian spiritual values and those of Kwanzaa for the holidays. The mother of two grown children, Irma Dolores and Shed William Hall Jr., she feels that the principles of Kwanzaa are good ones to live by. For example, she herself was raised to be self-reliant (a major Kwanzaa value). She doesn't wait for things to be given to her, but goes after what she wants.

Although she doesn't belong to an organized church, Irma is a very spiritual person who feels that just about everything is related to God. Her entire life is centered around God, and she sees everything that happens as something God has planned. She gives thanks every morning for a new day and every night for what unfolded that day.

When choreographer and author Ruth Beckford was growing up in Oakland, California, in the 1920s, home was a place of safety and love. Her father, Felix, was from Ocho Rios, Jamaica. A Marcus Garveyite, he taught that "Black Is Beautiful" a long time before the saying gained popularity in the United States. When I asked Ruth how we could make the holidays more ethnic she said, "If we sat down at dinnertime together every day you would not have to crowd it into one day. You learn by osmosis." Her father used to get the *Pittsburgh Courier* (a black newspaper from New York) and buy his kids black dolls. They learned about black pride and their ethnicity; every day and night they are living it. Some kids do not hear about their background except for those few days of Kwanzaa. Ruth's family lives the principles of Kwanzaa throughout the year.

"I came of age at a time when blacks were overly concerned with light skin versus dark skin and good hair versus bad hair," Ruth says. Her family, who were dark-skinned, never took that sense of beauty seriously, and because they didn't, the family was sought out by light- and dark-skinned people of all kinds.

Ruth describes her father, who always kept his Jamaican accent, as kind of a dandy. He wore starched collars with stickpins and always dressed formally for church, in spats and a homburg, accessorized by a cane and gloves. The family attended the Episcopal church, though they followed the Unity spiritual philosophy. (Unity Church accents the spiritual process more than the religious and believes there are many roads to God. Unity is a guide to improving your quality of life through practical spiritual principles.) The children were brought up on the daily spiritual guides *Wee Wisdom* and *The Daily Word*.

Ruth's mother, Cora, told her that when Ruth was in her womb she would hold her stomach and say, "You are God's most whole and perfect child." Ruth heard those words until her mother died at eighty-six. "When you have that kind of self-esteem brainwashed into you by mother and father, you have a strong core," said Ruth.

Why Celebrate?

"Why do we have holidays anyway? Because we know within us that we were born with the need to worship and celebrate. We have an inner need to do so. If you try to fill it with anything else it will not work. If you try to fill it with money, beauty, career, exploiting your life in any way, it will not work. Some people try to fill it up with drugs or alcohol or being abusive to others or self-destructive. It only can be filled with this spiritual aspect of your existence because that's what celebration is. Celebration is the spirituality of our humanity coming through, and that's why we set aside holidays—because we need this spiritual manifestation of ourselves. It is the empty part of our lives that must be filled," says Gwendolyn Goldsby Grant.

Both of her parents were born in Woodstock, Alabama, a little place outside Birmingham. They were products of a country life that has influenced their daughter's beliefs about survival and living off the land rather than shopping at the grocery store. She received a great deal of respect for her ancestors through her parents and their love for their parents. She uses these feelings in her work as a psychologist.

Gwen's maternal great-grandfather, born January 1, 1844, lived to be 110. He was twenty-one when slavery ended. After slavery he share-cropped until he could buy his own farm. His life was spent living off the land and proving one could survive without a handout, thank you.

Her great-grandfather worked a big farm where Gwendolyn remembers going for Christmas and every summer (that was her summer vacation as a child) from her home in Ohio. To get to the farm you had to drive through a creek—there was no bridge—so you prayed all the way from Alabama that it had not rained. The expression, "I will see you tomorrow if the Lord is willing and the creek don't rise" comes to mind. If that creek was too high she could not get to her great-grandpa's house.

Gwen remembers a smoke house with hams hanging and her great-grandmother cooking the cured hams for the holiday dinner. Her great-grandmother canned food and made fresh blueberry pies (from berries grown on the farm). She made ambrosia and pound cake for the holidays. She would cook in two different places, on the woodstove and at a fireplace. Her great-grandmother baked biscuits, cornbread, and other foods in the stove and if she ran out of stove space she put some sweet potatoes or unhusked corn in the white ashes of the fireplace ("they were closer to our soil and history" says Gwen). She would bake bread in the ashes—the ashes would purify it—and after it was baked she would take out the bread and brush it off.

Everything seemed better and tasted better to Gwen on the farm. Her grandfather built a spring house where you could keep everything you wanted cool. The water from the spring was so cold it made your jaws hurt. On Sunday morning her great-grandmother made lemonade in a steel vat and stuck it down into the spring. When they returned from church the lemonade would be deliciously cold. Gwen thought all butter came from a store until she saw them take milk, sour it a little bit, and churn it into butter.

Gwen says her mother did her such a favor to take her down into those woods so she could see some of this. Most kids from the city never did.

Gwen remembers her great-grandfather going into the woods and cutting down their Christmas tree. There was no electricity, so they attached live candles to the tree. She remembers sleeping with her great-grandmother and the feather beds and blankets, and the smell of biscuit dough on her great-grandmother's clothes. This memory is like a security blanket in her mind: When she gets worried, she closes her eyes and reminisces to center her spirit. Says Gwen, "All that great love and food assured you of an inner peace and was great medicine for life. Love is a great healer of our spirit. No one can stop me from going back there and finding in my mind the peace, love, understanding, and security."

She believes African Americans are compelled to honor our spiritual side, to maintain traditions, and to celebrate joyously: "Earth people come with some kind of celebration piece built into their psyches. This includes African Americans, Hawaiians, Native Americans, Malaysians, East Indians, and other ethnic peoples who are close to the earth in their history and evolution. Earth people understand that they must celebrate their source of the harvest—their nourishment—their life. They are the greatest celebrants on the planet."

I extrapolate from this that the further away we get from our spirit and our joyful celebration and into the technical impersonal world, the less we are of this earth. Once we are centered in God and truly appreciate all that we have as individuals and as a collective whole, it puts the holidays in their proper perspective. They are about enjoying each other and celebrating the existence of a higher being. As Father Jay always says, the holidays are another opportunity for us to come together in our fellowship with God and with our families and friends.

7

Holiday Recipes

*Food represents not just something for your stomach, food creates
a warm atmosphere—that turkey in the oven and those pots
boiling on the stove. . . . The children's chatter, the music, the
aromas of food—all build a portrait in the mind of comfort,
love, understanding, safety, fellowship, and family feelings of
togetherness. This creates the kind of atmosphere we have been
seeking all year long. One of* Let me go where somebody loves me
just as I am. *When we come together we're trying to re-create all
of those good times. (Mama's rolls cooked just for me, and from
scratch. She went through all of that trouble to make these for me!)
That nourishment for the mind and the spirit says that somebody
really loves me and went out of their way for me. It's a great
message to the human mind.*

*Making those rolls is symbolic of the bread of life. My mother
gave me life but she creates life right before my eyes. She does
it because she loves me. Her family goes back home to get the
emotional, spiritual, and psychological nourishment they need.
It works because these people accept you as you are. Here, served
on this plate, is not just food but unconditional love. Love has a
smell to it: a pot of greens and macaroni and cheese.*

Gwendolyn Goldsby Grant

Sometimes all the cooking and preparation necessary to feed our families properly just seems like so much hard work. Somehow, though, if we can share this effort with loved ones, the joy of continuing traditions and savoring celebrations makes it all worthwhile.

Many families make it easy on themselves these days, by having potluck dinners for the holidays. But some folks are still determined to do all the preparation, cooking, and serving themselves—a commendable ambition. Dr. Mona Lake Jones, educator and Seattle's poet laureate, eloquently summarizes the deeper meaning of the special room where people are inspired to go to great lengths to prepare these sumptuous holiday meals.

It wasn't the greens simmering on the stove, the smell of canned strawberry jam or the pies cooling on the countertop. It wasn't even the gravy being stirred to pour over the mashed potatoes. It was love that filled our kitchen! The kitchen was so full of love you could taste it when you licked the mixing spoon. You could feel it through the hot pads when you took the cornbread from the oven. You could see it on the faces sitting around the kitchen table. Love was the food being blessed and the sound of laughter when somebody told even a halfway funny story. Folks didn't just cook in the kitchen. They hugged and cried there. Broken hearts and cut fingers were mended right in the kitchen. Over the kitchen sink was a place to show off if you could sing, and many a dance was tried while waiting for what was being baked to turn the right color brown. Everybody in the family came through the kitchen to get a helping of love. Company would get enough love to take some home with them. There was hardly any left over because somebody was always coming back for seconds. Sometimes if you needed a refill of love, you could just go sit in the kitchen all by yourself, close your eyes, and help yourself to memories until you got warm and full. Our kitchen!*

*"Love in the Kitchen," by Dr. Mona Lake Jones is from *The Color of Culture II*, published by IMPACT Communications, copyright 1996 (reprinted with permission).

Desserts

Whenever my friend Brother Harold was a guest for dinner at someone's home, he would graciously ask the hostess if he could have his dessert first. He just wanted to make sure he had room for what he considered the most important part of the meal. So, in that spirit, I begin this chapter with desserts.

Dessert served with or right before the coffee service adds a finishing touch to a great meal—a completion before the curtain begins to close. Sometimes I offer more than one kind of dessert for my guests. I also like the desserts to complement each other in case my guests want to eat both. I might serve peach pie with rich vanilla-bean ice cream for one choice and, for the other, Christmas cookies and eggnog ice cream. Especially during the holiday season, it's great to have enough pie, cake, or cookies for leftovers guests can take home or your family can enjoy later. I especially look forward to dessert when you have good bakers in the house. The anticipation for me at a holiday meal is the dessert "spread" waiting to be tasted.

Southern Cream Cheese Pound Cake

Contributed by Matthew Green

My dear friend Matthew Green's paternal grandmother taught him and his brothers to cook as young boys. She told them, "If your wife ever gets sick you will be able to cook." One time when he was eleven, the people who were raising him—his grandparents and an aunt—were all ill at the same time, so Matthew, out of necessity, cooked his first meal. And he's been cooking ever since.

When he took a job as an apprentice baker at the age of twenty, he required no basic training; experience had taught him well. "One is very fortunate who can do both—bake and cook. One is not necessarily good at both," Matthew says.

Matthew believes cooking is an act of love. "You should not cook for anyone you do not like. Food prepared when you are angry or upset does not taste the same as when you are feeling loving about the process. The key to Grandma's cooking was that she had nothing but time and love."

Matthew says the love affair starts with the shopping process. Buy only fresh products. Measure all ingredients accurately; baking is a scientific process. When baking, all ingredients must be at room temperature.

3 cups cake flour
1 teaspoon salt
⅛ teaspoon baking soda
3 cups sugar
3 sticks butter (¾ pound), softened
1 8-ounce package cream cheese, softened

6 eggs
Juice and grated peel of 1 lemon, mixed together
1 teaspoon vanilla extract

Sift flour, salt, and baking soda 3 times. Cream sugar, butter, and cream cheese. Add eggs 1 at a time, as you continue to mix. Add lemon and vanilla. Then, gradually spoon in flour 1 cup at a time mixing slowly and thoroughly. Pour mixture into a tube pan; place in a cold oven and bake at 300°F for 1½ hours. *Do not* open the oven before baking time has expired.

Holiday Pumpkin Pie

Contributed by Gwendolyn Goldsby Grant

For a lower-fat, lower-calorie pie, use evaporated skimmed milk. You can also use 20 packets of Equal in place of the sugar.

2 eggs, lightly beaten
1 16-ounce can solid-pack pumpkin
¾ cup sugar or 20 packets Equal
2½ teaspoons ground cinnamon
½ teaspoon ground ginger

¼ teaspoon cloves
1½ cups undiluted evaporated milk (12-ounce can)
1 9-inch pie crust, unbaked

Combine filling in order above; pour into crust. Bake in preheated 425°F oven for 15 minutes. Reduce temperature to 350°F. Bake an additional 40 to 45 minutes or until knife inserted near center comes out clean. Cool; garnish, if desired, with whipped topping or ice cream. Serves 6–8.

My Grandma Jeanie's Prune Cake

From the author's kitchen

This is a recipe passed down to me from my grandmother. When we visited her on Christmas Day we usually had already eaten dinner at our own house. The first question on my brothers' and my lips was, "Did you by chance make that prune cake?" If the answer was yes, after a kiss for Grandma and Aunt Simonetta, we'd make a beeline to the kitchen.

Grandma Jeanie told me to make sure that the oven temperature was accurate and not to deviate from the directions. I also realize presentation is an important part of the process. Place your cake on a doily positioned on a pretty cake stand or on an attractive platter. Garnish the cake with flowers from your garden (pesticide free) after the frosting has been applied.

2 cups brown sugar, packed solid	1 teaspoon allspice
1 stick butter or margarine	1 teaspoon ginger
2 eggs, beaten	2¾ cups flour
1 cup pitted prunes, diced, with juice	1 teaspoon baking powder
	1 teaspoon baking soda
1 teaspoon cinnamon	1 cup buttermilk

Bring all ingredients to room temperature. Cream sugar and butter or margarine. Mix in eggs. Add prunes and all the spices; mix. Mix in half of the flour. Then add baking powder and baking soda with the buttermilk and add to mixture. Add remaining flour and mix. Pour into 2 greased and floured 9-inch round cake pans and bake in preheated 350°F oven for 45 minutes or until a toothpick inserted into the center comes out clean. Cool; remove from pans. Ice as explained below.

ICING
2 cups powdered sugar	1 teaspoon vanilla extract
2 tablespoons butter or margarine, softened	1 teaspoon almond extract

Cream all ingredients until smooth. Ice top of 1 layer, then put the other layer on top and ice top of cake, letting icing drip down the sides. Serves 8–10.

Café's Pecan Pumpkin Pie With Caramel Sauce and Whipped Cream

Contributed by Chef Donna Katzl of Café for All Seasons, San Francisco

This delicious alternative to traditional pumpkin pie is extremely easy to make.

1 29-ounce can pumpkin pie mix
1 5-ounce can evaporated milk
3 eggs, lightly beaten
1 cup sugar
½ teaspoon salt
2 teaspoons cinnamon

1 package yellow cake mix with pudding
1½ cups chopped pecans
½ pound butter, melted and cooled slightly

Preheat oven to 350°F. Line 2 9-inch pie pans with waxed paper. Mix together pumpkin, evaporated milk, eggs, sugar, salt, and cinnamon. Pour into pans. Sprinkle cake mix over the top. Distribute chopped pecans over cake mix and drizzle butter over all. Bake 1 hour. Chill. Invert and cut into wedges. Thin wedges can be eaten with the fingers. Large wedges can be served on a plate, topped with a dollop of whipped cream and warm caramel sauce drizzled over the top.

CARAMEL SAUCE

2 sticks (1 cup) sweet butter
2 cups light brown sugar

1 cup heavy cream

Cut butter into pieces and melt in a small heavy-bottomed pan. Stir in brown sugar and cream. Cook over very low heat, stirring constantly, until melted and blended. (Whisking the sauce will help bring it together.) Serve warm. Refrigerate any leftover sauce; reheat on low.

WHIPPED CREAM

2 cups heavy whipping cream
3 tablespoons powdered sugar

1½ teaspoons vanilla extract

In a medium bowl, whip cream into soft peaks. Add sugar and vanilla any time during whipping. Refrigerate until ready to use. Serves 6–8.

Pineapple Upside-Down Rum Cake

Contributed by Kimberly Elise Oldham

It's really a special time when her family spends the night Christmas Eve and cooks together at her parents' house, Kimberly says. Her mother makes the stuffing and cherry pie; her husband, Maurice, makes sweet potato pie and macaroni and cheese; and her dad roasts the turkey. Everyone participates, even if it's just to do some chopping. Kimberly bakes this cake, one of her family's favorite recipes, every holiday season.

CAKE
¾ cup margarine
⅔ cup granulated sugar
1 egg plus 2 egg whites, beaten
½ cup skim milk
2½ cups all-purpose flour
4 teaspoons baking powder
1 teaspoon salt

¼ cup brown sugar, firmly packed
6 slices canned pineapple

GLAZE
¼ cup water
¼ cup granulated sugar
3 tablespoons rum

Preheat oven to 350°F. Cream ¼ cup margarine in large bowl with electric mixer at medium speed. Add sugar gradually. Add eggs. Blend well. Add milk gradually. Sift flour, baking powder, and salt together. Gradually add to creamed mixture. Melt remaining ½ cup margarine and pour into 9-inch square pan. Sprinkle brown sugar over margarine. Place pineapple slices on top of brown sugar. Pour cake batter carefully over pineapple. Bake 50 minutes. Glaze right away.

For glaze, heat water to boiling in small pan. Add sugar. Stir until dissolved. Add rum. Cool. Pour glaze over top of hot cake. Cool slightly. Turn onto serving platter. Serves 8–10.

Vanilla Wafer Cake

Contributed by Phyllis Yvonne Stickney

Phyllis's mother passed this recipe to her. "My mother is an exquisite baker," she says. If this cake is being served, you know the holidays are in full swing.

1 cup sugar
1 stick butter or margarine
3 eggs
½ cup milk

⅓ teaspoon baking powder
4 cups crushed vanilla wafers
1 cup shredded coconut
1 cup chopped pecans

Cream sugar and butter. Add eggs 1 at a time, beating after each addition. Dissolve baking powder in milk and add alternately with crushed vanilla wafers. Add coconut and pecans. Pour into a greased and floured loaf pan or tube pan. Bake in preheated 350°F oven for 1 hour. Serves 8–10.

My Best Gingerbread
Contributed by Bernice Watson

When Mrs. Watson, a retired educator who also taught French to my etiquette students, comes over, we always hope she's bringing some of her wonderful home-made pastries. The widow of Tuskegee Airman Major Dudley Malone Watson, who died in a peacetime plane crash in Germany, she has baked for family and friends for years.

½ cup butter
½ cup sugar
1 egg
2½ cups flour
1½ teaspoons baking soda
½ teaspoon salt
1 teaspoon cinnamon

1 teaspoon ginger
½ teaspoon cloves
1 teaspoon lemon juice
½ cup each light molasses, dark molasses, and blackstrap molasses
1 cup hot water

Melt butter in 3- or 4- quart saucepan over low heat. Remove from heat and let cool. Add sugar and egg and beat well. Sift together flour, baking soda, salt, and spices. Combine lemon juice, all three molasses, and water. Add alternately with flour mixture to butter mixture. Pour into a greased 9-inch square pan or 2 standard loaf pans. Bake in preheated 350°F oven for 50 to 60 minutes. Cool 5 minutes. Remove from pan. Top with whipped cream or lemon sauce. Serves 8–10.

Tita Tessie's Apple Pie

Contributed by Melanie Austria Farmer

This is my daughter-in-law's great apple pie recipe. It comes from her Aunt Tessie.

4 green apples (Granny Smith or Pippin)
½ cup brown sugar
1 stick butter or margarine, cut into small pieces
½ teaspoon cinnamon
½ teaspoon nutmeg
1 tablespoon fresh lemon juice
2 9-inch pie crusts, unbaked

Peel apples. Spread thin slices of 1 apple on 1 pie crust. Top with some of the brown sugar, butter or margarine, and cinnamon. Repeat to make about 4 layers. On top layer, sprinkle nutmeg and lemon juice. Place second crust on top, and pinch edges together. Cut decorative designs on top; triangles are nice and simple. Bake in preheated 375°F oven for 30 minutes. Reduce heat to 350°F and bake 15 minutes more, or until top crust is golden brown. Cool at room temperature. Serves 6–8.

Melanie Austria Farmer
and Zahrah

Aunt Thelma's Lemon Meringue Pie

Contributed by Jacqueline Mitchell Rice

For filling, separate eggs. Set aside whites. Add condensed milk and lemon juice to yolks. Mix until creamy smooth. Pour mixture into pie crusts.

6 eggs
3 13-ounce cans sweetened condensed milk
1 cup lemon juice
2 graham cracker pie crusts

1 cup sugar
¼ teaspoon lemon extract
¼ teaspoon cream of tartar
powdered sugar for topping

For meringue, with electric mixer, mix egg whites at high speed. When they start to get fluffy, add sugar, lemon extract, and cream of tartar. Continue to mix until fluffy and smooth. Spoon over tops of pies. Bake in 375°F oven for 10 minutes or until meringue is golden brown. Sift a little powdered sugar on top. Refrigerate. Serves 12–16.

Side Dishes

Myrlie Evers-Williams remembers, "When I was growing up [in Vicksburg, Mississippi] we were poor, but we were not *po'*. We had my grand-mother's cooked corn—something she called spoon bread. Today you may recognize it as the Italian restaurants' polenta—boiled cornmeal. Somehow it has become a delicacy, just like chitlins became chitilinks. That's when you slice the chitlins into little pieces and deep-fry them and put them on toothpicks as hors d'oeuvres.

"They've gone from the throw-away food in slavery days to what those of us who grew up with no money could make to high society. So, there you have it: chitilinks pieces on toothpicks. At least when I go into an overpriced restaurant and they serve that, I can say, 'I know what that is.'"

Red Fried Tomatoes
Contributed by Myrlie Evers-Williams

4 large red tomatoes
Salt and pepper to taste

2 tablespoons cornmeal
Oil for frying

Cut tomatoes into thick slices. Sprinkle with salt and pepper. Coat with cornmeal. Heat enough oil to cover base of skillet. Fry tomatoes, turning once, until browned on both sides. Serves 4.

Creamy Cheesy Macaroni

Contributed by Cheryl D. Broussard

Everyone looks forward to Cheryl bringing over this dish. Macaroni and cheese is worshipped in my family!

2 cups (8-ounce package) macaroni
1 cup butter
¼ cup flour
2 crushed chicken bouillon cubes
2 cups regular or low-fat milk
3 cups Longhorn or Colby cheese
1 dash white pepper

1 dash red pepper
⅛ teaspoon onion powder
¼ teaspoon yellow mustard
¼ teaspoon nutmeg
1½ teaspoons seasoned salt
Paprika

Cook macaroni according to package instructions (without salt or fat); set aside. Melt butter in large saucepan. Add flour and bouillon cubes. Heat until bubbly. Add milk, 2 cups cheese, white pepper, red pepper, onion powder, mustard, nutmeg, and seasoned salt. Heat until cheese melts, stirring. Layer macaroni and remaining cheese in large casserole dish, then pour milk mixture over it. Sprinkle paprika on top. Bake in preheated 350°F oven for 35 minutes or until top is brown. Serves 6–8.

Cheryl D. Broussard
JIM DENNIS

Z's Sassy Green Beans

Contributed by Zahrah Farmer

The way my daughter, Zahrah, prepares these green beans, we all want to finish eating our vegetables. They're simply scrumptious.

1 pound fresh green beans
¼ cup butter
1½ cups finely sliced red onions
¾ cup fine sliced white onions

4 garlic cloves, finely sliced
⅓ cup garlic pepper
1½ teaspoons salt
¼ cup vinaigrette/salad dressing

Snip ends off beans and discard; rinse beans. Melt butter in skillet and sauté onions and garlic. Add beans, season with garlic pepper and salt, and cook on low for 15 minutes. Add vinaigrette and simmer at least 30 minutes. The longer it cooks, the deeper the flavor. Serves 3–4.

Zahrah Mallie Farmer

Brown Rice With Pine Nuts

Contributed by Marcia Carlson

Marcia Carlson began cooking seriously when she moved to Woodcliff Lake, New Jersey, in the late forties. Much to her family's delight, she continued to perfect her culinary skills throughout the time the family traveled to exotic locales, from Latin America to Africa, always improving on recipes she collected.

She offers these tips: "Always keep the pine nuts in an airtight container in the refrigerator and they'll last a long time. Use a good cast-iron saucepan—they're much better than the nonstick kind." She uses dried red pepper flakes instead of jalapeno peppers because they give her more control over the flavor and don't sting her fingers.

2 tablespoons butter
4 tablespoons chopped green
   onions
¼ cup pine nuts
1 cup brown rice
2 cups water

2 sprigs fresh thyme or 1/2 teaspoon dried thyme
1 Turkish bay leaf
Kosher salt and freshly ground black
   pepper to taste
¼ teaspoon red pepper flakes

Preheat oven to 400°F. Melt 1 tablespoon butter in a heavy saucepan and add onions and pine nuts. Cook, stirring until onions are wilted. Add all remaining ingredients. Bring to a boil, stirring; make sure there are no lumps in the rice. Cover with a close-fitting lid and place in oven. Bake 45 minutes or until all water has evaporated. Discard bay leaf. Using a fork, stir in remaining butter and blend well. Serves 4–6.

Roscoe Higgs-Dellums says Louisiana cooking is the tastiest food she's ever had, and the best dressing is made by her good friend Barbara Dorham, who has a Louisiana background and lives in Berkeley. After Roscoe moved to Washington, D.C., she and Barbara would get on the phone every evening before Thanksgiving Day and make their dressing together, sharing some great cooking tips and catching up on the latest news on both coasts.

"Nowadays most people don't stuff the turkey, because of health concerns," Roscoe says. "I recommend not stuffing the bird but baking the dressing in large roasting pans and saturating it with the turkey drippings two or three times while it's cooking. Bake the dressing in a preheated 350°F oven for about 3 hours, or until it's solid enough to eat with a fork. Don't let it bake too dry."

"Remember, since the turkey is not stuffed, place a stick of butter into the open cavity and pour melted butter and soy sauce (as a substitute for salt) over the bird with your other seasonings of choice before placing it into the oven. This will make rich, flavorful drippings."

"In deciding how much dressing to make, think about how many people you are planning to feed and how much you want for leftovers. When I make mine at Thanksgiving, I usually make enough to freeze for Christmas, too; you can freeze cornbread dressing for up to 6 months without changing the taste. It goes well with fish as well as poultry, so it's nice to have some on hand even when the holidays are over. This recipe makes a *lot* of dressing, so reduce amounts proportionately if you want less. For guidelines, look at the suggested amounts on the bags of prepared stuffing," says Roscoe.

Cornbread Dressing

Contributed by Roscoe Higgs-Dellums

Turkey parts: neck, heart, gizzard from 1 or more turkeys (an extra package of turkey parts can be added; chicken parts may be substituted

3 onions, finely chopped

4 bunches celery with leaves, finely chopped

4 bunches scallions, finely chopped

4 boxes Jiffy cornbread mix (or equivalent brand)

3 bags prepared cornbread stuffing

3 bags prepared herbal bread stuffing

Seasonings to taste: salt, pepper, sage, thyme, poultry seasoning, soy sauce

10 eggs, beaten

1 pound butter, melted

3 10½-ounce cans cream of chicken soup

3 10½-ounce cans cream of mushroom soup

In large pot, with water covering turkey parts, boil 2 to 3 hours. (You want a flavorful broth, so be generous with parts.) Sauté onions, celery, and scallions in a little oil, then add to broth. Make Jiffy cornbread according to package directions and cool. When ready to assemble dressing, crumble cornbread and combine with prepared cornbread stuffing and herbal bread stuffing. Season to taste. Add enough broth to make mixture moist enough to stir. In separate bowl, combine eggs, butter, and condensed soups. Pour soup mixture over cornbread mixture and mix together. Bake in a buttered or greased roasting pan or large glass baking dish in preheated 350°F oven about 3 hours, adding turkey drippings periodically so it stays moist but not wet. Test for doneness after 3 hours. If it stays on a fork—or if your nose tells you it's time—it's done!

Salmon Salad

Contributed by Denise Wilson

Denise Wilson is an excellent cook, a gracious hostess, and a dear friend. She serves this versatile salad as either an appetizer or a snack.

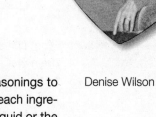

1 14¾-ounce can red salmon, drained well
2 or 3 stalks celery, chopped
2 scallions, chopped
Green olives with pimento, chopped
Black olives, chopped
Capers (optional)
Diced green chilies
½ cup sweet pickle relish, drained well

Garlic salt, to taste
Dash of curry powder
Dash of lemon juice
Cayenne pepper
Pepper
Mayonnaise
Macaroni (optional), cooked as on package

Denise Wilson

Using a fork, break up salmon in a bowl. Add other ingredients and seasonings to taste, using mayonnaise to moisten to desired consistency. As you add each ingredient, stir mixture with fork. Make sure to drain any ingredient that has liquid or the salad will come out soupy and taste like paste. Serves 4–6.

Corn Pudding

Contributed by Joyce Dinkins

Joyce Dinkins
JOAN VITALE STRONG

Joyce and former New York City Mayor David Dinkins have been hosting their Christmas dinner ever since they got married over forty years ago. This is one of Joyce's favorite recipes.

1 beaten egg
1 cup milk
16-ounce can creamed corn
1 cup bread crumbs
¼ cup finely chopped onions
1 tablespoon brown sugar

2 tablespoons butter or margarine
¼ teaspoon salt
Dash of pepper
1 teaspoon nutmeg
1 teaspoon cinnamon

Mix all ingredients together but reserve half of the breadcrumbs and half of the butter for topping. Pour mixture into a greased casserole; top with remaining butter and crumbs. Bake in a preheated 350°F oven for about 1 hour. Serves 6–8.

Sautéed Spinach With Mushrooms

Contributed by Marcia Carlson

1 pound fresh spinach
3 tablespoons extra-virgin olive oil
2 tablespoons chopped onion
½ pound portobello mushrooms, cut
    into 1/4-inch pieces

1 teaspoon freshly minced garlic
Salt and pepper
Pinch of nutmeg

From spinach, remove or discard any tough stems or blemished leaves. Rinse and drain well. In skillet, heat 2 tablespoons oil with the onion. Add mushrooms and cook, stirring, over high heat until brown. Add remaining tablespoon oil and spinach and cook, stirring until cooked, about 1 minute. Sprinkle with garlic, salt and pepper, and nutmeg, and cook about 3 minutes, or until spinach is wilted. (Do not brown the garlic.) Serves 2–3.

Mama Joyce's Hawaiian Potatoes

Contributed by Marcheta Q'McManus-Eneas

Marcheta Q'McManus-Eneas was born in Portsmouth, Virginia, raised in Annapolis, Maryland, and nurtured in the Carolinas. Her extensive family has passed to her recipes they have traditionally cooked for generations. This is one of them.

4 medium sweet potatoes	½ cup evaporated milk
½ cup butter	2 eggs, beaten
½ cup sugar	¼ cup shredded coconut
½ cup crushed pineapple	Marshmallows for topping
½ teaspoon allspice	

Boil potatoes whole until soft. Remove from water and let cool. Mix with all other ingredients, except marshmallows, until smooth. Place mixture in casserole greased with butter. Bake in preheated 350°F oven about 30 minutes, until well set. Remove from oven and top with a layer of marshmallows. Return to oven just until marshmallows are golden brown. Serves 6–8.

Main Dishes

Teriyaki Chicken Wings

Contributed by Claudia H. Farmer Perry

Claudia, my former husband's aunt, retired in 1997 after forty-seven years as an elementary school teacher in the Los Angeles school system. This was her husband, Jim's, favorite recipe. She was given this recipe nearly fifty years ago by a Japanese friend.

1 cup soy sauce	3 tablespoons sugar
1 cup water	1 tablespoon ginger
¼ cup cooking wine	20 chicken wings

Mix first 5 ingredients and pour over wings. Marinate in refrigerator overnight. Preheat oven to 350°F. Bake at 325°F for 1¼ hour. Serves 6–8.

Jessie's Haitian-Style Turkey
With Creole Sauce

Contributed by Jessie Leonard-Corcia

Jessie Leonard-Corcia

Jessie's catering features Cajun, Creole, and Caribbean cooking. The menu includes mouthwatering treats like Nineteenth-Century Crab Cakes, Haitian Bronzed Chicken Fettucine, Creole Ratatouille Pillows, Jambalaya, and Filet Mignon Lafayette. Here's one of her favorite dishes.

1 turkey, 15 to 20 pounds, giblets removed

MARINADE
4 cloves garlic, chopped
2 tablespoons kosher salt
¼ cup fresh chopped parsley
¼ cup distilled vinegar
4 tablespoons Lawry's Seasoned Salt
3 tablespoons Mrs. Dash

½ teaspoon chopped habañero peppers (or use Tabasco sauce to taste)
¼ cup lemon juice

CREOLE SAUCE
2 white onions
2 green bell peppers
2 red bell peppers
½ cup canola oil
½ cup tomato paste

Cut up turkey as if you were cutting apart a whole chicken. Clean turkey, rinse, and pat dry. Mix all marinade ingredients together well. Pour over turkey pieces and marinate in refrigerator at least 3 hours or overnight. To cook turkey, bake in preheated 350°F oven covered for 35 minutes or until golden brown and tender. Baste turkey with its drippings from time to time during cooking. While the turkey bakes, make the sauce.

For sauce, slice onions, green bell peppers, and red bell peppers julienne style. Heat oil in skillet. Add sliced onions, green and red bell peppers, tomato paste, and 1–2 cups turkey drippings and mix well. Cook for 10 minutes or until all vegetables are well cooked. Add salt, Lawry's Seasoned Salt, and Mrs. Dash to taste for more flavor. Serves 10–12.

Poached Catfish

Contributed by Marcia Carlson

½ cup chicken broth
½ cup clam juice
½ cup white wine
3 leeks
¼ cup chopped Italian parsley
¼ cup chopped cilantro

Kosher salt
Freshly ground black pepper
1 pound catfish filet (about ½-inch thick)
1 lemon, cut in quarters

Combine broth, clam juice, and wine in a large wok or skillet with a cover. Heat to boiling over high heat and allow to boil until reduced by half. Prepare leeks: Trim off the roots and green ends; cut white section in half vertically; rinse thoroughly; then cut into ½-inch-thick semicircles. Add leeks, parsley, and cilantro to boiling broth and cook 1 minute longer. Add salt and pepper to taste and stir. Add fish. Cover and cook 5 minutes. Test for doneness with a thin knife. To serve, spoon some of the leeks and broth over each portion of fish and garnish with lemon. Serves 2.

Festive Salmon Cakes

Contributed by Gloria Jean

In preparation for the Christmas celebration, Gloria's family discusses the menu, and "sometimes we draw names to determine who will bring what. We always try to prepare dishes that have been handed down from past generations."

1 8-ounce can salmon or fresh-cooked equivalent
1 teaspoon curry
½ cup cracker crumbs (whole wheat if possible)
½ teaspoon sugar (preferably raw sugar)
¼ teaspoon salt or seasoned salt or sea salt
¼ teaspoon red pepper or cayenne pepper

¼ cup chopped green-onion tops
1 tablespoon oyster sauce
1 tablespoon soy sauce
½ teaspoon lemon juice
¼ sesame-seasoned oil
1 egg
Vegetable oil or olive oil for pan frying
Flour for coating, optional

Drain and place salmon in medium bowl. Add curry, cracker crumbs, sugar, salt, red pepper, and green onions; blend. Add oyster sauce, soy sauce, lemon juice, and sesame-seasoned oil; blend, adjusting seasoning to taste. Add egg last, if using one. Shape palm-size balls and flatten into 5 or 6 patties. Dust in flour if desired. Fry in a skillet with enough oil to prevent sticking until golden brown. Serves 2–3.

Salmon Cornbread Cobbler

Contributed by Ruth Beckford

Ruth Beckford has written two recipe books all composed of practical, quick recipes of her own. Her recipes are designed for two to four people, with the single person in mind. Here's one of her favorites.

- 1 8-ounce can salmon, drained
- 1 cup onions, finely chopped, sautéed
- 1 8-ounce can cream of mushroom soup
- 1 cup frozen peas
- 1 package Jiffy cornbread mix
- 2 to 3 tablespoons grated Monterey Jack or Cheddar cheese

Put the salmon in a large bowl and break it up with a fork. Mix in onions and soup. Pour mixture into 9-inch square pan or casserole. Pour peas on top; do not stir. Prepare Jiffy cornbread mix as directed on box. Add cheese and pour cornbread mixture on top of salmon mixture. Bake according to cornbread package directions. Serves 4–6.

Manchupa

Contributed by Suzanne Costa-Castain

Suzanne Costa-Castain, raised in a rich Cabo Verde culture, has enjoyed cooking her entire life and here shares one of her family's favorite recipes. American Cabo (Cape) Verde are descendants from the Portuguese, Africans, Indians, Chinese, and Europeans who inhabited eighteen volcanic islands off Africa's West Coast many centuries ago. The language there was known as Portuguese Antigua (Ancient Portuguese) because it was under Portuguese rule. The Republic of Cabo Verde gained its independence from Portugal in 1975.

- 2 cups samp (dried corn)
- 1 cup large lima beans (dried, not canned)
- 1 cup kidney beans (dried, not canned)
- 1 large smoked ham hock
- 5 quarts water
- 1 tablespoon vinegar
- 1 large onion, chopped
- 1½ pounds beef (shank, neck bones, etc.)
- 1½ pounds pork (country ribs or neck bones)
- 1 tablespoon salt
- 1 tablespoon garlic powder
- 2 teaspoons pepper
- 2 teaspoons cumin
- 2 teaspoons paprika
- 3 bay leaves

Soak samp, lima beans, and kidney beans overnight in enough salted water to cover. Boil ham hock in 2 cups unsalted water with vinegar, until tender. Dump ham hock and liquid into a large pot. Add remaining water and bring to a boil. Drain samp, lima beans, and kidney beans and add to pot. Add remaining ingredients to pot and return to a boil. Cook over low heat for 3 to 4 hours, until samp is tender, stirring occasionally to keep from sticking. Makes about 8 quarts. Serves 16–20.

Chicken Cacciatore

Contributed by Mallie Helen Farmer

My in-laws used to own a restaurant in San Francisco's North Beach. Roy and Micky, the Italian brothers who ran the bar, would do the cooking on Sundays. They shared this recipe with my mother-in-law over forty-five years ago. You can use the mushroom-and-tomato sauce to make a gravy to serve over rice with the chicken.

- 1 frying chicken (2½ to 3 pounds), cut into medium size pieces
- salt and pepper to taste
- ⅓ cup olive oil
- ½ cup chopped celery
- ½ cup chopped onions
- ½ cup chopped green peppers
- 2 small garlic cloves, diced
- 1 8-ounce can tomato sauce
- 1 4-ounce can mushrooms
- 1 8-ounce can tomatoes with juice
- 2 or 3 15-ounce cans green beans, drained (optional)

Mallie Helen Farmer
J. K. PHOTOGRAPHERS

Preheat oven to 350°F. Season chicken with salt and pepper. Heat oil in skillet and braise chicken skin side down. Remove chicken and drain. Sauté celery separately. Sauté onion and pepper together and add garlic last. Arrange chicken in a baking dish with sautéed mixture, tomato sauce, mushrooms, and tomatoes with juice. Add green beans (optional). Cover with aluminum foil and bake approximately 45 minutes. Serves 4.

Gilda Howell's Lasagna Recipe

Contributed by Jacqueline Howell

Jacqueline Howell
and family

Jacqueline Howell and I have known each other since our birth; our families have known each other for over fifty-five years. Her mother, Gilda, was born and raised in Maglie Lecce, Italy. Gilda married Charles Howell during World War II and immigrated to the United States in 1946. Jacky is one of their three children.

Loved by all for her "Old World" charms and customs, Gilda was always entertaining friends and family. Everyone had a special "Italian" meal they wanted her to prepare, but lasagna was the most requested.

Olive oil for sautéeing
8 garlic cloves, chopped
1 medium onion, chopped
2 28-ounce cans stewed tomatoes
1 6-ounce can tomato paste
1 teaspoon salt
1 tablespoon pepper
1 tablespoon garlic powder
1 tablespoon onion powder
1 tablespoon Italian seasoning
1 pound ground beef
2 16-ounce boxes lasagna noodles

1 pound mozzarella cheese
1 pound Parmesan cheese
1 pound Monterey Jack cheese
½ pound Mortadello cheese
½ pound ricotta cheese
1 pound dry salami, thinly sliced
8 medium eggs, boiled and sliced

Cover the bottom of a skillet with olive oil. Sauté garlic and onion until tender. In large saucepan, combine stewed tomatoes and tomato paste. Add salt, pepper, garlic powder, onion powder, and Italian seasoning (add more to taste). Sauté ground beef. Drain and add to pan with sauce and cook for 2 to 4 hours.

When ready to assemble lasagna, cook noodles according to package directions and set aside. Grate the following cheeses: Mozzarella, Parmesan, and Monterey Jack. Combine with the Mortadello and ricotta cheeses.

Spread the bottom of a large rectangular baking dish with some of the sauce, then cover with a layer of noodles. Cover noodles with some of the cheese mixture, then top with some of the boiled eggs and salami. Repeat to make several layers, ending with cheese and sauce on top. Bake in a preheated 350°F oven 45 to 60 minutes, until sauce is bubbly and cheese on top is browned. Mamma Gilda! Serves 10–12.

Turkey 'n' Tacos

Contributed by Duriya Ali

Duriya Ali (a sister friend for over forty years) came from another one of those households where her mom, Nell Allen, was a superb hostess and cook. These traits passed on to Duriya; she makes sure to serve nutritious food to her family and friends.

2½ pounds lean ground turkey
¼ bell pepper, chopped
1 small red onion, chopped
1 clove garlic, chopped
1 stick celery, chopped
1 1.25-ounce package taco seasoning mix
1 teaspoon salt
1 teaspoon pepper
3 6-ounce bottles taco sauce
1 cup milk
1 cup tomato sauce
1 package soft corn tortillas (not tortilla chips)
2 cups grated sharp Cheddar cheese

In a skillet with a little oil, sauté turkey, bell pepper, onion, garlic, and celery with taco seasoning mix, salt, and pepper until turkey is browned. Drain and discard liquid. To make sauce, combine turkey with taco sauce, milk, and tomato sauce. Tear tortillas into quarters or eighths. In greased large rectangular pan, add some sauce, then some tortillas, then some cheese. Repeat in that order several times, ending with cheese on top. Bake in preheated 350°F oven 20 to 30 minutes, until sauce is bubbly and cheese lightly browned. Serves 4–6.

Chicken or Turkey Seafood Gumbo

Contributed by Roscoe Higgs-Dellums

4–6 quarts water

1 chicken, cut up, or 2 to 3 pounds turkey pieces (legs, wings preferred)

1 large onion, chopped

1 large garlic, finely chopped

3 tablespoons salt (may substitute soy sauce)

Black pepper, to taste

1½ cups sifted flour

Vegetable or olive oil (preferred)

4 ounces dried shrimp (optional)

2–3 pounds shrimp or prawns (peeled, deveined)

1 dozen crab legs (optional)

2 cups oysters (optional)

1 pound cooked sausage, 1/4 inch slices (andouille, linguica, or smoked sausage)

1 teaspoon curry powder

2 bay leaves

1–2 tablespoons poultry seasoning

1–2 tablespoons dried thyme

1–2 tablespoons dried sage

1 fresh hot pepper (or 1 teaspoon hot sauce), to taste

1 or 2 bunches parsley (remove stems), chopped

Gumbo filé for seasoning when served, or may be added to broth, about 1 or 2 tablespoons

FOR THE ROUX

4 tablespoons vegetable or olive oil (preferred)

1½ cups sifted flour

FOR THE OKRA

1 small can tomato sauce (approximately 8½ ounces)

1 small can tomato paste (approximately 8½ ounces)

2 pounds fresh okra

2 cups chopped green onions

3 cups chopped bell pepper

2 cloves garlic, chopped

4 tablespoons Worcestershire sauce

2 tablespoons cayenne pepper

Prepare broth by placing into a large pan two cups of water for every pound of clean chicken or turkey, the onion, and garlic, and bring to a boil. Turn down to simmering and cook about 45 minutes. Add salt and pepper. Soak dried shrimp in water (reserve water).

Meanwhile, prepare the roux by adding oil to a heavy skillet and browning flour as if preparing a gravy, stirring constantly over low heat. Continue to stir and cook flour slowly for about 45 minutes. Brown deeply but do not burn (to get rid of flour taste and maintain a uniform color) then add to simmering broth very slowly, stirring constantly to prevent lumps. Add remaining seasonings except filé. Reduce heat and add presoaked dry shrimp, washed shrimp or prawns, crabs, and oysters to broth. Add cooked sliced sausage. Add water from dried shrimp. Add parsley. Stir in herbs and spices and parsley. Serve over rice. Sprinkle filé on top. At least a dozen servings. *When making okra gumbo, do not make a roux. The tomato sauce in the okra serves as a substitute.

Prepare broth same as for chicken and turkey seafood gumbo. Wash and dry okra. Slice into small pieces. In large skillet heat oil, add okra, onion, garlic, and bell pepper. Fry until most of sticky substance is gone. Add tomato sauce and paste to ingredients in skillet. Add presoaked dry shrimp and shrimp water to cooking broth. Add fresh shrimp, prawns, and oysters to broth. Put ingredients in skillet into broth. Stir in herbs and spices and parsley. Add sliced sausage to broth. Cook down to taste. Serve over rice; sprinkle gumbo filé on top to taste. Serves 12–15.

Award-Winning Chili

Contributed by Roscoe Higgs-Dellums

4 pounds ground beef or ground turkey
3 tablespoons bacon drippings or olive oil
1 jalapeno pepper, seeds removed, chopped
2 tablespoons cumin
4 tablespoons chili powder
4 8-ounce cans tomato sauce
4 28-ounce cans whole tomatoes
2 8-ounce cans beef stock
2 8-ounce cans chicken stock
4 cups water
1 tablespoon Hershey's cocoa (or substitute brown or white sugar)

4 30-ounce cans red and/or brown kidney beans (optional)
2 large bunches scallions, chopped
2 large onions, chopped
2 large red onions, chopped
2 large green bell peppers, chopped
1 large red bell pepper, chopped
1 clove garlic, chopped
Louisiana hot sauce to taste
Salt and black pepper to taste
Cayenne powder to taste
Garlic powder to taste

In skillet, brown the meat in bacon drippings or olive oil. In large Dutch oven or stockpot, combine meat with all remaining ingredients. Cook on low heat for at least an hour. Season to taste as chili cooks for at least 3 hours. Serves 10–12.

Four-Flavor Chicken

Contributed by Amy Billingsley

This is easy to make and can be served hot or cold.

3 tablespoons orange juice	3 tablespoons sherry (optional)
3 tablespoons honey	1 teaspoon fresh grated ginger
3 tablespoons soy sauce	1 frying chicken, cut up

Pour sauce made of first 5 ingredients over chicken in bowl. Let stand 1 hour at room temperature or 4 hours in refrigerator. Turn occasionally. Place in single layer in shallow pan and roast in preheated 400°F oven until tender, about 50 to 60 minutes. Baste occasionally with sauce while cooking. Serves 3–4.

A buffet table of some of these savory delights would make for a splendid holiday celebration. Enjoy!

8

Christmas Eve and Christmas Day

To have a half dozen apples and oranges that were my own was one of the biggest things ever for a Christmas gift. But those six apples and six oranges were mine to have, to hold, to eat, and, from my parents' viewpoint, to share.

Myrlie Evers-Williams

When I think about Christmas I automatically think of home—it's truly where our hearts are. My heart is always with my family and friends.

My first Christmas away from home, I was working as a flight attendant for American Airlines. On Christmas Eve, I had a layover in Boston. The crew went out for dinner, and we had a great time. But something was missing for me, so I decided to look for a church. I don't remember the name of the cathedral I entered downtown, but in the dark and snow at 11:00 P.M., I showed up for the Christmas Eve service. Even though I was among strangers and felt weird being alone, it felt great being in God's house, and I found comfort there on this night.

On Christmas Day the planes were very crowded with holiday travelers, and I was miserably homesick. For me, this was a terrible way to have to spend the holiday. From that moment on, I vowed I would always do whatever it took to get home for Christmas. In that moment, I realized how important my family was to me.

When children first go off to college they feel eager to be on their own. Although they may enjoy their independence and not having parents always telling them what to do, the impact of missing their families, often for the first time, puts the meaning of *home* in perspective for them. They suddenly realize how important it is. When they return for vacations they've matured; they're also much more appreciative of home and its comforts.

When I worked for the airlines I chose New York as my base and I loved it, but I missed my connection to family. I was lonely, and I wished they lived closer to me. My mother, concerned as she always was about my well-being, said, "You can't just stay there because you're in love with a city; there has to be more dimension to it than that." I had gone to New York to find myself, but I had not figured that out yet. Eventually I returned to California.

Pauletta Pearson Washington has been in the music business since the age of five. She studied at Juilliard and appeared in numerous productions on Broadway before getting married and becoming the mother of four children. One year while she was living in New York, single and struggling, it didn't look like she would get home to North Carolina for Christmas. This would have been her first time away during the holiday. She tried not to let her friends know how sad she was, but some of them understood exactly how she felt. They pooled their money and bought her a bus ticket, giving it to her about two hours before the 8:00 P.M. bus departure. Pauletta got home at 6:00 A.M. Christmas morning, right before the family got up to greet the day. For Pauletta, her friends' act of kindness came to symbolize the Christmas spirit.

Furniture designer Cheryl R. Riley, who grew up in Louisiana, remembers the early-morning aroma of fresh biscuits. "My grandparents were Creole, and my grandmother was a major chef. There was a feeling of love and warmth that came from her cooking. The children were the focus of the holidays," she says. "Every Christmas my grandparents had a beautifully decorated tall tree, and my grandmother made fantastic gumbo, ham, and cakes and pies from scratch. The kids could put in a request and she would make it for them. She had a very large kitchen with a table that seated fifteen or more. The kitchen was the hub of activity. There was always someone sitting at the kitchen table snapping beans, drinking coffee, gossiping, or nursing or feeding a baby."

The kitchen is a place where we gather, talk, share, learn to cook, and carry on family traditions. It is where we bond together as family and friends. Restaurateur Mary Dulan, of Aunt Kizzy's Back Porch, says she has very fond childhood memories of cooking holiday meals with her mother (even though at the time she didn't look forward to doing the work). "Mom loved to cook, and she made homemade yeast rolls," says Mary. As a child Mary used to fuss because everyone wanted these rolls, and she and her mother would have to fix them. Now, each year at the start of the holiday season, it is Mary's grown kids and their friends who want to know if Mary is going to bake these rolls. Mary has them come over to help. "A lot of times you have family traditions that you do not realize you have, that have lasted for years," she says.

Sheila Frazier, who has volunteered her time at rescue missions during the Christmas holidays, spends her Christmas morning attending church. "Christmas is a time to reflect and meditate. It is Christ's birthday. A time that he really came so that he could die for us," says Sheila. She thinks about where Christ was born, how he was born with nothing, and how "we are all blessed because of Christ's incredible love," she says. Around Thanksgiving of 1998 Sheila's precious niece Dawn died. Sheila's perspective on the value of life has been changed forever. During Dawn's illness, Sheila saw a strength in her family that inspired her to have a greater appreciation for the holidays and life in general. Now, living has become so much more valuable and so has the importance of doing God's will.

Going to the mall on Christmas Eve, the jarring sound of horns blowing and the sight of frantic people rushing made me wonder: How did we buy into this crass campaign of commercialization? How many people were buying gifts out of obligation rather than enjoyment? How many people were going into debt? And out of all the gifts we buy, how many go to waste and how many are actually liked or used?

Gwendolyn Goldsby Grant, a mental health educator, and longtime advice columnist for *Essence* magazine, reminds us that we live in "a very advertising-oriented and materialistic society—we're in the midst of the commercialization of the American mind." She says, "We must guard our celebrations. These are very important passages in our lives, and we should not allow them to get sucked up by the commercialization."

My father, Ernest, was a postal worker and a real estate broker before he took on a supervisory role in the last few years of his life. He walked a mail route every day, even when he was ill. He often came home with many gifts from his route during the Christmas season, making him the one with the most gifts under the tree. He was also the least eager to open them, though he'd always be very grateful to his customers. He wasn't a materialistic person, just a genuinely nice guy who enjoyed his family's excitement and joy on Christmas Day.

When I think of home, I think of my parents and of a place that's always there, a place that's sacred. I think of my children and their role in my life. One year, a family friend gave us tickets to see *The Nutcracker*. We so enjoyed it, and for a long time we made it our Christmas Eve tradition.

When times were good financially, we'd go to the Fairmont Hotel's Crown Room for dinner after the ballet. When times were more challenging, we just scaled down. The most important thing to us was the pleasure of being together as a family. We all agreed—balcony seats would be fine. We don't always have to sit in the dress circle, we just want to experience Christmas Eve and the ballet together.

Mama Helen's Red Velvet Cake

Contributed by Zora Kramer Brown

Zora Kramer Brown is an outspoken advocate for minority and women's health issues, a seventeen-year-plus breast cancer survivor, and founder of Rise Sister Rise, a breast cancer support group for African-American women. The spiritual aspect of Christmas was very important to Zora's family while she was growing up, as it is today. They maintained the true spirit of Christmas by attending church. The Christmas pageants and songs, and returning home with apples, oranges, nuts, and candies, are wonderful memories for her today, and she still attends church on the holiday. Zora, the youngest of eight children, remembers the lingering aroma of childhood Christmases—which probably had to do with her mother's wonderful cooking.

Zora Kramer Brown
SYLVIA DUNNAVANT

½ cup butter
1½ cups sugar
2 eggs (room temperature)
1 2-ounce bottle red food coloring
2 tablespoons cocoa
2¼ cups sifted cake flour

¾ teaspoon salt
1 cup buttermilk
2 tablespoons vanilla extract
1 tablespoon baking soda
1 tablespoon vinegar

Cream together butter and sugar. One at a time, whip eggs and add to butter and sugar. Mix food coloring with cocoa and add to mixture. Add approximately half of the flour to the mixture. Add the salt to the buttermilk and blend with other ingredients. Add remaining flour. Add the vanilla extract and beat until smooth. Dissolve the soda in the vinegar. Add to batter and beat by hand until mixed well. Pour into 2 greased and floured 9-inch round cake pans and bake in preheated 350°F oven 30 to 35 minutes.

ICING

5 tablespoons sifted flour	1 cup sugar
1 cup milk	1 tablespoon vanilla
1 cup butter	

Mix flour and milk together. Cook over low heat until thick and smooth (stiff). Remove from heat and cool. Cream together butter and sugar and add to cooked flour mixture. Add vanilla and beat until smooth and fluffy. Makes enough icing for 2 9-inch layers, top and sides. Serves 8–10.

Always Together

Vivica Fox said that the year she was filming the movie *Set It Off*, they worked on Christmas Eve, unexpectedly, and had to be back on the set December 26. She kept the promise she'd made to her family, though, and flew home to Indianapolis for one day.

Fruit Trifle

Contributed by Joan Sonn

On December 10, when all the schools close in South Africa, Joan Sonn begins to prepare for the festive Christmas season. She prepares wreaths for the door and table from the beautiful indigenous flowers and shrubs that surround her holiday home outside Capetown where her family traditionally spends Christmas. She invites her entire family and friends for a day each holiday season as a way of saying thank-you to them for all their support. Some years this family tradition entertains over fifty guests.

Her Christmas menu usually consists of turkey, a leg of mutton (lamb), gammon (smoked leg of pork), a chicken or mutton curry, a fruit platter with a sweet melon, vegetables, and homemade applesauce. (Dried fruit—like peaches, prunes, and apricots, possibly pears—cooked to a boil with a little sugar and served as a salad with the meat is a South African favorite.) Trifle, one of her favorite desserts, found its way to South Africa via the British.

Joan and Franklin Sonn and family

1 sponge cake loaf
Sherry
1 8-ounce can fruit cocktail or
   thawed frozen fruit
1 small package fruit-flavored gelatin

¼ pint whipping cream
1 cup toasted slivered almonds
Chocolate flakes
Maraschino cherries

Slice sponge loaf into three layers horizontally and place layers in deep square dish. Soak with sherry. Add fruit cocktail. Mix gelatin and pour over. Allow to set in refrigerator about 1½ hours. Whip cream and top trifle with it. Sprinkle nuts and chocolate on top of cream. Garnish with cherries. Serves 8–10.

One Christmas most of the presents Roscoe Higgs-Dellums had bought for her children were stolen out of the car trunk at a store parking lot on Christmas Eve day. (Someone had drilled a hole right into the electric car lock.) Shocked and disappointed, the children made a big sign that read they had been robbed and put it up in front of the house. A few hours later, the doorbell rang, and it continued to ring all night long, with friends bringing them gifts to make up for their loss. This went down in family lore as "the Christmas we got robbed," but Roscoe says the outpouring of generosity and friendship made it one of their best Christmases ever, a time when her family experienced the true spirit of the holiday.

Myrlie Evers-Williams, who grew up with little in the way of material things, remembers: "My parents were never able to buy me toys. They were always hand-me-downs, and I had porcelain dolls passed down to me from the daughter of a white family my grandmother Alice had worked for—the girl was about two years older than I. My grandmother would sew the dolls' clothes for me by hand. And she would always save scraps of material from the dresses that she'd made for me and make me a rag doll of my own."

When she was growing up, Peggy Cooper Cafritz, a Washington arts activist, always got a surprise gift from her parents that encouraged her to learn something new. One year she got a dummy and learned to throw her voice; another year she got a polo stick. With choreographer Mike Malone, Peggy created Workshops for Careers in the Arts in 1968. It was renamed the Duke Ellington School of the Arts in 1974. The school's goal is to give underprivileged students gifted in the fine and performing arts an opportunity to develop their talents. The training helps them develop their self-confidence and social savvy while educating them and giving them a sense of opportunity along the way.

Christmas Eve is the time to be at Peggy's gracious Washington, D.C. home, when she hosts her annual Christmas Eve dinner for approximately seventy guests, "always family and closest friends, looking toward the New Year with hope and promise," she says. Her menu includes the traditional roasted turkey, a grilled turkey, grilled goose, oyster dressing, apple and walnut dressing, cranberry sauce, potato salad, Charlotte Creole rogue, greens, whipped sweet potatoes placed inside hollowed oranges, covered with marshmallows and rebaked, broccoli mold, pecan pie, pumpkin pie, biscuits, wine, hot cider and two eggnogs, one made with liquor and one without. At the end of the evening there is a champagne toast. Stockings for all the children fourteen years and under are hung on the mantels and in the windows, and Peggy stuffs them with gifts that she has picked up during the year. She has a twelve-foot Christmas tree and a large selection of African-American ornaments; garlands decorate the banisters, and there are candles everywhere. Peggy started this Christmas tradition when she was still a student and lived in an apartment. She says the key to making it successful is to invite people you feel a bond with; when the focus is on friendship the gathering can be as simple or as complicated and as inexpensive or as expensive as you want to make it, and can always be festive. Many of Peggy's guests have been her friends for more than forty years. "There is a sense of continuity that one could draw from that," she says, a way of watching families grow up, and a great time to interact and celebrate with everyone.

At the end of the Christmas Eve party, at about three or four in the morning, with the assistance of her older kids, Peggy brings out all the family presents from their hiding places to prepare for Christmas Day, when they traditionally open them together. Six children live with her, sons Zachary and Cooper, her daughter, foster children, and those she supports. One is in graduate school and two are in college. Christmas reminds her of the great joy she has derived from her children and renews her hopes for them. It is also, she says, a time for her to be grateful, give thanks, and count her blessings. She has had many challenges, so she is very aware of these blessings. Peggy has trained her kids to open their gifts slowly, to savor what each is, and to appreciate it. They spend literally hours doing this, and munching on the remaining goodies set out from the previous day's Christmas Eve events.

"Home has always been the place to be for Christmas," says Nancy Wilson. The elegant song stylist and actress has enchanted us with over sixty recorded albums of beautiful, memorable music. She has headlined Las Vegas shows and sophisticated supper clubs and has achieved outstanding honors, including the Essence Image award. Speaking of Christmas, she says it's always been "the day" that she enjoys most, as a warm family event. "It is the day we all get together."

Nancy's house is the gathering place for family and friends. Since she and her husband live in the mountains, the house and grounds make a natural spiritual setting. The place sits on acres of land that are studded with beautiful rock formations. The environment is so serene and uplifting that her Christmas tree needs no decorations, she says. Christmas is really about prayer, worship, family, and friends. "All of our Christmases are memorable. Just to see the people sneaking around trying to wrap gifts . . . it's the only day when we really go all out. It's just a wonderful time."

On Christmas morning Nancy's family and guests open their gifts and then have a big southern Christmas breakfast. She says it is a day of "serious food." Nancy is the one who does most of the dinner cooking, and the meal is quite a feast, with hams, turkeys, macaroni and cheese, greens, and other favorite southern side dishes. She and guests bake pecan pie, peach cobbler, cakes, cookies, and brownies, and a highlight of the evening comes when the kids go into the music room and sing, play music, and have a great time together.

When I think of home myself, I think of my own strong family foundations, what a lot of support there is among our family members. Before my children were born, both their grandfathers made their exit into the spirit world. And even though their father and I divorced, and he died, his mother and my mother have continued to remain at this family's core. In the same way, when my brother John and my then sister-in-law Cheryl divorced, her family and mine remained as one. Our families still celebrate Kwanzaa together.

When my son Jule married Melanie Austria, her family and ours joined ranks. Melanie's parents, natives of the Philippines who have lived in the U.S. since 1976, take Christmas very seriously; Christmas Eve is their big night of celebration.

As my kids and I like to say, "That Christmas in 1998 was the bomb!" We were invited to Melanie's parents' (Amelia and Martin's) house for Christmas Eve dinner that year. Along with our traditional gift exchange, everyone was told to bring a white elephant gift—an item you no longer wanted but *hoped* someone else could use.

The night arrived and we drew lots to determine who would get first pick from the array of wrapped white elephants before us. Knowing there were pranksters among us, we were cautious in choosing. Even so, the one we thought would be the worst turned out to be the best one—a huge pile of old collectible albums and books. The other gifts included a set of fairly new crutches, a used-but-working Walkman, some sewing patterns, and soaps, clothes, and aged perfume.

One of our favorite Austria family dishes is Jamon en Dulce.

Jamon en Dulce

Contributed by Amelia Austria

1 5–7-pound ham shoulder
1 cup vinegar
½ teaspoon thyme
½ teaspoon cloves
1 teaspoon cinnamon
¼ teaspoon laurel

½ teaspoon oregano
1 head garlic
1 cup sugar
1 cup Anizado wine or 1 8-ounce
   bottle Cerveza Negra beer
½ cup brown sugar

Boil ham shoulder for 20 minutes in vinegar and enough water to cover ham. Remove ham from liquid and scrape off all dirty parts. In enough water to cover, boil again, with thyme, cloves, cinnamon, laurel, oregano, head of garlic, sugar, Anizado wine or Cerveza Negra beer. Cook until ham is tender. Remove skin and coat with brown sugar. Brown top under broiler. Serves 6–8.

Our next Christmas Eve stop was the home of our dear friends Letha and Andrew Jeanpierre, whom we have known for more than twenty years. Letha and Drew's house is decorated with African and African-American spiritual artifacts, bestowing an air of authenticity and cultural enrichment to the occasion. The Jeanpierres always have two restaurant-size pots of steaming gumbo cooking when we arrive.

Letha hails from North Carolina. Drew is from Louisiana, and for him, gumbo is a Christmas tradition. They're both great cooks and wonderful hosts; every year at this event we get to see friends we haven't seen all year long, and we all enjoy the evening's main event, the hosts' delicious food.

Another Louisiana family, whose last two generations grew up in Berkeley, is Margot Dashiell's. Our families have been friends since our mothers were girls. Reminding me that Christmas gumbo is always served with French bread in southern Louisiana, Margot says she loves the warmth and inclusiveness of this tradition of drawing people in around food. As she puts it, "the sense that food is a centerpiece is such an enticement."

Another southern tradition is calling on people, and on Christmas, this tradition is highlighted. "You would always take something with you and there would always be food passed around. The host—whether expecting you or not—would always have something to serve, including cakes, cookies, and candies," Margot says.

Enormous pecan trees grow in Louisiana, and sharing foods laden with pecans over the holidays is another holiday tradition there. Louisiana people always serve pecan pies and pecan pralines. "In traditional southern style, you not only served your guests a treat, you also sent them away with something," Margot adds. She remembers a frail ninety-six-year-old woman from the Labat family, a friend of her grandmother's, gathering up pecans from her yard, roasting them, and sending them home with her guests.

Father Jay's (Father James Matthews's) maternal family roots are also in Louisiana. At a Christmas Eve reception he hosted for the parishioners in his Oakland, California parish, Father Jay was carrying on the tradition of serving gumbo after the midnight mass. Though he has since discontinued the practice because of the late hour it imposed on the families, he says some of his parishioners still keep the tradition alive.

Father Jay talks about his grandmother's sister, who hosted Christmas dinners during his childhood. "Very formal," he states. She worked for the Ghirardelli family and other wealthy families in Louisiana who influenced her style of entertaining. That flavor has been passed down through four generations and continues today.

Father Jay recently visited Spain and the Shrine of Monserrat, a Black Madonna shrine of the kind that sprang up all through Europe during the Middle Ages. He says the Black Madonna shrines and the artworks surrounding them are fabulous. "It is the Moorish influence," he explains. "Africa has had an influence on the life of the Christian Church from the very beginning. Christianity went into Northern Africa to preserve itself after the fall of the Roman Empire. The African influence on Christianity has been tremendous, and we are just waking up to it today. It is not a coincidence that you have these black shrines of the Blessed Mother. The Yoruba religion has really taken root in parts of Western Africa, the Caribbean, and Brazil. The two religions have developed in those places side by side for many centuries; there was no avoiding the mixtures."

Marcheta Q'McManus-Eneas says her most vivid memory of Christmas is of the one just before her father died in 1982. She had not been home to Maryland for Christmas since 1969, but nothing had changed—there were the same tree, the same smells, the same food, and her father, sitting in his chair, placed in the middle of the floor (his spot) at 4 A.M. on Christmas morning, directing what everyone should do. One child was in charge of the pie crust, another the batter for the cake, and so forth. That was how it was when she grew up—the hustle and bustle of preparing the food, everyone helping, and everyone waiting for the carloads of people coming from Baltimore and Washington.

I believe the beauty of a home comes from your peacefulness inside, which is all the more visible to your guests when you entertain at Christmastime. Your inner warmth will be reflected in the care you give to your home, decorations, and food. It can be simple and inexpensive, but the details must be attended to.

For Christmas, the table settings and decorations can set the mood. I enjoy beautiful china, but I don't like it to be so busy that it competes with the food and the atmosphere. For me, the china and the table accessories are part of a theater stage, set for the main event: the food, the people, and the conversation. The plate is only a picture frame for the food and its presentation. One very special approach is to use a lace tablecloth, white linen napkins tied with a silver satin ribbon as a napkin ring, mother-of-pearl silverware, and white china trimmed in silver. Sterling silver water goblets, crystal wineglasses with silver trim, and small silver doilies placed beneath them accompany this formal delight to the eyes. At each setting, you can arrange little silver dishes of candy, placecards, and a small wrapped individual gift. For the centerpiece, arrange a set of silver candelabras holding long, slender white candles, and petite silver vases of orchids in the center.

There are all kinds of things that you can probably find in your house to decorate your home and tables. Pull them out! It can be very simple; we have a lot more at our fingertips than we sometimes realize. One of my friends, a musician, had collected a lot of African-American jazz figurines over the years, and they became the intriguing centerpieces for his Christmas dining tables.

The colors for Christmas can vary, so arrange your dining tables with a color theme that establishes the mood. I was once at an estate sale at which they had a beautiful antique peacock blue china set with pictures of birds and flowers accented in a gold trim. It was a steal, reduced to half the original asking price. I resisted, though with its gold accents, it would have made a beautiful Christmas setting; it also could have been used year 'round. Another idea I like is using red-and-white striped cups and red saucers, and/or red salad plates, to go with solid white china. Or set an African-inspired set of china against a solid-color linen tablecloth that highlights the season's colors as well as the china, adorning the center of the table with small African objects of art and Christmas greenery. Or a piece of red print chintz fabric can be used as a tablecloth, with gold-rimmed red or white china and small vases of white chrysanthemums and eucalyptus as the centerpiece.

Create a Christmas dessert buffet table with a forest-green lining fabric made into a tablecloth and some red tulle placed down the center. Place your spread of desserts on top of the tulle. Find a guitarist, a piano player, or a harpist to play soft music while your guests eat. (He or she should be able to enjoy staying in the background.)

At a small family Christmas dinner party (I learned this from working with the airlines), provide your guests with white washcloths rinsed in lemon verbena water and rolled and heated in a microwave. They can be offered either before or after the meal, and don't even have to be scented to supply a refreshing and welcome touch.

When I think of home, I think about getting up on Christmas to a living room full of gifts and the smell of a turkey roasting. (Like many people, I get up very early on Christmas morning to put an already prepared turkey in the oven.) On a good day, I fix a Christmas breakfast of turkey sausage and scrambled eggs deluxe, accompanied by fried potatoes and onions (my mother-in-law Mallie Farmer's recipe from West Virginia) and cinnamon rolls. Of course there is coffee, tea, and juice. (You can substitute grits for the potatoes and peppered bacon for the sausage.) This is what my family loves to have on Christmas morning while we are opening our gifts.

Fried Potatoes and Onions

Contributed by Mallie Farmer

5 large russet potatoes
2 tablespoons bacon drippings or vegetable oil
1 medium onion, sliced
1 to 1½ tablespoons salt
1 to 1½ tablespoons ground pepper

Peel potatoes, rinse, and slice into medium thin pieces. Make sure they are completely dry. In a skillet, heat oil at medium high. Place potatoes in hot oil, and season with salt and pepper. Cook on one side until crisp and brown and then flip to the other side. Season again with salt and pepper and add onion. Cover until done; total cooking time is approximately 30 minutes. Drain on paper towel before serving. Serves 4 to 6.

Scrambled Eggs Deluxe

From the author's kitchen

1 tablespoon olive oil
1 small onion, chopped
½ green bell pepper, chopped
2 cloves garlic, minced
8 large eggs

1 tablespoon low-fat milk
1 medium tomato, chopped
3 tablespoons Cheddar cheese (or cheese of your choice), grated.

Heat olive oil over medium heat. Sauté onions and bell pepper, and add garlic last. In bowl, whip eggs with milk. Add to vegetables in skillet and add tomatoes. Scramble the eggs, stirring in grated cheese until melted. Serve hot.

The children who are currently living away usually sleep over at my house on Christmas Eve. As my kids get older (except for early-rising Melanie) they sleep in later, and after a while I find myself insisting that they get up. After all, someone has to drive the ten minutes to pick up my mother-in-law, because Christmas morning would just not be the same without her here. She has been part of our Christmas tradition since its inception.

Once Christmas Day is under way, we regroup and prepare for the family dinner. My mother-in-law goes home, to return a few hours later with my mother and brothers, the Austrias, Aunts Aisha, Cheryl, and my nephew Hasan. Friends who tell me they have no plans for Christmas Day are always invited too, as I hate the thought of people being alone on the holidays.

Dinner is served at three, though some of us are generally late (who wants to rush?). Exclaiming at all the wonderful dishes, we begin to lay out the buffet that has been so generously contributed to by the guests. My brother John always carves the turkey and the meat. It seems to be his role to perform this honorable task.

Last year, in addition to the turkey with cornbread dressing and giblet gravy, we served rib roast, cranberries, macaroni and cheese, bourbon sweet potatoes, steamed rice, southern-style green beans, tossed tomato salad, and rolls. We always make a holiday punch and serve champagne and other wine. For dessert, there's always Melanie's terrific apple pie or pecan pie, most definitely pumpkin pie, and sometimes sweet potato pie and French vanilla ice cream, too.

By dessert time, some of us are still seated at the dining room table sipping coffee or tea, or lounging in the living room in front of the roaring fire, deep in conversation. All the gift exchanging has taken place by now between family members. We might close the evening by playing a silly game like musical chairs or "freeze" (someone plays really hip music that you dance to, and once it stops, you freeze; if you move you're eliminated). My mother usually beats everyone at this one. It's truly a blessing being together.

Traditions Shared

Talking about traditions in her own family, political specialist Amy Billingsley says: "I think what is ethnic, in a sense, about our Thanksgiving and Christmas activities is community. I think that we as a people probably more than other people really do believe in extended family and adding friends to that extended family."

Amy offers this as a great brunch recipe that can be prepared in advance of your guests' arrival. Condiments may be added, or you can offer a "help-yourself bar" of mushrooms, onions, olives, meat, and raisins.

Egg Scramble

Contributed by Amy Billingsley

¼ cup green onion, chopped
2 tablespoons butter
12 eggs
3 ounces canned mushrooms,
  drained
1 cup ham or Canadian bacon,
  diced (optional)

FOR CHEESE SAUCE
2 tablespoons butter
2 tablespoons flour

2 cups milk
½ teaspoon salt
⅛ teaspoon pepper
1 cup cheese, shredded

FOR TOPPING
4 tablespoons butter, melted
2¼ cups soft bread crumbs (about 3
  slices of bread)
⅛ teaspoon paprika

Sauté onion in butter until tender but not brown. Add eggs and scramble until just set. Fold in mushrooms and Canadian bacon or ham. Set aside.

Cheese sauce: Melt butter in saucepan and stir in flour, making smooth paste. Gradually add milk, stirring constantly until sauce thickens. Season with salt and pepper. Stir in cheese until completely melted. Stir cooked egg mixture into cheese sauce. Pour into 12- by 7-inch baking dish. Combine melted butter with bread crumbs and paprika, and spread over eggs.

Cover and chill until 30 minutes before serving time. Bake uncovered in preheated 350°F oven for 30 minutes until topping is browned. Serves 6.

Broccoli Cornbread

Contributed by Amy Billingsley

1 box frozen chopped broccoli
1 stick butter, melted
2 cups sharp Cheddar cheese,
  grated

8 ounces sour cream
1 box Jiffy corn bread mix
4 eggs, well beaten

Combine all ingredients and mix well. Pour into 9- by 13-inch greased pan. Bake in preheated 325°F oven until bubbling and tender. Serves 6.

Gwendolyn Goldsby Grant's family focuses its holiday spirit on children. "The whole conversation is, 'What is the baby going to get?'" she says. "Through the celebration and holiday spirit, we are modeling the good life we want for their future. That's a great message for the holidays. We put on our best, buy our best, cook our best, talk and try to act our best. . . .

"Christmas is full of light. The light of life within us wants to be ignited again. Our lights do go out sometimes during the year. Each of us has a light, though, and by the end of the year, some of our lights are so dim that when we come together, this creates a kind of static electricity. We light each other up again," she observes.

To actress Kimberly Elise Oldham, it's important to open one's heart to people throughout the year. "That's why we invite people over who don't have families," she says. When Kimberly and her husband Maurice get the opportunity to go to her hometown in Minnesota for Christmas, it is traditional for her dad to dress up as Santa Claus for the younger kids. There's a big hill in front of the house, and everyone goes out and sleds in the snow.

Nancy Wilson says she knows people who don't have family but do have great friends. "There's no reason to be alone unless you choose to be," she says. "If you choose to be alone, don't turn it into something depressing. Once you deal with what Christmas is in terms of faith, you will not be depressed. If you go with what it's about, it should be very uplifting."

Kimberly Elise Oldham
MAURICE OLDHAM

Jessie Leonard-Corcia is from Haiti, and she remembers waking up to the wonderful aromas of her mother's fresh bread and Danish, her pumpkin soup, and the coffee being brewed on Christmas morning. Her mother now lives nearby. "I never really realized it, but just having my mother with me right now reminds me what a big role she played in my life when I was growing up," Jessie says. When she looks at her own two little boys, she hopes that she lives up to her mother's wonderful example, and is giving them a memorable Christmas experience.

Pumpkin Soup (Giraumon)

Contributed by Jessie Leonard-Corcia

2 ounces salt beef, chopped

1 pound beef, cubed (sirloin or any similar lean cut)

1 small pumpkin, peeled and diced

1 large onion, diced

3 bunches green onions, thinly chopped

3 bunches leeks, sliced

4 whole shallots, thinly chopped

2 sprigs parsley

2 sprigs thyme

2 garlic cloves, thinly chopped

1 whole habañeros (for flavor, not spicy); do not cut habañeros

Soak salt beef in cold water at least one hour. Place salt beef, meat, and 8 cups water in large pot and simmer for 1 hour over medium heat. Add remaining ingredients and continue to cook over medium heat until meat is tender, about 25 minutes, stirring occasionally; if soup is too thick, add at least 3 cups water. Remove thyme leaves and habañeras. Serve with garlic bread. Serves 4–6.

For his family, time has passed slowly since Commerce Secretary Ronald H. Brown was killed in a tragic plane accident that took the lives of several Clinton Administration officials and businesspeople. Now son Michael sits where his father used to sit at the dining room table on Christmas, opposite his mother Alma. His sister Tracey sits next to him, and together they serve dessert as Ron always did: Alma places the dessert china, silver, and three desserts, rum cake, apple pie, and sweet potato pie, in front of Michael and Tracey, who take requests. Tami, Michael's wife, sits with their twin sons, Morgan and Ryan, close to Alma at the other end of the table.

Christmas dinner for Alma Arrington Brown is a somewhat formal occasion. Her elegant table is set with white linen, Baccarat crystal, Christoflé sterling silver, and platinum-trimmed Heinrich white china. She uses placecards, and one year, the table boasted an enormous centerpiece made of assorted Christmas greens tied with a burgundy ribbon that rose from a deep pinecone basket, the ribbons cascading down the center of the table. Alma always hires someone to come in afterward to clean up, "a great investment that allows me to enjoy my guests," she says.

Kent Amos, head of the Urban Family Institute, a mentoring program for young adults, his wife Carmen, and their family are among Alma's guests. Kent presides over the blessing of the table, offering spiritual solace, just as he did when he presided over the memorial celebration honoring Ron's life. An eloquent speaker, he makes a moving tribute to Ron and others who have passed. "We always look toward the future and express gratitude for our blessings," Alma says.

Alma Brown and family

Fun and Surprises

As the youngest of four children, Ruth Beckford experienced Christmas Eve as a wonderful time. The family always got their tree on Christmas Eve, and decorated it after the children went to bed. The next morning their parents would lead them downstairs, blindfolded, to the kitchen for breakfast. "We couldn't eat fast enough," Ruth says. Only after finishing breakfast would they be allowed to open the sliding doors to the living room to see the sparkling tree, now decorated and surrounded by presents piled high. "We would be simply awestruck by its beauty," Ruth remembers.

Synthia Saint James says that one special Christmas Eve her mother dressed her and her siblings alike in white pajamas with red hearts so

Synthia Saint James,
age five

that they would wake up festively attired. Their dog Tabu had a red ribbon around his neck and their cat had two little red hearts tied around her neck.

Now Synthia enjoys a year-end vacation away from home. It's her time to rejuvenate, and she heads for sun, sand, and sea on a tropical island, returning in time to celebrate the New Year with close friends and family.

Blanche Brown finds a good deal to enjoy over the holidays, including live entertainment provided by her own family. "My aunt was a really great dancer," she says. "She was the one who got me interested in dancing. Now my son's age group will hear us dancing, and they'll come down and show us the latest steps. We roll back the carpet and dance."

Janet Langhart's husband, former Secretary of Defense William Cohen, recently surprised her with a treasure on Christmas Day: the book *Remembering Slavery: African-Americans Talk About Their Personal Experiences of Slavery and Emancipation,* edited by Ira Berlin (The New Press). The Smithsonian Institution and Library of Congress publication presents the voices of ex-slaves, and is packaged with twelve recordings made by the Federal Writers' Project. Janet says, "Their voices show the depravity they experienced in not learning the language. I could feel how deep their feelings were despite their inability to speak the language. I felt connected to these slaves, who exhibited great depth of soul, spirit, and intelligence."

Pauletta and Denzel Washington have hosted an annual Christmas Eve party in their neighborhood for many years. Friends and neighbors come over, and Pauletta serves eggnog, smoked turkey, gumbo, desserts, and more. Excitement grows when a Christmas caroler truck arrives to serenade them. "It started as a small pickup truck, with fifteen carolers, but now it's grown into a major production," Paulette says. "The carolers have a Santa, elves, reindeer, and lots of lights—they now use a semi plus five trailers to haul around up to hundreds of carolers."

Gwendolyn Williams's grandparents lived on a farm in Sacramento, California. It was a typical country situation, she says, where her grandmother always made everything from scratch. It seemed that everyone in the world would come for Christmas. She remembers them all sitting around a huge oak table. Everything came from the farm, including the toffee-coated nuts and the homemade pies.

Cheryl Riley enjoys putting together a Christmas Eve high tea, served from about 4:00 P.M. until 9:00, a British tradition. She invites her aunts and friends, and serves cucumber sandwiches, pâtés, caviar, and an assortment of teas. At the end of the evening she serves champagne with dessert tarts.

During the Christmas season of 1968, my close friend Margaret Jones and I were walking back to my New York City apartment from a trek along the East River. There had been a snowstorm the day before, and I guess we looked like easy targets, because three kids ambushed us with snowballs. Caught unexpectedly, and trying to defend ourselves, we got pretty wet from the work of these veteran culprits. We ran back to my apartment, quickly changed our clothes, and said "Let's go get them!" To their surprise—and joy—Maggie and I caught up with them, a few blocks away, and we all had the most fun-filled snowball fight!

Norma Jean Darden and her sister Carole wrote a cookbook and family memoir, *Spoonbread and Strawberry Wine* (Doubleday, 1978 and 1994). Now Norma, president of Spoonbread, Inc., a catering business in New York City, counts some notable celebrities and major corporations among her clients and specializes in healthy, traditional African-American cuisine. The catering business has also branched out to include the restaurants Miss Mamie's Spoonbread Too, and Miss Maude's Spoonbread Too, whose menus feature southern fried chicken, Louisiana catfish, North Carolina barbecue ribs, fresh shrimp, and meat loaf. She finds herself very busy during the holidays, and Norma says she spends her Christmas Day working, for many clients use their services to cater their holiday meals. Joyce Dinkins and former New York City Mayor David Dinkins are among them.

Christmas is when we come together as family and friends to preserve our bonds and our traditions and to reach across cultures. It is a time to remember what the reason is about: peace on earth and love for one another.

9

The Kwanzaa Celebration and Buffet

It is up to us to carry the meaning of Kwanzaa in our hearts.

Adwoa Afi Nyamekye

Kwanzaa is a series of cultural ceremonies and events that include the exchange of gifts (homemade is preferred), music, and food inspired by the traditional cooking of Africa, the Caribbean, South America, or wherever African peoples live. Begun in 1966 as an initiative to unite the African-American community through a celebration of its heritage, it has evolved into a celebration of roots, community, and family.

Kwanzaa is a Swahili word meaning "first fruits of the harvest." It's celebrated from December 26 to New Year's Day, and candles are lit each day in a sequence that corresponds with the discussion of the principle of the day.

The first evening, the black candle is lit for unity (Umoja). On the second night of Kwanzaa, the family gathers and the black candle for unity is lit along with the red candle for self-determination (Kujichagulia). On the third evening of Kwanzaa, the black candle and the red candles are lit, and the green candle for collective work and responsibility (Ujima). This sequence of lighting the candles and discussing the principle of the day extends through the seven days of Kwanzaa, continuing with the principles of cooperative economics (Ujamaa), purpose (Nia), creativity (Kuumba), and faith (Imani). The discussion each evening centers around what that day's particular principle means to every individual, and how each has applied it in his or her life that day. All the participants commit to practice that particular principle throughout the coming year.

Of the people interviewed for this book, all have expressed their appreciation for the intentions behind the concept—to formalize a way of honoring our ancestors and our culture. I have been especially impressed with how many people have embraced celebrating Kwanzaa out of their concern for our children and the community.

Our Family Kwanzaa Celebration

My family spends the evening of December 30 celebrating Kwanzaa at Sheila and Herb Fajor's home. Sheila, a cousin to Cheryl D. Broussard, the author of *Sister CEO* and *The Black Women's Guide to Financial Independence*, is president of the Bay Area United Way; Herb is CEO of a private company, National Graffiti Institute. Their home is where our extended family comes together to enjoy a time of recommitment to values and principles along with hours of laughter and joy. Many of the guests are dressed in African attire that, as Sheila describes it, "represents a connection with our heritage, a linkage with our ultimate roots and ancestors." The centerpiece of the room becomes the display of symbolic mazao (crops), kinara (candle holder), mkeba (mat), muhindi (corn), mishumaa saba (seven candles), kikombe cha umoja (unity cup), zawadi (gifts), and the bandera (flag). At the summoning of Herb's African drum, everyone gathers around it.

As this is the fifth day of Kwanzaa, the children light the black, red, and green candles in the appropriate order as we reflect on the principles which represent the nguzo saba, the seven principles of Kwanzaa. We also discuss Kwanzaa's history and meaning. The elders among us are acknowledged, and we pay tribute to those loved ones who have made their transition. Each person in the large circle calls out the name of someone dear to them who has passed. Then we drink our libations in unity; Herb pours a portion onto a growing plant as we drink, which symbolizes our growth and prosperity as a race and a community. Next, we discuss the principle for the day, and each person is asked to translate how she or he will employ that principle in goals for the coming year. The children are at the nucleus of the celebration and play an active role in the discussion. For example, one year, when the principle was cooperative economics, the children were handed savings account forms and money bags; they discussed how much money they would save, and its purpose. People of all ages are in attendance, and there are sometimes four generations of families present.

Remembering

Leola Clinton (Cheryl D. Broussard's grandmother), passed over a year ago. She had four children, four grandkids, and many great-grandchildren. She was the epitome of the black family. The way she loved her own family was exemplary. One of the most nurturing people I have met, she always had a kind word for me, and she is the essence of what Kwanzaa really means to me.

We adjourn with prayer and seven chants of "Harambee" (Swahili for "Let's all pull together"), and prepare to feast on foods of African and African-American origin. After we've eaten, Herb sets out tables for some competitive card games. African music and soft jazz play all night long. The children laugh and joke as elders and loved ones sit around enjoying the array of tantalizing desserts. We all talk to the gathered friends and relatives, who may get to see one another only a few times a year.

The setting for this serene night is a home beautifully decorated with furniture and exquisite black art. The mantel is set against a background of stone white rock decorated with African *objets d'art*, sculpture, African cloth, and paintings by black artists and craftspeople from different parts of Africa and the deep Diaspora. Nestled by the fireplace are two black iridescent reindeer and a black Santa soaking his feet and napping between deliveries, with a tray of cookies and milk set before him. Evergreen and twinkle lights decorate the spiral staircase that ascends to the second floor.

Some of the author's relatives pose in front of their fireplace.

Our hosts' seasonal decor includes a fresh, thirteen-foot Ponderosa pine tree, hung with antique gold ornaments, charms, iridescent icicles, bulbs, stars, bows, and crystal ornaments, many found during their travels. The buffet table is decorated with Sheila and Herb's color theme for the holidays, gold and white. When the evening comes to a close, everyone is given a gift of fruit to take home because, Sheila says, "it symbolizes prosperity and the sweetness, love, and harmony we carry into the coming year."

Sheila and Herb open their home to share the work of African-American and third-world artists and their contributions. They want to show a wide variety of artists who use various mediums of clothing, jewelry, sculpture, and home furnishings. They also want to educate African-Americans in the value of fine art and its investment opportunities.

Gifts for Kwanzaa are mainly given to children. I like to give them inspirational and motivational gifts and also to remember the elders of the family. For a young adult, I usually select a book written by an African-American writer or poet. There are so very many talented African-American authors our children can enjoy and benefit from reading.

Children often like looking through scrapbooks, and you can create an inspirational scrapbook containing memorabilia from your child's life, including photos, excerpts from projects for extracurricular activities, school papers, and other such items. Present it to the recipient in a binder covered with African cloth, with inspirational messages you have written on the inside cover. Such an album can be a documentation of your child's life the previous year or commemorate family events. And children can make gifts for their grandparents or other elders by creating quality color copies of favorite family pictures or of photos documenting a recent family event, framing the picture, or making a photo album. The frame or album can be decorated with African motifs and include African proverbs regarding the family and our roots.

Embracing Kwanzaa

Synthia Saint James, a distinguished artist, author, and book illustrator who lives in Los Angeles, designed the Kwanzaa stamp for the United States Post Office (see insert photo). She is the author of a children's book, *The Gifts of Kwanzaa*, and in collaboration with Grammy award-winning songwriter Bunny Hull, has written a song for children of all ages, "Happy, Happy Kwanzaa."

As we have noted, Actress Kimberly Elise Oldham, who won a Cable Ace Award for best supporting actress in the movie *The Ditchdigger's Daughters*, comes from the land of the White Christmas—Minnesota—and her husband Maurice, a photographer, hails from New Jersey. Moving to Los Angeles has meant adapting to new ways of celebrating the holidays for both of them. The family has recently begun celebrating Kwanzaa. "We haven't every year, but it's something we're just starting to do and we're learning more about. It's something we want to do to enrich our home. It provides an opportunity to teach the children about their heritage," Kimberly says.

Irma P. Hall, seen as Joletta in the movie *Patch Adams*, respects the precepts of Kwanzaa and shares her understanding of the holiday with her grandchildren. It has brought them closer together through its teachings, she says.

Over the years Myrlie Evers-Williams has also incorporated Kwanzaa into the family holiday traditions. Her daughter sets up the cloth and displays the corn on the mkeka (mat) along with the other symbolic objects of the holiday, the kikombe cha umoja (the unity cup), African art objects, and books representing a commitment to heritage and learning.

While Myrlie says she hasn't yet done a Kwanzaa/Christmas from beginning to end, the family makes a point of reading stories and books about Kwanzaa to learn more about it and incorporate it into their future holiday celebrations.

When Phyllis Yvonne Stickney, actress and president of Cocoa Girls Productions Company, Inc., thinks about the December holidays, personal growth comes to mind. In the old days, she and her grandmother and extended family would come together, usually "down South . . . it meant jelly cake and big red apples . . . fragrant oranges . . . candies . . . and sugar plums dancing in my head."

Today the holidays have taken on an entirely different meaning for her, "one that has evolved through reading and research as an adult, and as an Afrocentric person, with knowledge of myself," she says. "I hope we do not spend too much in the wrong places for the wrong reasons. I hope the first fruits that are gathered are shared in sacrifice and charity with the 'Cora Lees' of the block," she adds. It troubles her that Kwanzaa is in some ways devolving into a black version of Christmas. "If it really becomes that, then what's the point?" she asks.

Phyllis says her connection to her family makes her remember where wealth really resided, even "before we were brought to these shores." Kwanzaa brings her renewed laughter and healing for some of the things that have gone wrong during the year. It also allows her to reflect on the support and reinforcement she has received. She tries to focus back to a time before slavery changed the African world and put the Kwanzaa principles in place. "We have our own language and our own rituals to perform," she says.

For Tisha Campbell-Martin the holidays mean "a coming together of friends and family, especially out here where I don't have much family. My mom and brother live in California. In my household, when people come over, there are so many people of different religious backgrounds. Some are Christian, Buddhist, or Jewish. And, we try to make the atmosphere as inviting and loving and peaceful as possible so that everybody is as comfortable as possible.

"When the holidays come around, it can be a depressing time for a lot of people and that's why we try to bring so many people into our household from different backgrounds. They are all invited, so that they have a home; they have a place to go.

"I want to learn more about Kwanzaa. Sometimes, it's not the giving of Christmas, but it's the taking. I want to see if this is something I can celebrate in the years to come for my children's sake. I want to see how Kwanzaa can fit into our lives."

Adwoa Afi Nyamekye is an African-American woman on the board of directors of Kwanzaa People of Color, an organization that produces an annual Kwanzaa parade and festival in Los Angeles. The project represents an effort to practice cooperative economics and bring about advancement for the community. The parade features food booths and vendors selling their wares. It also features a daily program of speakers, music, and entertainment. Adwoa describes the group's Kwanzaa experiences: "We celebrate each day at a different person's house. Between seventy-five to a hundred and fifty people come to our celebration. It's a seven-day celebration. We begin on December twenty-fifth by lighting candles at night to celebrate the movement into our New Year—our Kwanzaa year goes from December twenty-sixth to December twenty-sixth. Then we do a meditation and prayer to move into this new time, and to reaffirm our acceptance of the principles of Kwanzaa, the nguzo saba. We utilize the principles in our daily lives—we create the type of atmosphere and energy needed to correct whatever is incorrect in our present; then we can shift into any direction we desire."

Adwoa explains that Kwanzaa is part of the living tradition of her group's daily life. "This is much like a traditional African value system. The values empower the celebrants. For the first six days we get together and discuss that day's principle and what it represents and we devise a project for the children.

"For example, to honor the concept of ujima (collective works), one year they constructed a toybox, which teaches them about collective work. Meanwhile, the men work together to prepare the music, and the women are in the kitchen preparing the food. We concentrate on unity and try to utilize a principle every day to do something constructive that relates to that principle.

"For ujamaa (cooperative economics), everybody may bring a certain amount of money and use it for something needed in the community, or give it to a family in need. For kuumba (creativity), everyone may clean their yard that day and prune their trees, to participate in the beauty of our community and in improving the face of our community. We dress in African attire. We want the children to become comfortable with their culture; the adults are proud of it, and they want the children to find a space in their hearts to love it.

"The last day culminates in a great big feast. There are dancers and drummers and the children light the candles, and we discuss all the Kwanzaa principles. The children talk about ways they can practice each principle in their daily lives. Then we recite a prayer, encouraging us to accept the principles and to recommit ourselves to the practice of those

Kwanzaa card, collage by Adrian Harper

principles. Then we take a piece of paper, on which each principle is written out separately, cut it up in pieces, and fold them and put them into a basket. Everyone pulls one from the basket, and whatever principle you choose, you are committed to evoking that principle in your community for that year. Although you practice them all, that becomes the one you focus on for your community. The children receive gifts of historical value, for example, books that teach them about their heritage, and they get the toys they want.

"The years also have significance. For example, 1998 was the year of nia (purpose), so everyone focused on that principle. We always use Kwanzaa as a learning tool. Even if you don't want to get together with a group, you can have a small ceremony.

"The feast is a harvest celebration—while this year the harvest was good, we pledge that the next one will be even better. We serve different dishes, for example, African dishes and African-American dishes, from fish chili and fried turkey to potato salad, nut stew, salads, akara (balls of black-eyed peas), and bean pie.

"On December thirty-first, the sixth day of Kwanzaa, a special ceremony for the Sister Circle takes place, ending at midnight with meditation. We give up the old and take up the new."

Finally, Adwoa says, "it's up to us to carry the meaning of this celebration in our hearts."

Part of Margot Dashiell's Kwanzaa ceremony involves going around the room and asking the children to indicate what they have achieved during the year in work and school. For her and her family, Kwanzaa really focuses on children, and on helping them progress. Then the adults commend the children on their progress and affirm the children's achievements. The family reflects about the future and its plans as they recognize together what their ancestors have sacrificed. Sometimes an historical figure and his or her accomplishments are cited. The ceremony concludes with a potluck—a sumptuous meal with food from the African world, such as ground nut lamb stew over white rice, sweet potato pie, black-eyed peas, greens, salad, and peach cobbler.

The Kwanzaa Buffet

Food plays an important role in this festival celebration of the first fruits of the harvest. Natural, healthy food is emphasized, along with traditional links to African, Caribbean, Creole, and Latin American cooking.

At my last Kwanzaa celebration at Sheila and Herb's home, my family and friends served the following:

- turkey and cornbread stuffing
- smothered chicken
- stuffed salmon
- chicken wings
- cornbread
- whole grain breads
- vegetarian lasagna
- macaroni and cheese
- spaghetti with meat sauce
- southern-style green beans and onions
- mixed green tomato salad
- black-eyed peas
- collard greens
- sweet potatoes
- red potato salad
- curried rice
- succotash
- homemade cranberry sauce
- fresh fruits
- lemonade
- hot apple cider with cinnamon spice
- chilled wine

The author's Kwanzaa table setting
LEWIS WATTS

This was followed by Herb's five-layer coconut lemon cake (he makes it every year), sweet potato pie, lemon meringue pie, chocolate cake, peach cobbler, pound cakes, and ice cream. The assortment of foods served up to fifty guests. All were presented in style on African-inspired dishes, in bowls made of gourds, on carved wooden trays, or in colorful African baskets. Don't worry, at the end of the meal we danced some of it off!

Sheila's sister, Joyce Matthews, makes the pilgrimage to the East Bay every Kwanzaa season from southern California. Joyce is assistant principal of the Maxine Waters Adult Vocational Training Center in Los Angeles, and her assistance to Sheila and Herb helps make our Kwanzaa celebration a success.

Vegetable Lasagna

Contributed by Joyce Matthews

1 medium onion, chopped
3 cloves fresh garlic, chopped
1 tablespoon olive oil
1 bunch carrots, chopped
1 bunch broccoli, separated into
   whole flowerets and chopped
   stems
2 medium zucchini, chopped
1 15-ounce can chopped tomatoes
Lemon pepper to taste
Spike seasoning to taste

1 package frozen spinach, or use
   fresh, carefully washed
1 12-ounce can tomato sauce
1 16-ounce package lasagna
   noodles
½ pound ricotta/cottage cheese
½ pound mozzarella cheese
½ pound Parmesan cheese
   (optional)

In large skillet, sauté onions and garlic in olive oil approximately 2 minutes. Add sliced carrots, sauté 5 minutes. Add chopped broccoli stems to mixture, then add flowerets and sauté 3 minutes. Add zucchini, sauté 2 minutes. Add chopped tomatoes and seasonings, simmer 5 minutes. Add spinach and tomato sauce. Boil noodles. Spread a little sauce on bottom of 9- by 13-inch baking dish, layer in noodles, add a layer of sauce, ricotta cheese, and mozzarella cheese. Repeat until last layer of noodles, sauce, and cheese, with Parmesan cheese on top. Bake 45 minutes in preheated 375°F oven. Serves 6 to 8 people. Enjoy!

Vegetarian Chili

Contributed by Joyce Matthews

2 medium yellow onions, chopped
6 cloves garlic, chopped
Vegetable or olive oil
3 green peppers, chopped into large pieces
6 medium carrots, chopped into small pieces
1 medium eggplant, chopped
3 ears corn, cut off the cob
5 14½-ounce cans red beans

2 28-ounce cans chopped tomatoes
2 28-ounce cans tomato puree
1 4-ounce can ripe olives, sliced
Spike seasoning, to taste
Oregano, to taste
Cilantro, to taste
1 package chili mix
Lemon pepper
Parmesan cheese, grated

In skillet, sauté onions and garlic together in oil for 2 minutes. Remove from heat and drain on paper towels. Sauté green pepper 2 to 3 minutes, remove from heat, and drain. Simmer carrots in water, add eggplant and then corn, simmering until all are slightly tender. In large pot, mix beans, tomatoes, and tomato puree, and simmer over low heat. Add carrots, corn, and eggplant to bean mixture, then onions, garlic, peppers, and olives. Stir and cook on low heat. Add seasonings and continue to simmer for 45 minutes. Serve over brown rice and top with Parmesan cheese and chopped green onions. Accompany with corn bread or garlic bread. Serves 10–12.

California artist and poet Gloria Jean weaves together her personal heritage—African-American and Cherokee. Her art includes her popular Kwanzaa card design. Gloria contributed the following reflection on her year-end holiday celebration:

"Holidays for us have always been family-oriented. This includes friends who might be without loved ones at holiday time. I host our Christmas family gathering. It's become one of a number of family traditions. Our holiday celebration took on a deeper dimension with the heritage movement that began to emerge in the latter part of the 1960s, which also meant the creation of Kwanzaa.

A Kwanzaa card by Gloria Jean

"Home preparation is a large part of our holiday ritual. . . . With traditional decorations, I make an effort to be mindful of African motifs, décor, and symbols in an attempt to blend our dual heritage. . . . Because my family is traditional in the 'Western' way, it has been difficult to completely change from Christmas to Kwanzaa, so what has happened is that we have incorporated some aspects of the Kwanzaa concept into our Christmas Day rituals. . . . I wanted to find a connection with our ancestors and to remember our bountiful heritage, lineage, and the beautiful legacy we've inherited."

All these voices reflect the different degrees and styles that mark our community's relationship with Kwanzaa. But while Kwanzaa was once considered untraditional, and those who celebrate it unconventional, its observance and rituals have become mainstream for black Americans. As we have seen, some African-Americans are even voicing concern that the holiday is becoming too commercial.

What I've observed is that the varying degrees of acceptance of Kwanzaa in our community have helped foster a craving for knowledge about ourselves as African peoples. In the next chapter, we'll take a look at how the age-old holy days of Ramadan are celebrated here and abroad.

10

Observing Ramadan

Ramadan is the month during which the Qur'an was revealed, providing guidance for the people, clear teachings, and the statute book. Those of you who witness this month shall fast therein. Those who are ill or traveling may substitute the same number of other days. GOD wishes for you convenience, not hardship, that you may fulfill your obligations, and to glorify GOD for guiding you, and to express your appreciation.

The Qur'an, 2:185

Islam is the major faith throughout large areas of Africa and Asia, and more than a billion Muslims throughout the world celebrate Ramadan. It's a time for inner reflection, devotion to God, and cultivating personal self-control. Some Muslims describe it as a kind of tune-up for their spiritual lives.

The designated times to observe the holy days of Ramadan are based on the sightings of the moon. In the United States, for example, Ramadan was observed from November 26, 2000 through December 25. Other countries may observe different dates.

Ramadan occurs during the ninth month of the Islamic calendar, a lunar calendar that is about twelve days shorter than the Gregorian calendar traditionally used in the West. Ramadan migrates throughout the seasons. These days the start of the month is often based on calculations in astronomy rather than on the naked eye. For Muslims everywhere, the average Ramadan day is approximately 13.5 hours long. The end of the month is marked by the celebration of *Eid-ul-Fitr*, a cultural practice rather than a religious one.

Muslims fast from dawn until sunset during the days of Ramadan. For them, the benefits of fasting include learning to maintain self-control while giving primacy to spirituality—the practice is a way of getting closer to God. Throughout this period, observers worship, read from the Qur'an, make charitable contributions, purify their overall behavior, and perform good deeds.

Fasting is also considered to be a way for those who have sufficient food to experience hunger, a discipline that helps to develop empathy for the less fortunate. It also teaches the worshipper to be thankful and to appreciate God's bounties. Fasting can also be beneficial physically (to those who are healthy), and provide a break from thoughtless habits or overindulgence.

The Moon Sightings

The last ten days of Ramadan are considered to have special spiritual power. This is when worshippers work to come closer to God through their devotions and good deeds. According to the Qur'an, the Night of Power (*Lailat ul-Qadr*), which usually falls on the twenty-seventh night of the month, marks the night the Qur'an was revealed to the Prophet Muhammad. This night is said to be superior to a thousand months, one reason many Muslims spend the entire night in prayer.

Traditionally, certain favorite foods are prepared during Ramadan. The holiday's celebrants reflect on community, so Muslims often gather together after sunset to share in the Ramadan evening meal.

Invoking the Spirit of Ramadan

Worshippers throughout the world use some of the following phrases to congratulate one another for the completion of their fasting and the *Eid-ul-Fitr* festival:

- ◎ *Kullu am wa antum bi-khair*: (Arabic) "May you be well throughout the year."
- ◎ *Atyab at-tihani bi-munasabat hulul shahru Ramadan al-Mubarak*: (Arabic) "Most precious congratulations on the occasion of the coming of Ramadan."
- ◎ *Elveda, ey Ramazan*: (Turkish) "Farewell, O Ramadan."
- ◎ *Ramadan mubarak*: The universal phrase for "A Blessed Ramadan."

In providing a special period in which to strengthen one's relationship with God and one's spiritual beliefs, Ramadan is not unlike Lent or Yom Kippur. It brings together a widely dispersed body of people, all striving for inner peace, and for African-Americans, reinforces our bonds as people of African heritage. There is a marvelous camaraderie among Muslims. Everyone helps each other. It takes a lot of discipline to change—or to maintain—our beliefs in a world where most people rely on the status quo. In this sense, those who embrace Islam also embrace each other.

During Ramadan Muslims extend special support to each other and encourage those who want to observe it to do so. As cleansing through fasting or abstaining from unhealthy foods brings one in touch with his or her higher self, it is very special when some of the older children decide to fast. Many experience a great sense of accomplishment because they meet this challenge. Muslims also make a concerted effort to spend time in prayer throughout the month of Ramadan—and every month—and to allow no quarreling or disputing, either in or away from home.

Muslim prayers begin at 5:00 A.M. every morning, so during Ramadan breakfast is eaten before the sun rises; dinner takes place only when the sun goes down. Many people who are not Muslims join the daytime fasting, affirming the concept of turning to God through abstinence. At the end of the thirty days of daytime fasting, Muslim brothers and sisters pray, reflect, and then feast to celebrate the end of the observance of this holy period.

Sister Rahiema Muslem has been a dedicated Muslim since 1967. She says: "Ramadan, the holy month, observes when the Qur'an was revealed to the Prophet Muhammad. Muslims cleanse their bodies by fasting, strictly as a dedication to God to show him that we can be obedient and mindful of him. Muslims call God Allah, and Ramadan is designed to let Allah know that we are in full submission to his will. Allah blesses you ten-fold when you complete Ramadan. Elderly citizens, the sick, or those taking medications are not expected to observe it. Ramadan is not supposed to be a hardship on anyone, but a blessing. At the end of Ramadan, *Eid*, there is a festive celebration, and we exchange gifts."

My good friend Gale Madyun says she participates in Ramadan about every other year. She believes that it's important to break the routine of our existence and to concentrate on the spiritual. "Sometimes I do Lent; I appreciate the discipline for focusing on what is important in this world."

A sample of the foods served at a Ramadan feast might consist of bean soup, barbecue lamb, curry chicken, fish and chicken gumbo, okra and fish sausage, fish loaf and crumb dressing, turnip greens, fried rice, fish chili, cabbage rolls, herb-steamed squash, baked broccoli casserole, cream of wheat bread, and a chef's fish salad. Dessert might be navy bean pie, chocolate and pound cakes, and homemade ice cream. The food is always healthy and delicious.

Three months after Ramadan, on the tenth day of the twelfth month of the Muslim calendar year, some Muslims go on the hajj, the pilgrimage to Mecca, the Saudi Arabian city that was the birthplace of Muhammad and is Islam's holiest city. The pilgrimage brings together Muslims of all races for a profound, uniting spiritual experience. If they are able, all devout Muslims make the pilgrimage once in their lifetime. When they return, they participate in the feast called the Eid-ul-Adha. Maryum Abdul-Shaheed, a devoted Muslim and good friend says, "Ramadan gives me a deep sense of unity. I feel light-hearted in spirit and dedicated to my belief in Islam."

Vegetable Chowder

Contributed by Maryum Abdul-Shaheed

½ stick butter or margarine
1 large onion, diced
2 cloves garlic, chopped
1 medium zucchini, diced
4 large russet potatoes, diced
3 large carrots, diced

1 11-ounce can creamed corn
1 11-ounce can corn niblets
1 quart milk
Cornstarch or flour to thicken
Salt and pepper to taste

In large soup pot, slowly sauté onion, garlic, and zucchini until transparent. In separate pot, boil potatoes and carrots until just tender. Drain and add to sautéed vegetables. Add creamed corn and corn niblets to soup pot. Stir in milk and heat to slow simmer. Add salt and pepper. Thicken with cornstarch and water or flour and water. Serves 10.

Gourmet Lamb Chops

From the author's kitchen

4 medium shoulder lamb chops or 6
   rib chops
1 cup Yoshida's Original Gourmet
   Sauce
1 tablespoon rosemary
1 teaspoon garlic salt

1 teaspoon pepper
6 large portobello mushrooms,
   sliced lengthwise
1 large onion, sliced
½ tablespoon olive oil

Clean lamb chops and blot dry. Brush both sides of chops with sauce, then season both sides with rosemary, garlic salt, and pepper. Place chops on a rack in a broiler pan. Broil approximately 10 minutes on each side or until done. (Pierce meat with a fork to make sure it is tender.) Sauté mushrooms and onions in a heated skillet with olive oil; drain. Serve mushrooms and onions over the lamb chops. Serves 2–3.

Baked Trout

Contributed by Ernest James Broussard

Ernest Broussard

This recipe, from my brother, is a family favorite.

2 medium whole trout (about
   ½ pound each)
1 tablespoon olive oil
1 tablespoon Cajun Creole
   seasoning

1 tablespoon rosemary or dill
1 tablespoon lemon pepper
½ tablespoon crushed red pepper
1 tablespoon Mrs. Dash
1 medium onion, thinly sliced

Preheat oven to 350°F. Remove heads from trout and rinse fish; place on a paper towel to dry. Rub olive oil over fish, then rub on seasonings. Cover with sliced onions. Place in an aluminum foil-lined pan. Bake approximately 20 minutes, until tender. Serves 2–3.

Marinated Green Beans

From the author's kitchen

1 pound of freshly steamed green
   beans
½ medium red onion, sliced thin
½ teaspoon garlic salt

½ teaspoon pepper
6 ounces Italian dressing
Parsley for garnish

Place the green beans and onion in a bowl and season with garlic salt and pepper. Mix in the Italian dressing. Marinate in the refrigerator for at least four hours or overnight. Before serving drain excess marinade and sprinkle green beans with parsley. Serves 4.

Navy Bean Pie

Contributed by Maryum Abdul-Shaheed

2 cups navy beans, cooked without
   salt
2 cups evaporated milk

1 teaspoon nutmeg
2 teaspoons vanilla extract
1 tablespoon vegetable oil

Drain cooked navy beans and mash to a fine texture through a food mill or ricer. Mix together with remaining ingredients and refrigerate 24 hours. The following day mix in a bowl:

6 eggs, beaten
4 cups sugar or honey
¼ cup flour

½ pound butter, creamed
1 teaspoon salt
1 teaspoon cinnamon

Combine and mix well with the navy bean mixture.

PIE CRUST
3 cups flour
1 teaspoon salt

½ pinch baking powder
1 cup vegetable shortening

Mix ingredients well and gradually add ½ cup of water to make dough. Roll out to fit 2 10-inch pie pans.

Pour mixture into unbaked pie shells. Bake at 375°F for 45 minutes or until a toothpick stuck into the center of the pie comes out clean. Each pie serves 6.

11

New Year's Eve and Day

If you're working on New Year's Day, you'll be working the whole year through.

Old African-American Saying

January 1, 1863, was the day President Abraham Lincoln signed the Emancipation Proclamation, the beginning of the end to slavery. New Year's Day is a time to be grateful for that act. It is a time to get my house in order. My temple (yes, my body) must be built upon a spiritual foundation in order to be at peace. Spirituality and good health work hand in hand for me—I know I can't do anything without my health, and I also know I can't achieve what I want in this life without being spiritual. This time of the year is like spring cleaning, except that it involves a spiritual cleansing. It is time to take an assessment of how I have been treating my life.

I need to listen to my inner voice as it tries to guide me. This seems simple, doesn't it? Just listen and do it. Just as God gave us all the other parts of our bodies, he gave us this inner voice as a way to provide direction and guidance. You cannot go wrong if you heed its positive whispers.

So this is a time for me to take inventory and readjust my roadmap, to think about where I have been and where am I going, so that when I look back on my life I'll be pleased about the direction I took and the choices I have made. As I reflect and reminisce, I see that I may have accomplished more than I have realized. Reflection puts things in the proper perspective for me.

"We are all just trying to make our way back to God," my friend Gale once said. I think we must all begin with the spiritual. Happy New Year!

Blanche Brown is a person who is deeply connected to her spiritual self regardless of the season. For New Year's, she does readings for the whole family in the tradition of African priests. "We have a way of talking to the orishas—God's intermediaries, who deal with the needs of the people on earth and manage the whole universe—through cowry shells," she says. "You throw the shells, and according to how they fall, you do a reading that attempts to see what's ahead for the coming year."

In a practice that resembles the Asian tradition of cleaning the house for the new year, Blanche focuses on cleaning: her altar water is changed; her orishas are polished; the area around her front doorway is cleaned; and incense and herbs are burned, cleansing the atmosphere. Then a flag representing a protective deity is put up. It will remain there, protecting Blanche's home throughout the year.

Launching the New Year

The sounds of rhythms from the drums in the neighborhoods around her mark the beginning of December for Marcheta Q'McManus-Eneas and her family. She can hear them practicing for Junkanoo, celebrated on both December 26 and on New Year's Eve.

"The majority of the African Bahamian culture comes from West Africa," Marcheta says. "They are for the most part of the Yoruba tribe. In Yoruba land, there was a religious practice that we call spirit-worshipping and is known as Egungun. The Egungun is a secret society, which is a burial society, or a society of the dead.

"If a person has a dead loved one that he wishes to communicate with during the celebration, he usually will have a mask made. It is the mask that will become a vessel through which the loved one enters the dancer. This is done through the Egungun societies. There are also, during the Egungun, other major or lesser deities present at the celebrations. These Gods have strong powers and are also masked. The masked entities, depending on the spirit, dance a certain way, and their costumes also represent particular spirits.

"With the exception of Brazilians and their Condomblé celebration, Junkanoo is the closest descendant of Egungun. It has become a popular tourist attraction in Nassau, Bahamas. The spectacle pulsates with the polyrhythmic sounds of the goatskin drums and cowbells cascading into the night air, supporting and sustaining the dancers in their frenzied, trance-like movements. With the rhythm of the drums, the spectators become more and more absorbed as they get into the spirit of Junkanoo. It is the drums that call the spirits, the drums that cause one to lose all worries and join in the new West African Bahamian phenomenon called Junkanoo.

"On some levels, the roots of Junkanoo are greatly misunderstood," Marcheta says. "Perhaps in the days when we did not know or understand our heritage, it could be conceivable that those who thought they understood actually misunderstood and thought that such a spectacle is because the Yoruba slaves were 'happy' folks, receiving a box of old clothes and leftover food the day after Christmas. To see Junkanoo in its present state shows the pride and love of the Bahamian people. Christmas in the Bahamas is not Christmas unless you can hear the drums awakening the spirits of long ago, to frolic with us before the year is over and before the new year begins," Marcheta explains.

"These rituals and dances also feature the beauty of the intricately handmade costumes and dazzling headpieces worn by celebrants. The participants dance in the streets to the rhythmic beat of drumming instruments, based on Nigerian Yoruba traditions. The festival starts at midnight and sometimes does not end until six in the morning. After the festival you go to someone's house for breakfast, and then another house for lunch, and then a party in the evening," Marcheta says. "It's not a time for a lot of sleep. My family is out all day and night. We have the advantage of a Bahamian-style New Year and an African-American style as well."

Marcheta's New Year's decorations include the Junkanoo dolls made of confetti that are placed on her dinner table, which is decorated in black and gold. Another tradition for New Year's that Marcheta inherited from her family is cooking chitlins (chitterlings) that she brings to the Bahamas frozen from the States—greens, for good luck, and black-eyed peas, for black people. She has incorporated all this into the Junkanoo celebration.

Janet Langhart's mother was born in Kentucky and raised in Tennessee, and Janet tells of a superstitious practice her mother brought with her. "The first person to come through your home on New Year's Day must be a male, and he had to go through every room before a female could come through. He would walk through the entire house to bring good luck." The year no male relative was available, Janet remembers her mother having to get a male neighbor to do the walk-through.

Janet Langhart and her sister (with their mother) as children

Preparing for the New Year on New Year's morning, Roscoe Higgs-Dellums always begins the meal by serving buckwheat pancakes; according to black southern tradition, the "buck" in buckwheat symbolizes prosperity, "so we eat buckwheat pancakes for breakfast New Year's morning with the hope that we'll have lots of bucks throughout the year," she says. "Later that day we'll have greens to symbolize greenbacks, and black-eyed peas to symbolize coins." Apparently this practice derives from handed-down post-slavery mythology.

When the Dellumses came to Washington, D.C., they learned the traditions of southern blacks, including how they celebrate New Year's. Cooking for family and friends, Roscoe began to prepare mustard and collard greens, black-eyed peas, ham, chitlins, candied yams, cornbread, rice, and sweet potato pie—not bad for a third-generation girl from the northwest!

Roscoe Higgs-Dellums and family members

When I was a child, Aunty (Roscoe's mother) always held a New Year's Day open house, and that's where my family would go. Homemade eggnog was served in a silver punch bowl, and we would help ourselves to candied nuts and fruit cake while the five Higgs sisters related their New Year's Eve party stories about the night before. Roscoe says, "When we became teenagers and started to get crushes on boys, my mother placed mistletoe all over the house for New Year's Day, and it became a day for first kisses as well as a time for celebration."

"If this is good, a little more must be better," Roscoe observes about the ingredients in her favorite recipes. Her mother's eggnog became all the richer because her mother used an extra dollop of ice cream in it. Roscoe splits the eggnog in two so those who don't drink can sample it alcohol-free.

Holiday Eggnog

Contributed by Roscoe Higgs-Dellums

1 dozen eggs
2 pounds white sugar
1 quart half-and-half
1 quart heavy cream, whipped, or
    softened vanilla ice cream

Rum or whiskey to taste (optional)
Nutmeg

Separate egg yolks and egg whites into separate bowls. Beat yolks until they become light. Beat whites and gradually add sugar as mixture continues to thicken. Stir in half-and-half and liquor. Fold in whipped cream or ice cream. Chill. Dust with nutmeg. Serves 6–10.

Candied Nuts

Contributed by Roscoe Higgs-Dellums

1 cup sugar
⅓ cup milk
½ teaspoon cinnamon

½ teaspoon vanilla
2 cups pecans or walnuts

Mix sugar, milk, and cinnamon, and bring to slow boil. Continue boiling until mixture thickens and forms a soft ball. Remove from heat. Add vanilla. Quickly stir in nuts. The result: individualized candied nuts. These can be spooned into decorative holiday tins and given as gifts. Makes about 2 cups.

"Parties are given so we can laugh and enjoy friendship and music. They are always a celebration of life," says Roscoe. With all the formal New Year's Eve parties given in Washington, D.C., friends still remember the year that Roscoe and family decided to have a jogging party that night. About two hundred people showed up, many of them couples dressed in matching jogging clothes, and when the clock struck midnight they jogged around the block. Where there was snow on the property, champagne was packed all around the trees; every couple got its own bottle and went in to dine on soul food. They danced to the sounds of a disc jockey playing music on one level of the house and a live piano player at another, playing on the same white baby grand that Roscoe's father had given her mother as a wedding gift.

When I go to a party I always try and take the host a gift of liquor or food—wine, coffee, teas, candies, or dessert. I usually had difficulty wrapping the gifts that I gave on New Year's Eve; then I started using pieces of decorative fabric, tulle, or even a brown paper bag tied with colorful ribbons. You can buy a variety of beautiful craft paper at an art supply store for wrapping gifts.

The author's New Year's Day table

If you are planning a New Year's party yourself, start early. Send your invitations out a month in advance, and don't get caught with the last-minute frenzies. The earlier you start planning and organizing, the more relieved and relaxed you'll be. Shop for groceries early. And remember that there is so much demand at this time of the year for musicians, caterers, servers, housekeepers, babysitters, etc., that you may have to book them well before your party. You will enjoy Christmas more if you know you have your New Year's bash all ready to go. I used to work with a woman who planned her parties literally months in advance. When it got close to party night there was never a last-minute rush, and she was calm and collected. She enjoyed her parties.

Wanting to find herself "in a place of serenity on New Year's Eve," Gwendolyn Goldsby Grant usually goes to church. She is challenging herself to be the best she can be for the New Year. Through meditation and prayer and "a kind of consecration," she prepares for the challenges ahead. "Our life is serious business," she says. "I used to think that life was a bowl of cherries, but I found out that there are some sour grapes in it, too."

She, too, must have black-eyed peas on New Year's Day, She prepares a big pot to serve the day's visitors in anticipation of all those she expects to arrive. "Those legumes represent our ancestral struggle. Those peas were part of sustaining my ancestors' lives, because they were not privy to a diverse menu in the world. Beans and ham hocks were their staples. And we did survive, even in the face of poor diet . . . and all the other things that go along with an oppressive life. . . . On New Year's we're trying to build up the fellowship that we are going to need for the rest of the year with the family and the community."

Newswoman Belva Davis celebrates New Year's Day in the general tradition of Gwendolyn Goldsby Grant and Roscoe Dellums, but with a twist. In her Louisiana tradition, "you can't go to somebody else's house and get their luck—you have to come to your own house and cook there." Though she usually goes to enjoy gumbo at the home of a good friend on New Year's Day, she cooks her own greens—collard greens or Chinese mustard greens "dollar bills" and black-eyed peas "small change", as she calls them.

"When we lived in Berkeley," Amy Billingsley recalls, "New Year's represented a time for 'down-home doings.'" She and her friends, including Roscoe Higgs-Dellums, gathered around an ethnic potluck, and "really talked—we'd be talking about people's dreams for the New Year."

Joan Sonn and Mary Braxton-Joseph are friends, and both have marked the New Year by attending the same fundraiser—an event in South Africa to benefit a charity in Cape Town. One year the theme was roaring twenties; the next year the theme was New York City, and the guests with the best costume were awarded a trip to New York. Both Joan and Mary's families enjoy the event and have the pleasure of contributing to a good cause.

Sheila Bridges spends New Year's with her close friends, and she usually hosts a dinner party; she finds that this has greater significance than going out to large parties. So six to eight people drop

Mary Braxton-Joseph

by for a late potluck dinner, and everyone brings a bottle of bubbly. Most of all, Sheila says, she enjoys the intimacy of these gatherings.

For Patricia Russell McCloud, this is a time for reflection. She goes to church for "watch night" services, a tradition that harks back to the day abolition was announced. Over the course of the evening there is praise to the Lord and private prayer; then the service begins, the pastor speaks, and there's altar call, with numbers of people invited to go to the altar to say their prayers. By midnight, more and more people have crowded into the church, and the congregation begins the New Year together.

Ruth Beckford chooses to be alone on New Year's Eve. First of all, she enjoys her own company, she says. It's an introspective time for her—to put her papers in order, create an "I want" list, and to take stock. Ruth says that too many parties she has been to for New Year's Eve have seemed to hinge on forced gaiety. She does love to party, she adds,—just not on New Year's Eve.

In 1938 Hattie Mosley moved from New Orleans to Saratoga Springs, New York. At first she sold chicken and biscuits to stable boys who worked at the racetrack. Her great cooking eventually led to her establishing a restaurant that focuses on southern- and New Orleans–style food.

One day Christel Albritton MacLean stopped in for dinner, and Hattie's husband, who was waiting tables, invited her back to the kitchen to meet Hattie, then ninety-one.

She told Christel, "You're gonna buy this restaurant." At the time, Christel worked for Salomon Brothers on Wall Street, and certainly had no plans to open a restaurant. She changed her mind about a year and a half later, though. When Hattie and her husband both passed away in 1998, Hattie was at peace about one thing, at least: her restaurant was in good hands.

For their New Year's Eve buffet, Hattie's offers a menu of southern and particularly Louisiana cuisine. It includes smothered pork chops, Hoppin' John (black-eyed peas), Creole oyster pie, sweet potato pie, pecan pie, bread pudding with whiskey sauce, holiday punch, and champagne. They start serving late in the afternoon and toast in the New Year in the restaurant's new outdoor patio. Designed by Christel's husband, Colin Scott MacLean, who oversaw every aspect of the project, the brick courtyard and garden setting is enchanting, enclosed with a tent decorated with midnight-blue fabric and gold stars. When you look up at the ceiling, you can see the red chili pepper chandelier hanging down the center of the tent, illuminating the room.

Christel says Saratoga is a community-oriented town—they call New Year's Eve "First Night," and local businesses sponsor puppet shows, finger-painting, and other events.

Christel Albritton MacLean and
Colin Scott MacLean

Bourbon Shrimp Mandeville
From Hattie's Kitchen

Contributed by Christel Albritton MacLean

8 jumbo shrimp, peeled and
  deveined
3 ounces Cajun seasoning
1 ounce olive oil
1 red bell pepper, sliced
1 green bell pepper, sliced

3 ounces Kentucky bourbon
4 ounces heavy cream
¼ stick butter
2 cups cooked rice
1 bunch scallions, chopped

Lightly dust shrimp with Cajun seasoning. In a sauté pan, heat olive oil. Add shrimp and red and green peppers, and sauté until shrimp is cooked. Flame with bourbon and remove shrimp. Add heavy cream and reduce, simmering until sauce thickens. Add shrimp and butter. When butter has melted, pour shrimp mixture over rice and sprinkle with scallions. Serves 2.

Peggy Cooper Cafritz says that she always spends the New Year's holiday with the kids. She has many happy memories, and mentions one year, when she was renting a friend's house in Palm Beach, Florida, and she and her children jumped into the Atlantic at midnight on New Year's Eve.

Friends will be glad when Cheryl R. Riley resumes a tradition she maintained for twenty years. Cheryl's New Year's Day open house started at two in the afternoon, with the last guest usually departing at ten in the evening. She observed the old southern tradition of inviting good luck and money by preparing two restaurant-size pots of black-eyed peas and two big pots of collard greens, one for vegetarians. Cheryl provided cornbread and guests brought homemade cobblers and one even brought homemade ice cream. All of her friends, business associates, and family—sometimes as many as one hundred fifty people—came through the house during the course of the day.

Margot Dashiell remembers laughter, too, and being with family on New Year's Day, the high point of the year for them—and celebrated at the home of her mother's godmother, Aunt Nita.

"Anita Boziner Johnson and her mother's family came from Louisiana," Margot says. "Aunt Nita would serve all the traditional foods: a sumptuous table was set, featuring fine lace and china, and crystal goblets. She served turkey and cornbread dressing, hog headcheese, black-eyed peas, ham, bourbon balls, and homemade fruitcake. You realized what tremendous work went into this—the talent, love, and commitment.

"At family holiday celebrations we don't consider a meal complete without my sister Merryl's cranberry sauce. Sometimes she thoughtfully prepares extra sauce, which becomes a cherished present for a family member or friend when it's placed in an attractive jar. The cook doesn't have to worry about anyone getting tipsy from the wine that's in it since the alcohol content evaporates in the cooking," she adds.

Merryl's Cranberry Sauce

Contributed by Merryl Dashiell

1 package cranberries
1 cup good red table wine
2 cups sugar
Pinch of cloves

Pinch of allspice
½ to 1 tablespoon orange zest
   (grated outer peel of fresh
   orange)

Pick out any remaining stems of cranberries and rinse. Mix wine and sugar in 3-quart (or larger) pot. Bring to a boil and add cranberries. Turn down flame to a low simmer, stirring occasionally. Cook for 30 minutes; during the last 5 minutes add spices and zest. Cool, place in container, and refrigerate overnight. Water can be used instead of wine, but wine adds a nice depth of flavor.

During slavery, African-Americans referred to New Year's Eve as "heartbreak day," for it was a time to say goodbye to their loved ones, with whom they had been briefly reunited after a year apart, many having traveled across enormous distances to be together for the Christmas holidays.

Our lives are vastly different today. Fortunately, most of us can rejoice in the blessings of the past year, no matter how hard our struggle. With courage and vision, we can look forward to accomplishing new goals, limited only by our own reluctance to reach for the stars.

12

The African Renaissance Comes Home

Together we keep ties alive, life spirits, and spread hope.

Margot Dashiell

During Black History Month, I went into my local bookstore and looked at the African-American book section. I found an absolutely wonderful array of books. If only I had time to read them all, or even to listen to the tape versions, I know I could tap into a wealth of knowledge. Seeking self-knowledge through history, spirituality, and other education, and shepherding myself to a higher plane of existence, is a goal I cherish.

You can't grow if you don't know your history. How can you reach your highest potential if you don't know where you have come from?

Celebrating Dr. Martin Luther King Jr.

All humanity is involved in a single process, and all men are brothers. To the degree that I harm my brother, no matter what he is doing to me, to that extent I am harming myself.

Martin Luther King Jr.

As I write this, we in the United States have recently celebrated Dr. Martin Luther King Jr.'s January 15 birthday. Since the official holiday fell on a Monday, this year the observance encompassed an entire weekend of tribute. Schoolchildren had Monday off, many businesses and all government agencies closed, and television producers appeared to be more focused than usual on the culture of African America, a kind of a warm-up for Black History Month, perhaps.

Reverend Dr. Martin Luther King Jr., one of the greatest American leaders of the late twentieth century, has deeply affected us all. He stands out vividly today, for there is such leadership vacuum in our community. A leader of the Montgomery Bus Boycott (1955–56), keynote speaker at the March on Washington (1963), and the youngest Nobel Peace Prize laureate (1964), King and his policy of nonviolent protest were dominant forces in the civil rights movement from 1957 to 1968. In 1957 he brought together a group of black leaders and launched what would become the influential Southern Christian Leadership Conference (SCLC).

At the historic March on Washington on August 28, 1963, King delivered his now-famous "I Have a Dream" speech on the steps of the Lincoln Memorial. "Let us be dissatisfied until that day when nobody will shout 'White Power!'—when nobody will shout 'Black Power!'—but everybody will talk about God's power and human power," he implored.

When he later rallied behind the anti-war movement, he antagonized many civil rights leaders and others by calling the United States "the greatest purveyor of violence in the world." In announcing his opposition to the Vietnam war, he was able to open the eyes of many apolitical citizens, black and white. He forced the white middle class to concede that no movement could dramatically affect the course of government in America unless it involved deliberate and restrained aggressiveness, persistent dissent, and even militant confrontation. These were the very ingredients of the civil rights struggle in the South during the 1960s.

To King, poverty was the single domestic issue that directly related to the Vietnam struggle, so he launched an inspiring campaign against them both. His death by gunshot in 1968 on the balcony of the black-owned Lorraine Motel in Memphis, Tennessee, caused a wave of violence in Washington, Chicago, and Baltimore as grief and anger engulfed the black community. How could a man so dedicated to the pursuit of nonviolence become the victim of violence?

To me, Dr. King is a symbol of peace. My daughter Zahrah reminded me of her early elementary school years, when she was one of two blacks in her predominantly Caucasian class. On Dr. King's birthday, I would deliver a lecture to her classmates on black history and of course, Dr. King's contributions. Zahrah remembers that her classmates were captivated and very attentive to the information; this made my daughter very proud. When my son Jule entered elementary school, I did the same thing; I felt it was important for all children to be exposed to the true historical facts regarding African Americans.

Alma Arrington-Brown, Chairman of the Board of the Ronald H. Brown Foundation, says she remembers when Dr. King spoke at Fisk University in 1961, where she was a student. They had to move the event to the gymnasium because of the standing-room crowd. It was phenomenal, she says, and people were mesmerized by Dr. King's voice.

Father Jay, the recipient of numerous awards including the Martin Luther King Jr. Award for Outstanding Community Services, calls the King birthday weekend another opportunity for families and friends to honor their bonds and come together. He celebrates Dr. King's birthday with a family of parishioners and tremendously enjoys being part of their celebration. They discuss Dr. King, African-American history, and contemporary politics. Adults of all ages participate.

My friend Gale Madyun, a retired geologist and writer, says, "When I realize the significance of Dr. King's birthday, I am hopeful that mankind is moving toward greater understanding, though it may be coming too slowly for my lifetime."

When Reverend Bernice King, the youngest daughter of the late Dr. King, spoke at the Ebenezer Baptist Church service commemorating Dr. King's birthday on January 18, 1999, she told the audience about an incident that took place a few days before the recent New Year's Day. An assistant in her pastor's church found herself having to cancel an order they had placed for balloons they would be using for their church's New Year's Eve service. No cancellation policy had ever been explained to her by the company, and the man who answered the phone and received the cancellation order, needless to say, was upset. As she describes it, he went on to say that "when blacks order he expects them not to follow through on their commitments. 'That is how your people are. That's why I don't deal with black people.' " Then he hung up. Telling the story, Reverend Bernice King concluded by adding that "although the physical manifestations of racism are gone, they are still etched into the hearts and minds of many and still pour from people's lips."

She says she is often asked, where she thinks we are in terms of her father's words, "I have a dream that my four little children not be judged by the color of their skin, but by the content of their character." Her reply this day was, "Your presence here today is indicative and makes me hopeful that there are men and women committed to the ideals of what my father fought to eliminate, that being the final vestiges of racism."

When I asked my mother, Maybelle Broussard, about her impressions of this great man, she replied that she always had admired his stance on nonviolence. She has seen some progress as far as jobs for black people go, she says, as well as some improvement in the African-American economic base, but we need to keep pushing, she believes, to continue to help ourselves by becoming both more business-oriented and less materialistic. Blacks are still not where we ought to be economically because we don't push hard enough, she says.

I know that we need to continue to unify our race and be positive role models for future generations. Our youth are our responsibility. Furniture designer Cheryl Riley once said that if we don't document our own history and tell our own stories, we certainly can't expect anyone else to do it. She believes that Dr. King is the reason we can still say that the United States is a democratic country: "He helped to bring this country to its senses and made this a livable country for everyone. We are living through the legacy of Dr. King, one of the most brilliant orators of his time. We need to keep his name forward for the younger generation. We must pass our history on to them and teach them how much we have contributed to this country. There was free labor to build this country . . . where would America be if there were no black people ever here? . . . African Americans have contributed tremendously to the strength and viability of America."

Generalizing these thoughts to address commercial products based on black experience, Margot Dashiell, president of Frederick Douglass Designs, says, "when our pictures or products give someone joy, provide pride in our history, remind a man or woman, boy or girl, of their value, we are lifted too. We are proud to be a part of a large circle of people who believe that pictures are mirrors that remind us of who we are. The reflection in the mirror lifts people up or puts them down. As our partner, you take the words and pictures, which you have encouraged us to gather, and send thousands of these little mirrors across and beyond the United States. Together we keep ties alive, lift spirits, and spread hope."

The son of an educator and a domestic worker, South African Bishop Desmond Tutu won the Nobel Peace in 1984 and the Martin Luther King Nonviolence Peace Prize in 1985. President Nelson Mandela appointed him chairman of the South African Truth and Reconciliation Committee. Himself long the target of repressive measures and threats by the former

South African government, Bishop Tutu has been unrelenting in his advocacy for non-racial democracy and human rights in South Africa. When he rose to speak at the service commemorating Dr. King's birthday at Ebenezer Baptist Church on January 18, 1999, he said, "the victory in South Africa was your victory here in America." That victory would not have happened without the prayers, love, and support we sent. Bishop Tutu thanked the congregation and the audience for them.

"It is a great privilege to thank you," he said. "We want to give a special birthday present to Dr. King, to say he inspired us. Dr. Martin Luther King Jr. inspired us, and our gift to you is our freedom. Our victory, in a very real way, is your victory, a monument we want to build to Dr. King. Our victory is entirely due to you. Thank you to all the black and white people who supported us," he said.

Having waited for decades to vote in his own country, Bishop Tutu was sixty-three years old—and Nelson Mandela was seventy-six—when they first cast their votes.

Bishop Tutu gave recognition to the strength of African-Americans and the fact that we emerged as strong as we are from slavery. This gave his people faith that God would deliver the South Africans from their bondage. "If God be for us, who be against us?" he asked.

Bishop Tutu calls America a caring country. He thinks the United States could reach greater heights if we give ourselves the opportunity to tell one another our stories. He believes that we should draw out the poisons and the pain that still linger in the pit of our stomachs. America has not yet come to grips with the legacy of slavery and the Civil War, he observes. He encourages us to risk opening these festering wounds in order to cleanse them. The split along racial lines during the O.J. Simpson murder case was part of this unhealthy, festering silence, he notes.

We must get all the hurt out, he believes, and learn the skill of really listening, even if every word burns: "God has a dream, like Dr. Martin Luther King, that America will become more compassionate, gentle, and forgiving, more inclusive of all, especially of those with different sexual orientation. The wonderful people of this land realize we are all members of one human family. Then maybe this country would be able to say truly, 'we are free at last, thank God almighty we are free at last.' "

When my children were young, we belonged to the organization Jack and Jill of America, Inc. At the time, San Francisco didn't offer the social and cultural exposure for African Americans that I believed my children needed to fulfill their lives. The schools they attended were predominantly white.

This nonprofit organization's mission is to enhance the social, cultural, and intellectual development of our black children, and it provided a way for my children to participate in productive educational, cultural, civic, and social activities with other black children their age. I so wanted them to have the same exposure to the kind of strong community of African Americans I had when I was growing up in Oakland.

While activities at Jack and Jill include the entire black family, it was founded as a mothers' organization, and it is the mothers who are responsible for the organization's day-to-day work. The San Francisco chapter always presented a Black History program for the family each year. Our children, divided into groups according to their ages, practiced long and hard to make their presentations on stage memorable. We always produced staged readings and performances of plays that focus on our history and on black historical figures. Afterward, we always celebrated the African-American family by having a dinner that recognized and celebrated the strides we have made as a people.

The Pleasures of Family and History

Family history is precious. As I write, I'm looking forward to inviting my family over for dinner and to playing a few instructive games relating to our own black history. Through my son Jule's marriage to Melanie Austria, a Filipino-American, we are now a mixed family, so of course I'll be inviting the Austria side of the family to join us. Together we can share our cultures and enjoy some short presentations about people from all of our backgrounds.

Throughout February, Black History Month, network and cable television now present some wonderful programs documenting African American history. And there is a flowering of African-American historical museums, festivals, and exhibits all over the country. (See *Pathfinders Travel*, a travel magazine for people of color, for lists of historical and social events for African Americans year round).

You might be able to gather a group of elders in your family before it's too late, and tape or otherwise document as much information about your ancestors as you can. Copies of the tape or a synopsis of its contents make wonderful gifts for Black History Month, Kwanzaa, or any time of year.

For many years I saved all my African-American wall calendars that contained African-American history and pictures. I plan to make it into a black history scrapbook and present it to my grown kids.

Joan Sonn, born in George, South Western Cape, South Africa, is a teacher by profession. She says her family keeps their history alive by telling stories. When the family comes together, her husband's father tells stories about apartheid, and about other historical aspects of their country. Joan's husband Franklin tells stories about his own childhood. This has helped the children understand how their parents had suffered in the past.

Until the very recent past, Joan and Franklin lived mostly for the sake of their community and the struggle against apartheid, as opposed to focusing on material wealth or other such pursuits. According to Joan, we should do the best we can without expecting to get anything back; we should not give in order to receive. She is grateful that they were chosen to represent their country when Franklin was made ambassador to the U.S. under President Mandela.

Many African Americans are compelled to affirm our history. In recognition of Joyce Burrows Dinkins's concern for literacy, the Joyce B. Dinkins Children's Collection was established at the Schomburg Center for Research in Black Culture, in New York City. A research library of the New York Public Libraries, the center's purpose is collecting, preserving, and offering information that documents the history of peoples of African descent. As the former first lady of New York City, she promoted education, health care, and the arts for children. She is convinced that our youngsters deserve to know as much as possible about our heritage, and that we as adults have a responsibility to pass this information on to the next generation.

The value of her blackness was instilled in her at a very early age, says Janet Langhart, president of Langhart Communications. In her role as first lady of defense, she is a particularly active advocate for the needs of American soldiers and their families. Her values came from her mother and the experience of growing up in Indianapolis, traditional headquarters of the violently racist Ku Klux Klan. She says that her black consciousness was intensified by having known and touched a slave, her great, great grandfather, a man born into slavery who died when she was seven. Janet was very aware of hearing stories told by him, in the old African grio tradition. In those days there was no television, of course, so folks related to each other. Janet remembers the beautiful way these stories were told, and now, she says, she lives her culture every day.

An avid collector of African art, Cheryl R. Riley is a designer of Afrocentric furniture and loves going to the Museum of African Art in New York's Soho district. She particularly enjoys the way the museum's exhibits take the visitor through ceremonies, practices, and lifestyles in a fully thematic show, which adds another important dimension to the art on display. She says there is a profound reason that these things have survived in people's cultures for centuries; they feed a deep human need for people to express themselves.

The San Francisco Museum of Art recently acquired Cheryl's folding Hunter Screen, inspired by the original which was shown recently in New York. Designed for use in a ceremony to protect the hunter, the African screen was hung with amulets, mirrors, animal teeth, skin, and claws. Cheryl's screen has different elements, and its purpose is purely spiritual, she says.

Black History, Oakland Style

The observance of black history is very important to employees of the City of Oakland, a longtime African-American stronghold. Formal celebrations were launched in 1988 by a committee headed by Doris Peeler-Brown, an administrative analyst in the city's Community and Economic Development Agency. An educator at heart, she believes it's vital to understand our history, rituals, and ceremonies. The event is always upbeat and of unusual quality. One year, the celebration theme was "Moving Higher"; in another, it was "Walking Tall Through It All." Among the important historical facts always discussed is why Carter G. Goodson, the father of Black History Week a precursor to Black History Month, in 1926 selected the colors black (for the people), green (for our land), and red (for the bloodshed during our struggle) to represent our flag. (In 1976 the observance became Black History Month.) Also discussed is the meaning behind the African-American national them, "Lift Every Voice and Sing," before the celebrants join into sing it. (It was written by attorney and author James Weldon Johnson, an African-American, to celebrate the birthday of Abraham Lincoln.) Each year, the program is dedicated to someone who made a contribution to the historical progress of the black community—not necessarily someone famous.

· Speakers at the celebration have included Judge Horace Wheatley of the Alameda County Superior Court. Judge Wheatley is one of the creators and sponsors of a non-statutory drug diversion program that is used by the court as an alternative to the incarceration of young adults between the ages of eighteen and twenty-four who have been arrested and charged with the possession or sale of illegal substances. This Mentor Diversion Program allows those who qualify an opportunity to participate in a very structured and closely monitored program in which one of the specific requirements is that the offenders go to school. Rather than giving jail time to some of those who appeared before him, Judge Wheatley gave them "school time." Many of the defendants, several of whom are African-American and Hispanic, have successfully completed the program.

Another program speaker was Don Houston, an African-American architect and owner of the company Cyclops in San Francisco, whose self-assigned mission is to document on CD-ROM and video the contributions made by blacks to architecture, from the time of the ancient Greeks.

Another year, Doris Peeler-Brown presented a narrative on the slave trader John Newton, who wrote the popular spiritual, "Amazing Grace." Having mistreated his slaves for twenty-eight years, he eventually had a change of consciousness and wrote this song. His own atrocious history is documented in the lyrics.

The celebration wouldn't be complete without good food, Doris observes, so the City of Oakland's employees cap off the day with a sumptuous meal chowing down on fried chicken, greens, macaroni and cheese, cornbread, black-eyed peas, and peach cobbler.

Honoring our history, embracing our culture, and valuing ourselves—they are all part of solidifying our strength as African Americans as we gear up for the future. This survey has touched only the surface of how we might continue to affirm these values as we celebrate and nurture the occasions to come.

13

Let the Good Times Roll–
It's Mardi Gras

*In other places, culture comes down from on high. In New Orleans,
it bubbles up from the street.*

Ellis Marsalis

Settled by the Spanish, sold to the French, home of my brethren
(and various branches of the Broussard family), La Nouvelle
Orleans is a North American jewel, and the home of Mardi
Gras, the French term for "Fat Tuesday." The celebration, from
January 6 to Ash Wednesday, marks the culmination of the carnival
season before Lent. It's estimated that the Mardi Gras parade draws two
million people to New Orleans.

Located on the banks of the Mississippi, where jazz and the blues
were born and bred, the splendid streets of New Orleans' French Quarter
remind one of European cities. The city's cultural riches include European, African, and Native American influences, all on constant display
and brought to life in the city's music, dance, religion, architecture, interior décor, tropical gardens, and, of course, the fabulous food and lavish
entertaining.

Enter the city of New Orleans, and you're likely to hear violins, banjos, tubas, trombones, clarinets, tambourines, and drums joining together in a wonderful fusion of brassy beats—it's the legendary New Orleans sound, whose influences are mainly European and African. New Orleans was also home to such great musical stylists as trumpeters Buddy Bolden and Louis Armstrong, ragtime pianist Ferdinand "Jelly Roll" Morton, (who played in the Storyville brothels district along Basin Street), and rhythm 'n blues pianist and singer Fats Domino.

Go to New Orleans for Mardi Gras, and you'll be awash in the drama of the event's fabulous parades, imaginative floats (financed by local private clubs), marching bands, and dazzling masquerade balls. Revelers crowd onto Bourbon street in the French Quarter, dancing and shouting, and others beg for beads and trinkets tossed down from the floats. Krewe (club) members dressed in colorful costumes made of exquisite fabrics throw favors to the crowds along the parade routes, and "throw me something, mister," is a common plea from the celebrating crowds.

The Zulu is a predominantly black krewes. Riding on the Zulu floats, dressed in grass skirts and made up in blackface, lipstick, and wigs, the costumed Zulus throw to the crowds the prized possession of decorated coconuts. This version is called the Zulu coconut or "Golden Nugget," beautifully designed with sequins and paint.

When our family friends, J. Garfield Broussard Jr. and his wife Pamela Herman Broussard attended Carnival in 1999, the event marked the first official meeting between Zulu, the African-American king of Mardi Gras, and Rex, the Caucasian king. With their godlike demeanor, the two kings affirmed one another and toasted their city.

Garfield and Pamela's family and friends in New Orleans had arranged for them to attend various balls and festivities. One of these was the Zulu ball, held since 1909, where many of New Orleans's black middle-class come decked out in their finery. No invitee dressed in less than strictly formal attire is permitted entry. The ball begins with a formal coronation of the King and Queen of Zulu and a presentation of the royal court. Eighteen debutantes were also presented, wearing fabulous gowns

Changing Times

Recent controversy surrounds some of the older white krewes whose members were not willing to abide by a new city ordinance declaring that they would have to open their membership to minorities and women or would not be allowed to use city streets and services. Some of these krewes canceled their parades in protest, refusing to abide by the new integration laws the city has set forth. The older clubs' view on the matter is that family bloodlines and their historical accomplishments are the defining prerequisite to membership, perceptions that seem quaint indeed in a democratic society.

and dramatic headdresses. With the great food and drinks, Garfield and Pamela joined in the fun and danced the night away with The Gap Band and Gladys Knight.

Beverly-Anna Broussard, Garfield's mother, is a native of New Orleans who now lives and works in Oakland, California, as a pharmacist. She recalls the Original Illinois Club Ball, held during Mardi Gras in the early 1950s, where she was crowned queen of the ball. New Orleans is famous for its social clubs, and in this one, the male members escorted the local debutantes, who were invited only by special invitation.

Beverly remembers that her gown was made of French sequins and lace, and how exciting it was to attend the era's elaborate debut parties with other girls all wearing beautiful formal gowns. Each girl's debut party was as big a production as a lavish wedding, she says.

Garfield and Pamela attended the one hundreth Original Illinois Club Ball. It was like a cotillion with a lot of pageantry, they report: The king of

Beverly-Anna Broussard

the ball was dressed like a king in medieval times; there was an Alice In Wonderland theme, and the club members were dressed like the characters.

New Orleans is also the epicenter of the masked ball, a tradition begun in the 1740s, and inspired by classical themes and the French theatrical tradition of the masque. These days, well over a hundred masked balls take place during the carnival season. One was the 47th Country Club Sports Ball that Garfield and Pamela attended, in costume, dressed as an African couple.

Describing the festive atmosphere, Garfield says, "There were lots of parties and parades. On the final day of carnival season, Fat Tuesday, everything is closed, but people are giving you presents and inviting you to barbecues—the city is like one big party. Everyone lines the parade routes to see the final parades. The meridian, on St. Charles Avenue where the floats pass, is packed with people picnicking and barbecuing, waiting to view the parade."

Voodoo, "Tribes," and "Gangs"

To experience this city is to feel as though you're in another country. The voodoo religion that had been worshipped openly in New Orleans by African slaves and their offspring is still alive in some quarters, and the rituals are practiced in several local churches.

Marie Laveau, the most famous and powerful Voodoo Queen, is still heralded in song and fable. Born in New Orleans around 1794, she died there in 1881. She was a free woman, a Quadroon (African, Indian, French, and Spanish). She proclaimed herself Pope of Voodoo in the 1830s. Respected and feared, she was also a devout Catholic who disturbed the Catholic Church.

Laveau attended mass daily, and got permission to hold rituals behind St. Louis Cathedral. She had started out as a hairdresser, then a nurse. She had fifteen children by her second husband, and her daughter, Marie Philomene Laveau Glapion, eventually became almost as powerful as she.

Today, if you roam the back streets away from the main parade along Canal Street, you will find the "Mardi Gras Indians," named "Indians" mostly by outsiders who did not understand their history. (Michael P. Smith has written a wonderfully illlustrated and informative book about the Mardi Gras Indians.) Approximately twenty "gangs" or "tribes" exist today, with names like Wild Tchoupitoulas and Yellow Pocahontas. These African Americans—black Indians or maroons—are descended from fugitive slaves who escaped their plantation lives, many of whom hid out and survived in the swamps and marshlands outside New Orleans. A number of these slaves escaped from the West Indies and Guiana in the seventeenth and eighteenth centuries; other Mardi Gras Indians are descendants of African slaves who came directly to New Orleans from Senegal. Many formed their own "gangs" or tribes, and for Mardi Gras they dress in fabulous costumes of elaborate beadwork, rhinestones, and feathers. The different tribes challenge each other in a variety of rituals and competitions with elaborate performances of dance and chant. Year 'round they are curators of their own heritage and cultures, having preserved their families' African traditions, folklore, and art. They participate in the small spiritual church services, jazz funerals, and brass band parades within their own black working-class community. The black Indian tribes are testimony to a spiritual connection between Native Americans and the African slaves who received their help early in this country's founding. For Mardi Gras their costumes are one of a kind, hand-sewn in exquisite fabrics and feathers. The outfits take all year to make, and those who strut around in them glory in their costumes' meticulous attention to detail and in dedication to their culture.

Father Jay, pastor of St. Benedict's Roman Catholic Church in Oakland, California, whose mother is from Louisiana, was raised in the Louisiana tradition. "There are strong religious overtones for Mardi Gras," he says. "Coming out of Christmas, we will prepare ourselves to go into Lent, but have a good time as we do it. There's that old Creole saying, *laissez les bons temps rouler*—let the good times roll! Having a good time is another great opportunity to spend with our loved ones. The Mardi Gras carnival season ends on Ash Wednesday. January sixth is the feast of Epiphany, the day the three kings encountered the infant Jesus."

Epiphany

Epiphany, Little Christmas on the Twelfth Night, is a festive time for exchanging gifts and celebrations. In honor of the three Kings who brought gifts to the Christ child, all over the world it is celebrated twelve days after Christmas. One Mardi Gras tradition is to serve the king's cake. Baked with cinnamon, filled with dough, and glazed with sugar, it's sprinkled on top with a rainbow of traditional Mardi Gras colors in purple (representing justice), gold (symbolizing power), and green (representing faith). It also holds a surprise—a tiny plastic baby. According to tradition, the person who finds the baby inside his or her piece of cake continues the celebrations by hosting the next party.

Dirty Rice

Contributed by Beverly-Anna Broussard

1 large onion, diced
1 green bell pepper, diced
3 stalks celery, diced
2 cloves garlic
2 tablespoons cooking oil
1 pound chicken liver or beef liver, or 1 pound chicken gizzards, ground

1 tablespoon poultry seasoning
½ teaspoon thyme
½ teaspoon rosemary
salt and pepper to taste
4 cups rice
Fresh cilantro (optional)
Parsley (optional)
Green onion, chopped (optional)

Sauté onion, bell pepper, celery, and garlic, in oils. Mix with ground liver and poultry seasoning. Add thyme, rosemary, and salt and pepper. Cook four cups of rice in a rice cooker, and fold the liver mixture into the cooked rice. Garnish with fresh cilantro, parsley, or green onion stirred into the mixture. Serve hot. Serves 8–10.

Oyster Poor Boys

Contributed by Beverly-Anna Broussard

1 loaf French bread	2 eggs, beaten
1½ tablespoons butter or margarine	1 cup shredded lettuce
20 extra-small oysters, shucked	1½ tablespoons mayonnaise
Vegetable oil for frying	½ cup pickles
½ cup corn meal	2 tablespoons ketchup
½ cup flour	

Cut bread in half lengthwise. scoop out insides, and discard. Butter bread and toast in oven. Drain oysters and dry well on paper towels. Preheat a deep fryer to 375°F. Whip eggs. Mix corn meal and flour. Dip oysters into beaten eggs and coat with flour mixture. Fry oysters until crispy brown. Shred lettuce. On one side of toasted bread loaf spread mayonnaise, shredded lettuce, sliced pickles; on the other spread ketchup. Spread oysters, close loaf, and slice like a submarine sandwich. Serves 4.

A visit to New Orleans is not complete without sampling some New Orleans culinary delights or understanding the distinctions among cuisines. Jessie Leonard-Corcia, former owner of Jessie's restaurant in San Francisco, contributed the following description of the common New Orleans terms for cooking.

Cajun/Creole cuisine was formed from French recipes, livened with Spanish spices, and inspired by African vegetables and general magic. "Caribbeanized" by West Indian hands, it was yet laced with black pepper and pork by the Germans, infiltrated with potatoes by the Irish, blasted with garlic and tomatoes by the Italians, and even touched in some ways by the Swiss, Dutch, and Malaysians. Small wonder that what emerged was a unique and savory cuisine.

Beignet: (been-yay) A raised, rectangular dough (similar to a doughnut, without the hole), which can be stuffed and served with a savory sauce, or sprinkled with powdered sugar as a dessert with strong coffee.

Alligator: A large lizardlike reptile indigenous to southern Louisiana swamps and sometimes seen crossing Route 1-10 between Baton Rouge and New Orleans (no kidding!). Its snow-white meat looks much like chicken, but has a delicate fish flavor. It's farm raised, quite plentiful, and a favorite food of the Cajuns.

Blackening spices: A blend of the following dried seasonings: garlic, allspice, salt, paprika, cayenne pepper, pepper, and onion.

Cajun cuisine: The "rough around the edges" robust food of the country people, it is most often characterized by its spiciness. The deep rich color and flavors are arrived at by using a dark roux (made of browned stock and flour thickening agent). Cajun cuisine is a totally indigenous American cuisine.

Crawfish (never crayfish): A fresh-water crustacean resembling a small lobster. Also known as "mudbugs" and "crawdads." Crawfish are an important ingredient in many Cajun/Creole dishes.

Creole cuisine: (cree'ol) A more refined cuisine than the Cajun. Referred to as "city food," it traditionally uses more butter and cream in its sauces.

Dirty rice: A rice dressing with ground pork and giblets made with all those wonderful Cajun spices.

Etouffée: (ay'too'fay) A thick, dark tomato-based, spicy sauce with either shrimp or crawfish. It is usually served over long-grain rice.

Filé: (fee'lay) Dried sassafras tree leaves, ground into a powder and sprinkled on the top of a bowl of gumbo just before serving.

Gumbo: A delightfully rich, savory soup made with either shrimp, crabs and crawfish, or with poultry and andouille sausage.

Jamaican jerk sauce: A Jamaican barbecue-style sauce. It's hot! Made with vegetable oil, vinegar, Scotch bonnet, chilies, scallions, allspice, nutmeg, bay leaves, black pepper, garlic, cinnamon, and peppercorns.

Jambalaya: (jam'bull'eye'a) A spicy rice dish that was created when the Spanish came to Louisiana in the 1700s; it's a descendent of their paella. A New Orleans specialty.

Pain perdu: (pain'do) Creole version of French toast.

Po'boy sandwich: Another famous New Orleans original sandwich, often made with oysters. The name po'boy has nothing to do with poor folks; it is derived from the French *pourboire*, meaning a tip or gift for service rendered.

Red beans and rice: The beans are cooked first and their broth is used to cook the rice, hence the "dirty" color. Oh, but what flavor! The late Louis Armstrong used to sign all his letters, "Red Beans and Ricely Yours."

Remoulade: A cold sauce of mayonnaise, mustard, pickles, and chopped herbs.

Zydeco: Dance music that originated among the blacks in Louisiana. It's a lively, toe-tappin' music with its roots in blues and white Cajun music. An accordion and washboard give the music its rhythm-sound. We use the term in reference to that feel-good, toe-tappin' feeling you get when you eat the foods we describe as Zydeco.

As the sirens sounds on Bourbon Street and the carnival season comes to an end, we greet Ash Wednesday, which begins a season of abstinence and rededication to God, a time of rebirth and recommitment.

14

When Easter Comes Around

It wasn't until my first experience with my husband's family that I really had a true Easter experience. I always looked forward to it. The Easter egg hunts were so funny, especially when it was time for the grandmothers, Ma and Nana, to find their prizes, and then when my mother, Amelia, came to one that was even funnier—imagine a bunch of older women hunting for an Easter surprise in their best Easter threads in the backyard. . . . I always love the fact that my mother-in-law NEVER remembers where she hides the eggs, so there must be hundreds of accumulated hard-boiled eggs scattered in her garden after all these years. The meal is always impressive; the aroma of baked lamb is unbelievable. We always have the best trimmings—Ma's salad, Cheryl's mac and cheese, pie, yams, yum yum yum. And, I LOVE the festive Easter decorations on the piano.

From an E-mail sent to me by my daughter-in-law,
Melanie Austria Farmer

When I was a child, my mother dressed me for Easter in fancy white knee-highs, or lace anklets with white patent-leather Mary Janes to set off my splendid new dress, sewn by my godmother, Aunt Eva. The dress, usually a soft calico print, was complemented by a straw bonnet, a matching patent leather purse, and white cotton gloves.

Girls always came to church looking their prettiest, with their hair curled or braided, and tied with colorful satin ribbons. The boys attended Sunday school wearing spanking-new suits, polished shoes, shirts, and ties. The women at church wore ornate Easter bonnets, and the men always sported handsome hats. And, of course, all of the children brought Easter baskets for the long-awaited egg hunt afterward. Then we went to Easter brunch, or maybe to an early afternoon dinner with our respective families.

The author and Melanie
J. K. PHOTOGRAPHY

The senses awaken and the spirit rises to the delightful melodies of songbirds and the sweet fragrance of jasmine growing in my yard. I rejoice seeing the soft pink roses and the passion vines, climbing toward the sun. The healthy, flowering trees—cherry and apple, and my neighbors' fuchsia azaleas and purple rhododendrons—all remind me of how glorious spring is in San Francisco. From my dining room I see camellias and tulips. The window boxes off the rear deck are alive with scented geraniums and sweet alyssum. In the coming weeks I anticipate tasting home-grown vegetables and herbs. Easter is a time of rebirth. It's also proof of the natural world's everlasting beauty.

In our hurried times we sometimes forget the historical context of Easter and its true meaning. Christians throughout the world celebrate the resurrection of Jesus Christ at Easter. The holiday originated with the pagan celebration of Eastre, the goddess of spring and fertility. That's where the Easter bunny, a symbol of fertility, got his start. We decorate Easter eggs to symbolize spring's sunlight.

The Last Supper was served on Holy Thursday, the night before Jesus was crucified. The next day, Friday, commemorates Christ's crucifixion. His rebirth on Easter is one of the most triumphant holidays in the modern Christian calendar.

For Lent, Christians are called to fast for forty days, as Christ is said to have done in the desert. This becomes a time of discipline, reflection, personal examination, spiritual atonement, and prayer. Fasting begins on Ash Wednesday and in the Roman Catholic Church concludes on Holy Thursday. Palm Sunday, a week before Easter, marks the beginning of Holy Week. The palms of Palm Sunday represent the fronds placed at the feet of Jesus when he entered the city of Jerusalem in triumph.

According to Father Jay, "The tradition was that Lent ended at twelve noon on Holy Saturday. Then you would really prepare for Easter. You could go eat your favorite foods that you gave up for Lent. This was a practice that probably first started in Louisiana. In actuality Lent ends on Holy Thursday, because the next three days leading to Easter Sunday commemorates the Passion and Death of the Lord. On Holy Saturday evening, Christians would gather for the Easter Vigil as soon as the sun set (the Vigil cannot be celebrated until the sun sets); that is when Easter begins."

Easter and Passover share the season. The eight days of Passover begin at sundown and represent the Israelites' flight to freedom from slavery in Egypt. On the night of their escape they were ordered to eat roasted lamb, unleavened bread, and bitter herbs—the first Passover Seder.

Years ago, I was cast in a play about the crucifixion of Jesus Christ. In rehearsal on Holy Thursday in preparation for our Good Friday performance, the play's director, Edward Blair, kneeled and carefully washed each cast member's feet, symbolic of Christ's last rituals. We performers were deeply moved by his act.

As a young child, Pauletta Pearson Washington elected to follow her mother's tradition of observing Lent. Today, Pauletta and Denzel Washington's children, John David, Katia, Olivia, and Malcolm, also follow the tradition. The family observes Lent through Easter Sunday. After Easter Sunday church services, they indulge once more in their favorite foods.

Pauletta says how rewarding the observance of Lent has been for her family, and how it has taught her children the value of sacrifice. Early in their lives, Pauletta explained the rationale behind Lent to her children. When the twins, Olivia and Malcolm, were six, one gave up ice cream and the other cake for Lent. This coincided with the end of a school sports program, when the children's respective teams became champions and the teams planned to celebrate by serving ice cream and cake. Pauletta was asked if the twins could join their teammates in eating the food. After their teacher realized that the twins were observing Lent, she left the decision up to the twins, and she was very gratified that both chose to maintain their commitment to Lent.

What Easter Means to Me

I asked my good friend, Matthew Green, a licensed practitioner in The Church of Religious Science in San Francisco, about his perception of Easter, and here is what he wrote:

Easter represents a time of rebirth. At Easter time, we see evidence of the rebirth process in almost every aspect of nature. Individually, Easter is twofold. First there is a sense of joyfulness and renewed interest in our chosen purpose. Spiritually, Easter is the rebirth of our consciousness. It's a time when we purposely engage in some sort of spiritual growth activity that allows us to heighten our spiritual awareness. For example, we often attend religious services to celebrate the consciousness that was demonstrated by the Christ. Or we spend quiet time in nature for the purpose of reflecting and recommitting ourselves. To me, it's necessary that we recognize this if we want to stay on a moral course in the affairs of our life, for our consciousness is a forever-expanding process by which we continually develop our awareness of who we are and what our purpose is. It's at Easter time that we Christians universally celebrate the Christ consciousness. The Risen Christ is symbolic of this rebirth.

Easter Egg Magic

Easter, a time of joy and renewal, brings my own family together to celebrate nature's bounty—the flowers, fruits, and vegetables growing in our gardens, a wonderful leg of lamb roasting in the oven, and the famous ultimate egg hunt for everyone.

Since ancient times, the egg has been a symbol of birth and resurrection. Egyptian tombs have been discovered with eggs placed in them, and the Greeks placed eggs on the top of their graves. The custom of people exchanging white, painted, or gold-leafed eggs at springtime emerged many centuries ago, predating Easter.

Years ago, a friend of mine reported taking her small children to a remote town on the Mendocino coast for an extraordinary Easter party. Her friends have a modest farm, including a petting zoo and a dozen chickens. Each child delighted in going into the chicken coop and picking out a couple of eggs, some brown, some white, others blue. They painted them in pastels, coded the eggs with their initials, and hid them. The child that found the most eggs got a prize—a golden egg.

I dye my Easter eggs with food coloring and dry them in an open egg carton. You can also use brown eggs and decorate them with non-toxic crayons and paint, drawing funny faces and imaginative designs. I also use stencils with floral, plant, or other decorative design outlines to decorate the eggs. Children love to draw their favorite cartoon friends on eggs. If you use a white birthday candle to draw some decorations, and then place the egg in dye, the markings will stand out from the color, leaving a beautiful design. When your decorated eggs are ready, you can place them in egg holders or colorful baskets or bowls for decorating the mantel or the center of your Easter dining room table. For a lovely table, arrange the egg displays among candles and small floral bouquets.

When my kids were young, they used the same decorated Easter baskets year after year. Luckily for me, they had a special attachment to their own baskets and it was certainly cost effective. I always kept extra baskets on hand for other kids who joined us on our egg hunts.

My children are grown now, but we still enjoy family Easter egg hunts. My children, my eleven-year-old nephew, Hasan, my six-year-old granddaughter-in-law Annalyn, and all the adults get into the hunt, with the grownups hiding treats for the kids and the kids hiding surprises for the adults. Our favorite candies, including healthy treats like popcorn, nuts, and dried fruits, are wrapped in colorful cellophane bags, pastel-hued tissue, papier-mâché, and colored plastic eggs, which I decorate with Easter motifs. There are plenty of edible eggs to be found, too. The treats are tied with colored ribbons and each person is assigned a color. A vow of silence keeps the hiding spots of the other person's surprise secret—sometimes forever.

Easter-egg hunt ideas include hiding and digging up hidden treasures, like a collection of gospel CD's or tapes for the family, books, bookmarks, or puzzles about black history for the children, or pen and pencil sets and other educational toys. It's also fun to hide and find things the children really need—for example, girls' ribbons or hair barrettes or boys' neckties or a pair of socks, which you can roll up and stuff handily into a hollow plastic egg. Or you can use the colorful plastic eggs to hide Afrocentric treasures like cufflinks, pendants, bracelets made of cowry shells, and African beads.

After Easter dinner, the Dellums family used to invite their friends to participate in their family egg-decorating contests. Erik Dellums, now grown, and a seasoned professional actor, told me that when he was a young boy his family had great fun competing to decorate the funniest, cleverest egg. First they dyed their boiled eggs, and then they considered the baskets they had, filled with cotton, toothpicks, buttons, beads, glue, scotch tape, crayon, paints, and little paintbrushes. Different ideas would be written and placed on separate papers in a basket, and whatever one pulled out instructed the person to decorate his or her egg. If it said Harriet Tubman or Josephine Baker, it would be up to you to somehow transform your egg into that character, using the materials supplied or whatever else you could think of.

One year the family had a peace and freedom egg, and then there was a feminist egg. Congressman Ron Dellums made a Frederick Douglass egg with hair and a beard. Sometimes they would break into teams; the girls might compete against the boys, for example. At the contest's end, everyone voted for the best eggs, and individual prizes were awarded.

One spring day, as I took a walk, at the center of a neighbor's beautiful backyard behind a white picket fence, I spotted a tree whose branches were hung with multitudes of gorgeous, colorful eggs. Impressed by the scene, I went around to the entrance of this white colonial house, where I found the threshold decorated with lavender garlands and white silk flowers. A beautiful Easter basket hung from the front door. I asked the owner about her egg tree, and she told me how for many, many years she and her friends and neighbors have decorated her Easter egg tree. They used L'Eggs' egg-shaped stocking containers, which they had collected over time and then decorated as Easter eggs.

To make your own egg tree, take plastic or decorative paper eggs, drill or punch a small hole in one end, and string a colorful ribbon through the top center. Tie a know on the inside end of the ribbon (to secure it) and make a loop on the other end to hang it from an indoor plant or miniature indoor tree.

Recently, at a garage sale, I paid a small amount for a variety of baskets that had been colorfully decorated by an artist. One was a small periwinkle painted basket that was decorated with purple flowers, berries, and pink tulle. I stuffed it with gold tissue paper and filled it with colored eggs and with all of my daughter Zahrah's favorite treats. Then I attached an Easter card and left the basket out on Easter Sunday to surprise her. Since her siblings were out of town and no egg hunt would take place that year, I wanted to let her know that I cared. She was delighted. It was also a lot of fun to do.

Easter Table Settings

I like to set the Easter table with a white cotton embroidered tablecloth and some pastel blue linen napkins. My dinner china has a spring-colored floral pattern, trimmed in gold. I also use a set of soft blue glassware and some lemon glass plates on which to serve the dessert. My center-pieces include cobalt blue miniature vases filled with spring bouquets. Sometimes I float gardenias or candles designed to float in water (made by my daughter-in-law, Melanie) in lemon glass custard dishes, and arrange them along the center of the dining table. Or I arrange small, charming Easter baskets filled with edible, decorative eggs and bunny rabbits over palm leaves, which I scatter along the table center.

Other ideas can come from nature's palette, incorporating pastels for Easter décor. Shades of violet, yellow, green, blue, or ecru, or floral themes are ideas for the table. Tablecloths and napkins are made of chintz, gingham, or another textile with a lively spring theme. Recently, I found glass dessert dishes decorated with bouquets of pink tulips and cups to match, a sparkling addition to the Easter display.

For the center of the table, you can use herbs, African violets, minia-ture roses in decorative small pots (you can plant them outside later), or small framed photos of family and friends extending down the center of the table. Anything colorful can make a centerpiece, no matter how simple.

Easter Recipes

Here are a few of my favorite Easter recipes. I like to garnish the platters with edible spring flowers like viola, geranium, or pesticide-free roses, or with fresh herbs like parsley and mint, or fruits like sliced melons and small bunches of grapes.

Leg of Lamb

Contributed by Gale Madyun

Gale Madyun

"As with everything in life, it is all in the preparation when it comes to this dish," says my friend Gale Madyun.

5–6-pound leg of lamb
2 tablespoons extra virgin olive oil
8 cloves garlic, coarsely sliced
5–10 bay leaves
Pinch of marjoram
Pinch of thyme
Salt and pepper to taste

1–2 bottles Italian dressing (any kind)
8–10 half slices pears, canned or fresh
4–8-ounces mint jelly
Parsley for garnish

The night before cooking, clean lamb well under cold running water. Pat dry and rub lamb with olive oil, then cut small slits all over it. Stuff garlic slices into the slits. Crush bay leaves, and sprinkle along with the marjoram and thyme over lamb. Add salt and pepper. Place lamb in large bowl or pan which can be covered tightly, or use oven cooking bag (such as Reynolds Brown-in Bag). Pour Italian dressing over lamb, and marinate, covered and refrigerated, overnight. The next day remove lamb from bag and clean off marinade but reserve. Place meat thermometer in the thickest part of lamb and place lamb in roasting pan. Roast, uncovered, in preheated 350°F oven, until done to taste. Keep enough water or leftover marinade to constantly cover bottom of the pan while lamb is roasting so meat does not stick. Remove from oven and place lamb on cutting board. Serve either whole or sliced, on a pretty platter surrounded with pear half slices filled with mint jelly and garnished with parsley leaves. Serves 4–6.

Summer Squash

Contributed by Gale Madyun

8–10 pieces firm summer squash
1 large onion, chopped
1 large bell pepper, chopped
2 tablespoons olive oil
1–3 scallions
1 teaspoon marjoram

1 teaspoon thyme
1 teaspoon basil
Salt and pepper to taste
1 pound Monterey Jack cheese, sliced

Clean squash thoroughly, and boil in hot water until tender. Remove from hot water, and save liquid for later use. Sauté onion and pepper in oil in large skillet. Mash squash in bowl with potato masher and place in skillet with onion and bell pepper; stir. Continue stirring and add other ingredients, using squash broth as needed, to prevent burning. Reduce heat and simmer 10 minutes. Place cheese on top of squash, and place in preheated oven to brown or cover with a lid to allow cheese to melt. Use remaining liquid if needed. Serve in skillet or pan. Serves 5–6.

Mixed Vegetable Platter

Contributed by Gale Madyun

1 bunch fresh broccoli, cut into florets
1 head fresh cauliflower, cut into florets
8 medium carrots, skinned and sliced
1 red bell pepper, cored and sliced
1 green bell pepper, cored and sliced
1 yellow bell pepper, cored and sliced

1 medium onion, sliced
2 tablespoons olive oil
1 teaspoon salt
1 teaspoon marjoram
½ teaspoon thyme
½ teaspoon rosemary
½ teaspoon basil
½ teaspoon oregano

Remove stems from broccoli and cauliflower florets. Mix all vegetables in bowl or wok with salt and herbs. In wok or large skillet, heat olive oil over medium heat until hot. Cook vegetables until crisp but not soft. Serves 6–8.

Asparagus Supreme

Contributed by Matthew Green

1 pound asparagus
1 teaspoon salt

1 teaspoon butter (optional)

Using a vegetable peeler, lay asparagus spears on flat surface and peel from midway down, removing tough skin. Cut about an inch off bottoms and discard. In skillet large enough for spears to lie flat, boil 2 cups cold water. Place the spears into the boiling water and add salt. When water boils again, turn off heat. Let asparagus sit in the hot water for 15–20 minutes. Pour off hot water and melt one tablespoon butter over asparagus.

More Easter Traditions

My neighbor, Edgar Kolm, had the nicest tradition of giving his neighbors a box of chocolate candy for Easter. He would go to Shaw's, a candy store in our neighborhood, and buy us boxes of assorted chocolates. The store's owner, Kathryn Claitor, says these chocolates are among the most popular Easter candies, along with chocolate Easter bunnies, decorated eggs, candy carrots, and marshmallows.

Other ideas for gifts found in Kathryn's store include picture frames, vases, ceramic cookie jars styled as African-American jazz musicians, and decorative teacups and saucers. Every year my mother gives me a potted plant—white Easter lilies. It makes a lovely centerpiece for my coffee table, and after it finishes blooming I plant it in my yard for next year. Sometimes I make a bouquet of flowers cut from my garden to give as a gift. Giving a flower journal, a Bible, or an inspiring book of affirmations or daily meditations also tells friends or relatives that you are remembering them at this special season.

For me, Easter is a time to celebrate the blessings of life, family, and friends. It's also a time to review my progress concerning the goals I vowed to achieve at the year's beginning, and time to have fun with my family. Most of the things I use to celebrate Easter at home are items I have accumulated over the years. Those I buy are small, and because we always do potluck, no one person has to absorb the cost of the meal.

Family Circle magazine once (April 1994) featured a beautiful spring wreath made of yellow and pink roses, lemon branches, bay and quince, blue and pink hyacinth, heather, and dried purple larkspur. Wreaths always make inviting door decorations, and, of course you can buy them at your local flower mart, florist, or make them yourself.

Inexpensive Easter cards that have the simplest and most thoughtful messages are also sometimes ways to convey your fondest thoughts. Sealing them with stickers of bouquets of flowers, a seal with your initials, or Easter stickers is a nice way to personalize them.

What I love about growing my own flowers is that for a little bit of painstaking labor, I will have the joy of gathering them to decorate my home and also give as gifts. Sometimes on Easter morning I make bouquets from my garden and leave them on my neighbors' doorsteps.

Another way to scent and decorate your house at Easter is to buy a couple of pots of jasmine (Jasminum polyanthum), put them in plant stands, and enjoy seeing them wind their ways gracefully down the legs of the stands. Jasmine is a hearty plant and needs a cool, bright location. It grows quickly, and the leaves are real climbers.

Easter Memories

Marcheta Q'McManus-Eneas remembers Easter at Arundel-on-the-Bay along the Chesapeake River, where she lived as a child. There was only one Caucasian family in the community, and the wife, who was a German immigrant, designed and decorated beautiful Easter eggs. She had a huge yard, and all the kids in the neighborhood were invited for the egg hunt. Only children under the age of thirteen could participate. Whoever found the egg wrapped in gold paper, always the hardest one to find, turned it in for the prize of a silver dollar.

Marcheta also remembers how uncomfortable her crinoline petticoats were under those frilly Easter dresses, with their rolls of lace and a big sash tied in the back, the small pocketbooks that you couldn't fit much of anything in, and the Easter candy that you dared not eat in church. She savors the memory of Easter dinners of ham and goose, the special time to open Easter baskets, going to the movies with her family and friends, and the excitement of traveling to Baltimore and Washington to visit with family and friends during the holiday.

Gale Madyun loved hearing her grandmother's piano on Easter morning "In the Easter Parade," a tune so frequently heard on Easter morning. She remembers going to sunrise services at the Hollywood Bowl. On Good Friday she has a barbecue with her children because this kicks off spring. She periodically observes Lent or Ramadan, both involving sacrifice, the recommitment to one's spiritual life.

Sheila Frazier remembers when she and her two sisters wore their new Easter clothes, hat, gloves, and shoes. They each had their own godmothers take them to church—the women were responsible for teaching them about God. As Sheila got older, around fifteen, her perspective became more spiritual. She understood Christ's crucifixion and His resurrection.

As I write this today I recall the fiftieth wedding anniversary celebration for my dear friends, Hildred and Pat Chevalier. The event left me with the feeling that being able to spend time with family and friends, to really enjoy them, is one of the greatest blessings we can receive. There were people in the room whom I had known for most of my life. I also felt the joy of seeing neighbors I had grown up with and had not seen since we were kids. No matter how much time had gone by, the bonds were still there. Words were not necessary. Pat has since passed on. His legacy speaks in our hearts of the closeness and camaraderie all of us shared, and I think this spirit is what inspires us on holidays.

15

Cotillions, Beautillions, and More Great Party Ideas

As a younger person I liked to do it all by myself. Now that I'm older I like to get all the help I can get. It's insanity to want to do all of the work yourself. You're trying to take care of everybody's needs and they're all happy and you're dead tired.

Mary Dulan, owner of Aunt Kizzy's Back Porch

It's been an honor to meet and talk to the wonderful, multifaceted women and men who contributed to the making of this book. I have been so impressed with their sense of style and entertaining that I'd like to share a few more of their ideas with you. They can all stimulate new concepts for a wonderful party at any time of the year.

Ruth Beckford's Favorite Parties

Dancer and writer Ruth Beckford has a true sense of theater, and lots of flair. The best party she ever threw, she says, took place one December 7, for her seventieth birthday, at Geoffrey's Inner Circle, a private club in Oakland. She rented the entire top floor to accommodate two hundred friends for the black-tie affair.

Entertainment was provided by the velvet voice of John Turk and his one-man band. A year before the event, Ruth personally called to invite her guests, warning them that they wouldn't hear from her again until a month before the party. "Look sharp," she said, intimating that she would arrive wearing a dress with a train! She did not want her guests to bring her gifts, she said, but to put their money "on their backs." She told all the women to wear their finest full-length dress and to look glamorous.

The buffet tables were arranged so that people could walk along down both sides rather than having to stand in line forever for their food. Since her birthday falls just before the Christmas holidays, Ruth made sure there was a poinsettia on every table and a lavishly decorated Christmas tree in the room. Her concern for her guests' comfort also included making sure that the champagne flowed freely all evening.

About that dress: Ruth wore a dramatic, floor-length, fitted silk velvet gown in mustard gold with a turtleneck, long sleeves, and yes, a train.

One talented friend from Los Angeles, Cle Thompson, surprised her with the gift of song, performing her favorite tunes as a touching honor.

When Ruth was married she threw lots of parties. She would rent a boat docked at Jack London Square in Oakland for Sunday brunch, inviting friends to dress as though they were going for a cruise. She wrote clever invitations in rhyming poetry providing instructions. Music was played by Art Fletcher, a jazz and classical pianist.

Not long ago, Ruth hosted a ninetieth birthday party for dance legend Katherine Dunham, her mentor and friend of fifty-eight years. Ruth turned the event into a kind of living birthday card, and people from all over the United States and Europe who danced with Katherine Dunham or studied with her participated in the celebration at the Radisson Clayton Hotel in St. Louis. According to Ruth, who is also Dunham's biographer, all those who have been inspired in the field of dance and anthropology owe their livelihoods to the legacy of Ms. Dunham, the first dancer to incorporate anthropology with dance. During the celebration the guests all toasted her and let her know that they are her living legacy. (One gave her ninety long-stemmed red roses.)

Organize, Organize

As with any grand production, total organization, early planning, and contingency thinking are the basic keys to successful entertaining. While the following might seem obvious, you'd be surprised at how many people don't think through the essential details of preplanning that is needed to throw a great party.

Is there enough food and drink?

Will your guests fit around the table(s) comfortably?

Have you thought about providing appropriate background music?

Will your friends get along? Have you invited a good mix of personalities to stimulate enthusiasm and conversation?

Blanche Brown's Favorites

"The best party I ever attended was my own sixtieth birthday party," says Blanche Brown. It was a black-and-white party—everyone dressed in either black or white. The celebration was held at a private club. Blanche had it catered and invited everyone she had ever known, including family and friends from the realms of dance and religion. There was a great mix of ages, and over the course of the evening everybody made it to the dance floor. This time, the hostess wore red.

"My second favorite party," Blanche adds, "was one I had in honor of the fifteenth anniversary of my being initiated into the Orisha tradition. It was a garden party, and all the women came dressed in beautiful garden clothes—lovely dresses, and hats and gloves. A string quartet played traditional African Orisha music, and the thirty-five guests reveled in the pleasures of nature.

Mary Dulan's Talents

For the last three or four years, Mary Dulan has been putting together a Christmas party for a ladies' group she belongs to. It always begins at her house with hors d'oeuvres. Then, the group of women and a valet get into a rented bus. The entire vehicle is laid out like a living room, with leather sofas, coffee tables, twinkling lights, and even a refrigerator. More food is served.

The destination? To visit Mary's friend, owner of a restaurant in San Juan Capistrano. Next stop, Laguna Beach, to see the enchanting Christmas decorations at the Ritz Carlton Hotel. After viewing the rooms, everyone has a drink at the hotel and they take the bus back, having covered a lot of ground in great comfort and style.

Mary also had the greatest time putting together her daughter's wedding—for four hundred people. A traditional affair, it was also a bit unusual in that she did her flowers in a variety of rich colors, dominated by hues of purple and yellow. A special vase was designed for the long-stemmed flowers which, once arranged as table centerpieces, appeared to explode at the top like fireworks. The celebration featured both live music and break music provided by a DJ. There was an open bar, and hors d'hoeuvres, and dinner were served. The real surprise? The reception was held at a secret location.

Mary also loves theme parties, and once put together a Caribbean rum punch party, inviting four friends whose birthdays are close together; she had guests celebrate in island attire.

Sundays With Vivica A. Fox

Sundays are Taco Sundays at Vivica Fox's, and she serves mimosas to a gang who love to kick back and watch football. For Vivica, entertaining doesn't have to be elaborate and expensive—good fellowship is more important than a fancy scene. "People just like good down-home cooking. You can choose inexpensive foods that people enjoy, even if it's just spaghetti. Later in life, when you 'make it' and are freer, you can have the more elaborate parties," she says.

Gwendolyn Goldsby Grant's Favorite Style

A dinner party with music, conversation, coffee, dessert, and laughter . . . breaking bread together . . . intimate, quiet dinner parties with six people—these are Gwendolyn Goldsby Grant's favorite ways to get together with friends.

"Make it simple," she advises, "and learn to organize well in advance. Do some pre-cooking for whatever you are doing." She suggests doing all your slicing and dicing two to three days in advance and keeping the food fresh in plastic bags. Her mother used to cook on Saturday nights, she says, so there would be "no fooling around" in the kitchen on Sunday other than the last-minute things like frying the chicken.

Themes With Phyllis Yvonne Stickney

Phyllis Yvonne Stickney likes theme parties where everybody has to do something, be something, or bring something. There is a sense of collectiveness and community in most things that she does. "You, too, are a participant." This brings a sense of union to her parties, she says. Since she's often on stage, she likes to bring people to the stage for celebrations.

Leola "Roscoe" Higgs-Dellums's Way

Roscoe's grandmother was active in civic organizations and social clubs, which is how Roscoe's mother learned to be a great hostess, and Roscoe has inherited her mother's and her grandmother's great entertaining style. One year she threw an Alice in Wonderland birthday party, and another, a peanut party where all the games the children played were with peanuts;

the prizes were small toys and peanuts, and the invitations were designed in the shape of a peanut. Her playful imagination and creativity are always inventive and witty.

Roscoe's children also had "character" parties—they'd ask their guests to dress up like their favorite cartoon characters, and the invitations were like the decorations, made out of comic strips.

When Roscoe turned fifty, her son Erik gave her a fifties theme party, to which everyone came dressed in vintage 1950s clothes. The décor featured posters of the pop stars of that period, including James Dean in *Rebel Without a Cause*. A disc jockey spun records of the era by artists like Chuck Berry, and an Elvis-like male stripper appeared.

When Roscoe threw a bon voyage party for her eldest son, Brandy, and his new bride, Lizzie, the games included "musical guys," with the men sitting on the floor and the women moving around them to the music's beat and then dashing to sit on their laps when it stopped. Another featured game was based on the character "Cinderfella": The women were blindfolded and the men took off their shoes and socks, rolled up their pants legs, and sat in a circle. One at a time, a blindfolded woman had to attempt to find her mate. When she thought she had found him, she had to kiss him and remove the blindfold. Laughter filled the room, for invariably she would have picked the wrong man.

Gwen Williams's Way

Gwen's fiftieth birthday party invitations featured a picture of her at age five, dressed in her favorite red and white dotted Swiss party dress, dancing. An interior designer offered her studio showroom space for the party, and she decorated it like a house, divided into groups of rooms that were furnished with antiques and other items the studio had for sale. Guests could both socialize and shop.

Numerous family members and friends contributed something, from wine to cake, and Gwen's brother-in-law flew in a friend from L.A., who, together with another musician friend, sang especially for Gwen. As she sat in a beautiful Renaissance Revival chair, her friends celebrated her, and while she was blowing out her candles (flickering in an unusual five-candle candelabra), she was presented with red roses. Gwen's daughter Dorian and her friends acted as hostesses and servers, all dressed in coordinated white and black outfits. A birthday banner hung outside the entrance, and as the guests arrived, dressed in their elegant attire, they stepped from their cars onto a red carpet.

Tisha Campbell-Martin's Favorite Entertaining

One year, for the birthday of her husband Duane Martin of *Scream II* fame, Tisha Campbell-Martin invited a large crowd to a karaoke party at home. For her own birthday, she put on a big scavenger hunt, eliciting lots of enthusiasm by telling her guests that they'd find money: instead they found counterfeit of sorts—bills with her face on them.

Partying With Christel Albritton MacLean

Entranced by faraway places, Christel Albritton MacLean once threw a party with a Moroccan theme. She spent time in practicing to prepare the traditional Moroccan dishes beforehand, and accompanied the evening by playing the traditional evocative music of the region. Even the invitations had a touch of exotica—they were printed in a leopard pattern.

Fortunately for Christel, she works well with her husband, who also has a background in food preparation and entertaining, and he really enjoys devising the menu, doing the cooking, and adding just the right lighting and other finishing touches.

My Memorable Party for Maybelle

For my mother Maybelle Broussard's eightieth birthday, my brothers and I cooked a wonderful dinner for forty guests. Later we played a game: Who

Knows Maybelle Best? It was a way to tell my mother's story and share her life and accomplishments with those who love her. We gave a prize to the guest who had the most correct answers.

Toy Heaven

Because my son Omar's birthday falls on December 10, I gave his fourth birthday party a Christmas theme. For special fun for the little ones, I rented a preschool with a playground fully stocked with all the toys, jungle gyms, and tricycles a kid could ever want. I also rented a Santa Claus costume for my husband Jule to wear, and he had a great time trying to convince the older kids that he was really Santa Claus.

Cotillions

Many years ago a true debutante was defined as a young lady who did not date until she was eighteen and was not otherwise exposed to society until she made her debut. Instead of the expensive debutante balls, families had private parties at which these young ladies made their debuts in society. "They were really coming out," Ruth Beckford remembers. The first cotillion in Oakland, California took place at the Oakland Parks and Recreational's Defermery Park, under the supervision of Dorothy Pitts. Defermery was an intense recreational center located in the heart of the African-American community, and the cotillion was sponsored by a local chapter of the Links. In-service training sessions regarding jobs and careers were offered. Ruth taught the girls to waltz, bow, and promenade in the grand march with their escorts. She has been a mentor for black women since she began teaching modern dance in 1947 and founded the first recreational modern dance department in the United States at Oakland Parks and Recreational. "I had the teacher gene and that was my gift," she says.

Cotillions are sponsored by individual chapters of the Links, Inc., The Girl Friends, sororities, and civic and social organizations. For the Links, Inc., the cotillion is part of a philanthropic program that helps the organization raise money for scholarships and other community causes. These women are committed to improving their African-American communities.

Fred Harold Ferguson was the longtime choreographer for the Oakland Bay Area Chapter of the Links, Inc. cotillions, and for other cotillions sponsored by other groups for over twenty-five years. He was always in demand. "He was a special person, a free spirit," says Ruth Beckford, with whom he studied dance for many years, loved and appreciated by many. Fred was a master of dance and choreography, and when the debutantes and their escorts hit the dancefloor to African-American-rooted music, it was evident that he and his team had rehearsed and prepared them well.

Marijo, a drama coach, worked with Fred on the cotillions since 1981 and subsequently on the beautillions, the parallel events for young men. With her background in theater, she guided all the participants through a series of improvisational exercises and theater games. Fred wanted to warm up his young charges not only physically but mentally. He wanted them to be at ease in life as much as in social dancing, the box step, and the cha-cha.

Marijo says, "Fred also wanted the participants to feel there was a purpose to what they were doing, not just an empty effort." He tried to convey to them that they were crossing over into another realm. They were partaking of a rite of passage. Through the theater exercises, Fred and Marijo taught the young adults to present themselves like young kings and queens. There was a pride in their attitude, and they carried themselves with a positive and self-affirming demeanor.

I knew firsthand what refinement, exposure, and involvement could do for a girl's growth and confidence, but this experience is not for everyone. Participation is an individual decision, and what may be good for one child could be an absolute turn-off for another. A young woman—or her escort—should not be forced into the experience; if it is not their own expressed desire to participate, then don't pressure them to do it. And a family may consider spending their time, money, and resources in a different direction.

Today the cotillions are very expensive—thousands of dollars. As Ruth Beckford says, "that money could be better spent for college, travel, or a down-payment toward a house or business. Some parents took extra jobs just [so their children could be in] the cotillion."

When my daughter Zahrah came of age at seventeen and was a senior in high school, she expressed her interest in this rite, and we were invited to attend a tea for the prospective participants sponsored by the Oakland Bay Area Chapter of the Links, Inc. My concerns were the cost and the time, but once we went through the beginning processes and I realized how much it would mean to my daughter, I agreed that we would participate. A series of rehearsals started in September 1988, held on Sunday afternoons for the girls and their escorts to learn the waltzes and dance routines. Sometimes they practiced in their long skirts and petticoats, the ones they would eventually wear under their ball gowns. On we went, through a process of teas, receptions, a fashion show, rehearsals, fittings, debutante parties, workshops, and other preparations, all working up to the big event, a week before Christmas. There was the debutante enrichment symposium, which focused on growth, etiquette, interpersonal communications, and appropriate dress. I had the privilege of being one of the facilitators for this event.

The day of the ball was a flurry of activities. Debutantes, escorts, and parents had the final rehearsal. Afterward everyone returned to their booked suites to make final preparations for the after-ball parties.

On the evening of the cotillion, the mothers of the debutantes put out the place cards on their designated tables. On entry a beautiful program booklet was presented to all the patrons, which included a page of each girl's formal picture and recognition of her family, achievements, and her desired goals. The escorts were also highlighted in the souvenir program.

The evening opened with an invocation, and then there was a welcome by the president of the local chapter of the Links, Inc. and acknowledgments and philanthropic presentations. Dinner was served. After dessert the cotillion began. There was the presentation of the debutantes as they curtsied in their exquisite white formal gowns for their very proud parents and the audience; then there was the elegant debutante waltz with their escorts, and the finale was the presentation of the girls, escorts,

The author's daughter Zahrah Farmer with her father at the cotillion ball
ESCHENBACH AND RUBIOLO

and parents. The final moment of the cotillion was absolutely joyous, and very significant to all the families involved. Dancing followed, and at the conclusion the debutantes received gifts of flowers, jewelry, and other keepsakes in recognition of their debut from family and friends. Many of the families and friends partied through the rest of the night at the after-parties and into the early morning.

My daughter has said that she gained from being exposed to positive brothers and sisters, friends she made for life. She loved the formality, loved getting dressed and putting on her jewelry, her long white gloves, and her white formal gown. Excitedly Zahrah said, "It was off the hook."

This is a special evening for the escorts as well as the debutantes. They participate in all the activities and benefit from the same process, and their families get involved as well. But please remember: The experi-ence—and the expense—should be carefully considered in advance, and no one should be pressed to participate.

Beautillions

A wonderful series of events for young African-American males culmi-nates with a beautillion. Its purpose and process is the same as the cotil-lion for the girls, and on the final evening the Beaus, young men who are predominantly seniors in high school, are escorted by belles (young ladies). Fred Ferguson also provided the choreography for the Jack and Jill, Inc.–sponsored beautillions in San Francisco for many years. He styled them to be masculine and appealing, with an African theme. The sharp routines the boys performed in their white tails and top hats were very impressive; basically the Beaus "got down," in a wonderful presentation of young men at their best. Marijo, who worked with Fred, says: "Those beautillions had a particular magic—the theatrics in the presentation, and how it all came together." The escorts, who were the belles, were dressed in lovely evening gowns in uniform colors and styles, selected each year. A junior beau, a younger African-American male who hoped to become a

beau, participated in the promenade with them. The souvenir program described their achievements and their goals. Some of the young men were sponsored by local African-American businessmen. It was a glorious celebration honoring the achievements of young African-American men.

Beautillions are sponsored throughout the United States during different times of the year. Marcheta Q'McManus-Eneas and her husband

The author's son Omar at his beautillion

Dr. Judson Eneas are the founders and chairpersons for the Nassau Bahamas Beautillion, and Marcheta says that sometimes more than fifty young African Americans have participated in the annual event.

As we've observed, the cotillions and beautillions take a lot of dedication: time, money, and energy, provided by parents, loved ones, and the sponsoring organizations' membership.

I want to commemorate my childhood friend Fred Harold Ferguson and dedicate this chapter to him. For many cotillions during the Christmas season and the beautillions during the spring, I have witnessed Fred's marvelous choreography and human skills at work. Fred left us a legacy of continued commitment and devotion toward our African-American youth.

The cotillions and beautillions should leave our kids who participate with a feeling of confidence and self-worth, a jump-start toward the future and a memory of a positive rite of passage. Tradition also has its responsibilities, and we hope those who participate in this one will want to express gratitude to those who made this memorable event possible for them.

16

Juneteenth—A Celebration of Our Legacy

The people of Texas are informed that in accordance with a Proclamation from the Executive of the United States, all slaves are free. This involves an absolute equality of rights and rights of property between former masters and slaves, and the connection heretofore existing between them becomes that between employer and free laborer.

On June 19, 1865, Union soldiers led by Maj. Gen. Gordon Granger brought word of freedom to slaves in Galveston, Texas—about two and a half years after President Lincoln's Emancipation Proclamation, which had ended slavery in the U.S. on January 1, 1863. Stories abound about why it took so long for word to reach Texas following the Emancipation Proclamation. Was the messenger killed on the way to Texas? Or were the plantation owners determined to yield one more crop of cotton before telling our people freedom was at hand?

Today, Juneteenth is celebrated as African Americans' Independence Day. On April 10, 1997, the U.S. Senate adopted legislation officially recognizing June 19 as Juneteenth Independence Day and encouraging its observance.

Juneteenth Celebrations

I not only celebrate and commemorate the freedom of our ancestors, I also celebrate the progress of my family. I always say a prayer of thanks that my ancestors survived the institution of slavery, that my family has done well for itself in America as free people, and that each generation has made a better life for itself.

This holiday reminds me of my paternal grandmother, Eugenia, and her migration from Texas to California in 1917. At the age of nineteen, she traveled to the west coast on the segregated trains of Jim Crow days with a newborn baby, my father Ernest. My father was the eldest of five, and as a young man during the Depression he worked to support himself and help support his family. As my grandmother was widowed twice, the family worked hard to make it My father worked as a cook on the railroad.

Juneteenth also brings back memories of my maternal grandfather's journey to California, from Missouri. He and his five siblings were born into slavery in Missouri, children of their black mother and the English plantation owner. My grandfather lived to be ninety-four years old; he worked as a dining car waiter on the Southern Pacific Railroad and later as a City of Oakland employee.

One Juneteenth, my family celebrated with a barbecue with family and friends. I served barbecued beef ribs, grilled chicken, and corn on the cob, biscuits, fresh green bean salad, potato salad, hamburgers and hot dogs, lemonade, homemade fruit cobbler, and ice cream.

Every year, a variety of Juneteenth celebrations are held around the country. In San Francisco there's always a traditional Juneteenth parade. In the 1970s, Bill Picket, the late nineteenth-century cowboy, was the first black inducted into the National Cowboy Hall of Fame, and his legacy continues to remind African Americans to salute the unhailed work black people did in the West.

This year's Juneteenth festivities included a fashion show, a film festival, and, at the famous Fillmore Auditorium, a gospel concert. At Wildcat Canyon Ranch in nearby Oakland, there was a rodeo, staged by cowboys who recognize that African-American men, too, broke horses and trained them in the Old West. There was barrel-racing, calf-roping, bareback riding, steer-wrestling, and bull-riding. Adding perspective to the scene, animal rights activists point out the irony that freedom could be celebrated by oppressing animals; I don't disagree, and it pains me to think of some of the techniques used to subdue animals in the rodeo. But when we celebrate our history, I think we must be realists, and view the good with the bad, taking pride in where we came from, the hard work we've done, and our contribution to our country's economic growth.

Our Legacy

My legacy is still in progress. As I learn to use my insights and creativity, and share my perceptions with others more widely through my work, my contribution to this world begins to be measured by those around me. I am the sum total of all the peoples who have come before me to create the woman I am: Africans, French, English, Native Americans—all the slaves, the free men and women, the students and teachers, the strivers, and the workers who became Broussards, Guytons, and Craigs. With luck, my legacy will emerge from the totality of the work I leave behind, from the knowledge and emotions I have shared with my children and the goals I achieve.

To have helped a few people along the way, to have lived an honorable life, to have loved deeply and well, to have become my best self—these are the essentials I hope to leave behind, to be spun into the atmosphere.

The next few pages document the replies of some of the other people I've asked to describe what they hope their legacies will be.

Maybelle Broussard

My mother Maybelle told me she wants to be remembered as a good mother. She hopes she has given her children some guidance. She'd like to be remembered as one who had a lot of friends and was a kind and compassionate person. She hopes that through her volunteer work she contributed to others.

Mary Braxton-Joseph

"There's one thing that would characterize my approach to life, and that is the idea that 'the only difference between a stepping-stone and a stumbling block is how high you pick up your feet.' But I like that because I think that's characteristic of many of us, particularly black people. That captures sort of my philosophy in life—you can be knocked down by your obstacles, or you can be strengthened by them—and it really is about how high you pick up your feet."

Myrlie Evers-Williams

Here is how Myrlie Evers-Williams hopes people might describe her: "She was real. She cared about people, particularly *her* people. She fought for justice, equality and opportunity. . . .

"What you see is what you get. I'm a good, human being who recognizes her strengths and her weaknesses and works daily to improve those strengths and eliminate the weaknesses. I used to tell my children, 'Look, I am not perfect. Don't even try to take me there.' But I'm tough. I'm a deeply religious person, but I like to have fun. I like to laugh. I embrace life and living. And I have lived long enough to realize that all of the things that have happened in my life, those that we categorize as good and those as bad or evil, have all come together to make me the person I am today. And there's always room for improvement, so I'm constantly in

◆◆◆◆◆◆◆◆◆

"I never let prejudice stop me from what I wanted to do in this life."

Sadie Delany
at age 105

◆◆◆◆◆◆◆◆◆

search of that. Whatever life has to offer, I greet it with open arms, knowing that I'm gonna make it. As long as I keep my hand in His hand and that's where I am."

Patricia Russell-McCloud

Patricia Russell-McCloud says she hopes to be remembered in part for her life as a professional, "one who has been dedicated to being unselfish and giving and meeting people at their point of need." She tries to be really clear about who she is, to be humble and willing to give because she has been so blessed. She wants to be remembered "as a person who is at home in the world."

Belva Davis

She hopes, Belva Davis says, that if she and her husband Bill were not here, one of the children "would continue the tradition—to always have the family gather together and to feel good about the holidays." She has instilled in them the idea that no matter who might have differences with whom, one gathers as part of a family and comes together with the other members during the holidays.

Cheryl R. Riley

Cheryl Riley's legacy is inextricably linked to her work with children. In her mentoring, she encourages them "to see the world from a perspective larger than themselves." She treats each child as a special individual who has much to contribute to the world.

She also strives to set an example of a life well lived, she says, of a person who gives back to the community, of one who is true to her own spirit, ability, and heart, and of someone who experiences the beauty of

"Life can only be understood backwards, but it must be lived forwards."

Søren Kierkegaard

each day. It's important, she says, "to surround yourself with things that make you feel good and to treat yourself as a guest in your own house."

Cheryl takes enormous pride in being the first African-American to have a show at the Cooper-Hewitt Museum. She leaves her designs for posterity.

Joyce Burrows Dinkins

"Reading is the most important skill a child can learn," says Joyce Dinkins, former first lady of New York City. Through her encouragement of children to read, and through the distribution of books to them, she hopes that she has made a difference in the lives of many young people.

Synthia Saint James

Synthia Saint James, artist and author, says, "My hope is that my legacy will be the body of my work, both paintings and books, left behind for the joy, knowledge, and encouragement that I have always intended for them to bring to the universe."

Marcheta Q'McManus-Eneas

Marcheta hopes her children will be understanding and strong. No matter what profession they aspire to, she says, "do it well."

Kimberly Elise Oldham

"I strive to do pure work from the heart. I try to live honestly, spiritually, and positively."

Christel Albritton MacLean

"I hope to be remembered for having integrity . . . for being one who does what she says she's going to do, with all the gusto she can possibly muster. I try never to say I'll do something if it's something I don't want to do. If I feel I have to do it out of a sense of duty, I'll do it with integrity. And I hope I'll be remembered as trying to live in unity and avoiding divisiveness."

Jacqueline Mitchell Rice

Jackie Rice wants to be remembered as a giving person . . . as a strong woman who helped her family to be stable, as a great mother, an excellent wife, and a person people come to and rely on.

Peggy Cooper Cafritz

The founder of the Duke Ellington School of the Arts in Washington, D.C., hopes she leaves "a beacon of opportunity for kids from all strata of society."

Sheila Frazier

"Someone who made us stronger and healthier as a people—that's the legacy I'd like to leave, that I made somebody's life permanently changed for the better."

Margot Dashiell

She would like to be remembered by her community and students "as a loving person who shared and gave generously of her time and resources."

Phyllis Yvonne Stickney

"I would like to be remembered as a strong, positive black woman who sought to free herself and her nation family from the bondage of self-hatred by using healing laughter and love."

Alma Arrington-Brown

Life is short, and it's up to you to make it sweet."

Sadie Delany

Alma Brown says she wants to be remembered as someone who cared very deeply about her children and grandchildren. She hopes they know she will always be there for them, and that they were loved unconditionally. It's important to her that they feel good about themselves.

Alma says she has come face to face with her own mortality since her husband died. She realizes that everything can be taken from one in a split second, and she takes nothing for granted anymore. While she plans for the future, she lives each day as if it could be her last, and tries to get the most out of each moment.

Her children and young twin grandsons help keep her husband alive for her, she says. When they come to spend the night, they see photos of him in the room, constant reminders of the happy days they spent as a family.

Cheryl D. Broussard

"My mission and purpose has been to provide financial educational empowerment information to African-American women; to help black women improve their quality of life through wealth building," says Cheryl.

Ruth Beckford

Isn't it wonderful to be honored while you're still alive? Ruth Beckford, modern dancer and teacher in the tradition of Katherine Dunham, is a recent recipient of the San Francisco Foundation Award for her contribution as a community leader. She says her greatest joy comes not from the audiences she has thrilled over the years with her gift, but "when people stop and thank me for the meaningful input I have had in their lives." She is also proud of having taught many women to be "free spirits."

Leola "Roscoe" Higgs-Dellums

My dear friend Roscoe says she wants to be remembered "as someone who was sincerely grateful for her gift of life; as someone who recognized the awesome responsibility that comes from being a citizen of the world community and tried to meet that challenge; as someone who wanted to be an active participant in this life and not merely an observer; as some one who wanted to share her humor, laughter, understanding, and tolerance with the people she came in contact with; as someone who grew to know that she was a spiritual being having a human experience, and that therefore, armed with this knowledge, she would have the ability to love unconditionally and to have a forgiving heart; as someone who wanted to live her life in such a way that she made a positive contribution so that when she kissed this earth goodbye it would be a better place for her having been here; and finally as someone who left a legacy worthy of her precious children and their children to inherit."

Amen.

Celebrating

It has been my pleasure to share the meaning of holidays and celebration with you—that sense of kinship, spirituality, and humanity innate to my family and friends. It has brought me enormous joy to demonstrate the deeply woven sense of celebration our families have clung to through so many generations of duress, upheaval, and, ultimately, accomplishment. Of course we African-Americans are not alone in this, as all cultures experience it to one extent or another. But I felt a deep need to express our way, especially since today, more than ever, our culture crosses so many color barriers.

Isn't it important to understand the meaning behind Mama's rolls, and why she really baked them? And to acknowledge that she might need help sometimes? I wanted to demonstrate our warmth and express our strength as a people, to show our commitment to family, culture, community, and tradition. I also hoped to reinforce our values, and to connect the past to the present as we carry on positive traditions for ourselves and future generations.

I have been truly blessed over the years to experience so much love, support, and direction from my family and friends. It has kindled my life, and given me the ability to write this book. I was continually moved by the participants' stories and by their many contributions. People brought me into their lives, sharing their triumphs and their tragedies. Women brought me into their kitchens and shared recipes and memories passed down through generations. The process of recalling word and deed was not only fun, but healing.

When Ruth Beckford talks about her Oakland childhood and how the family gathered on Sunday evenings at her grandmother's house for dessert, listening to radio programs, and entertaining one another with their stories and talent, it is obvious how important a part of communication with other people this had become, and how special it made her feel as a girl. This tradition reinforced her support base for life, not only on holidays. Ruth's story reminded me of how I grew up, too, and how important the family structure has always been for my own sense of self.

When Jessie Leonard-Corcia told me about her childhood in Haiti and how she so delights in having her mother nearby today to help her bringing her culture, food, and traditions on the long road from Africa to Haiti to Northern California, I understood.

Sheila Frazier's words brought home a particular moment for me, too. Her natural sensitivity and caring translated into charity, and helping someone in need.

And what can compare to the excitement I felt when my daughter Zahrah and I drove to Los Angeles to interview Synthia Saint James and

Pauletta Pearson Washington? They were gracious enough to trust me, a complete stranger, to spend time with them and share their intimate, cherished feelings about their homes and their lives.

When I started this project, I felt that it's women who carry the culture. Now, after meeting so many family-oriented men through my gathering of people's stories, I see "it ain't necessarily so." I hope in the future to give men more of an opportunity to express their styles and perspectives on living.

I hope this book has given those who sought it a sense of direction and pride, and reminded you that our work isn't in vain. After all, every day can be a celebration, and every challenge beckons us to conquer it, to evolve, and to move forward. Thanks for reading my book. May God's light in your house forever shine!

Resources

Artists

Synthia Saint James
Atelier Saint James
P.O. Box 27683
Los Angeles, CA 90027
(323) 769-4388
(818) 845-3998 fax
www.synthiasaintjames.com
    Artist/author

John Broussard
(510) 633-2170
Broussard/art@aol.com
    Artist

Beverly Heath
P.O. Box 6017
Altadena, CA 91003
(626) 797-8652
(626) 791-7147 fax
www.beverlyheath.com
rootwoman@beverlyheath.com
    Root artist/cultural therapist
    Constructs altars in celebration of
life and identity

Books and Communications

Cyclops
Don Houston
(415) 759-9032
    Documents black people's
contributions to architecture, going
back to the first century and the
ancient Greeks, on CD-ROM and
video

Impact Communications
Joe C. Jones, president
4029-51st Avenue South
Seattle, WA 98118
(206) 723-1926
(206) 723-1927 fax
    Publisher of *The Color of Culture II*,
by Dr. Mona Lake Jones

Marcus Book Stores
3900 Martin Luther King Jr. Way
Oakland, CA 94609
(510) 652-2344

Marcus Book Stores
1712 Fillmore Street
San Francisco, CA 94115
(415) 346-4222
(415) 931-1536 fax
www.Marcusbooks.com
info@Marcusbooks.com
    Marcus has sold books by and
about black people for 40 years and
counting!

Sister 2 Sister Magazine
Jaime Foster Brown, publisher
P.O. Box 41148
Washington, DC 20018
(301) 306-0100
(301) 306-0104

Fine Arts and Fine Crafts

Dolls by Quarana Davis
(707) 642-1427
www.dealersweb.com/Quarana.htm
Qdoll@AOL.Com
  Authentic African-American dolls

Fajorian Fine Arts Gallery
Sheila and Herb Fajors
(510) 351-3955
  A fine arts gallery that shows a
wide variety of artists of color, who
use various media, including clothing,
jewelry, sculpture, and home
furnishings

Gloria Jean
P.O. Box 21077
Piedmont, CA 94620
(510) 531-5442
(734) 758-2071 fax
heritage7@yahoo.com
www.virtualcolony.com/gloria_jean/
  An interactive site dedicated to
quality-of-life amenities, cultural
heritage, cultural arts, and fine art
investments and financial options.
Introducing the Ancient Black
Christian Fine Art Collection; publisher
of *The Ancient Black Christians: Our
Story Revealed*.

Marijo
(510) 562-6928
marijotells@aol.com
  A professional storyteller/
playwright/actress

Flower Growers and Landscape Gardeners

Perata Brothers Wholesale
644 Brannan Street
San Francisco, CA 94107
(510) 235-0487
(510) 235-5598 fax
www.dryflowerlink.com
  Flower growers

Ellen S. Edelson
(415) 731-5924
  Landscape gardener

Gifts

DBW, INC.
Just Like Me Coloring Books
Yaba Baker
President and CEO
P.O. Box 4494
Washington, D.C. 20017
(202) 526-1725
emailybaker@justlikeme.net
www.justlikeme.net

Mythic Gifts
Poly Karayianni Reif
107 West Portal Avenue
San Francisco, CA 94127
(415) 731-6665
  Timeless gifts for all ages

Plain Jane's Old-Fashioned Gift
  Emporium
Erik Holte and Lloyd Sanner, owners
44 West Portal Avenue
San Francisco, CA 94127
(415) 759-7487
(415) 759-7559 fax

Shaw's Candies
Kathryn Claitor, owner
122 West Portal Avenue
San Francisco, CA 94127
(415) 681-2702
shawssf@slip.net

Greeting Cards

Frederick Douglass Designs
Margot Dashiell, president
P.O. Box 8738
Emeryville, CA 94662-0738
(800) 399-4430
(510) 420-3615
(510) 420-3625 fax
www.fddesigns.com
  African-American greeting cards,
art prints, calendars, and gifts

Etiquette, Home Accessories, Interior and Furniture Design

Sheila Bridges Design, Inc.
(212) 678-6872
(212) 932-2514 fax
SBDesign@aol.com
www.sheilabridges.com
  Interior design

Janine and Jacqueline Beachum
Bumbershoot
Richmond, CA 94806
(510) 243-1533
  Interior and garden design studio
with a strong emphasis on African-
American and ethnic pieces; furniture,
accessories, antiques, and gifts
available by appointment or mail
order

Antoinette Broussard and Company
(415) 431-5235
(415) 431-5236 fax
BroussardA@aol.com
  Etiquette/protocol and interior
design

Sandra B. Jimenez, Allied ASID
(415) 831-2312
(415) 831-2319 fax
SJimenezDesign@juno.com
  Architectural interior designer

Cheryl R. Riley
Right Angle Designs
(201) 413-0094 x211
(201) 413-1119 fax
cherylrenee69@hotmail.com
  Public art and custom furniture

Brian Charron
briancharron@IX.Netcom
  Creative furniture and interiors

Photography

Lewis Watts Photography
Department of Architecture
University of California
232 Wurster Hall
Berkeley, CA 94720
(510) 235-1825
Lwatts@socrates.berkeley.edu

Penn Design Photo
Eric Penn, owner
3589 Flint Creek Drive
San Jose, CA 95148
(408) 274-9174
(408) 274-4954 fax
EMPENN@IX.Netcom.com
www.penndesign.com
   Photographic design of products
for publications

Restaurants/Catering

Aunt Kizzy's Back Porch
Mary and Adolf Dulan, owners
4325 Glencoe Avenue
Villa Marina Center
Marina Del Rey, CA 90292
(310) 578-1005
(310) 306-1715 fax
   Down-home southern-style food

Hattie's
Christel Albritton MacLean, president
   and owner
45 Phila Street
Saratoga Springs, NY 12866
(518) 584-4790
(518) 584-9980 fax

www.hattiesrestaurant.com
hatties@hattie'srestaurant.com
   Landmark restaurant serving
authentic southern and Louisiana
cuisine since 1938

Jessie Leonard-Corcia, Caterer
(415) 681-7367
(415) 437-2980 fax
   Cajun, Creole, and Caribbean cuisine

Miss Mamie's Spoonbread Too
Norma Jean Darden
366 West 110th Street
New York City, NY 10025
(212) 865-6744
(212) 865-0854 fax

Miss Maude's Spoonbread Too Cafe
Norma Jean Darden
547 Lenox Avenue
New York City, NY 10037
(212) 690-3100
(212) 690-3879 fax

Spoonbread Catering Company
Norma Jean Darden, Carole Darden
(212) 865-0700
(212) 865-3960
   Gourmet catering for all occasions
Specialty: healthy, traditional African-
American cuisine

Sweet Georgia Brown Restaurant
Myrna Williams, owner
Downstairs at Kym's
70/71 Wilton Road
Victoria
London SW1V1DE
0-207-828-8931 tel and fax

0-771-982-1008 mobile
Londonmyrna@aol.com

Authentic American cuisine with a soul food specialty

Professional Resources

Cheryl Broussard and Company
P.O. Box 27287
Oakland, CA 94602
(510) 482-5129
(510) 482-3541 fax
sisterceo@aol.com
www.cherylbroussard.com

Professional speaker, financial and small business information consultant

J. Garfield Broussard, Jr
Insurance broker
P.O. Box 2698
Toluca Lake, CA 91610-0698
(818) 973-1020
(818) 973-1024
JGBBis@aol.com

Professional liability insurance and commercial insurance for California professionals and owner

Group Petit La Croix
Blanche Brown, artistic director
(415) 626-0678
(415) 863-8344 fax
odiche@aol.com

Drum and dance company that performs traditional Haitian dance

Zora Kramer Brown, Founder and Chairperson
Breast Cancer Resource Committee, Inc.
(202) 463-8040
(202) 463-8015 fax
www.afamerica.com/bcrc
zorbrw@aol.com

The Breast Cancer Resource committee (BCRC) is a not-for-profit, 501(c)3 organization located in Washington, DC. BCRC is dedicated to reducing the incidence and mortality from breast cancer among African-American women, particularly those who have little or no access to adequate health care and treatment.

Harisse Davidson and Associates, Inc.
Harrisse Davidson, president
1516 W. Estes
Chicago, Illinois 60626
(773) 743-3444
(773) 743-3505 fax
HDTalent@aol.com

Agent/Manager to actors

Leola "Roscoe" Higgs-Dellums, Esq.
(202) 686-5155
(202) 537-5848 fax
estherleo@aol.com

Sole practitioner: government relations, small business development and government procurement; general practice.

Zahrah Mallie Farmer, president
Jule Television
The Jule Farmer M.D. Film Company
(818) 623-9655
Zfarmer@JuleFilms.com
www.JuleFilms.com
  Television station and film
foundation that supports first-time
filmmakers of color

Sheila Frazier
Director Network Talent
8306 Wilshire Blvd, PMB 135
Beverly Hills, CA 90211
(323) 938-2917
(818) 526-1580
(818) 845-8643 fax
dsl777@aol.com
Sheila.Frazier@Bet.net
  Train on-camera talent in media and
on-camera techniques. Also oversee
the talent needs of the network.

Matthew Green
Practitioner
Church of Religious Science
280 Claremont Avenue
San Francisco, CA 94127
(415) 731-3887
  Religiousscience.org

Donna Katzl
Executive chef
Cafe for All Seasons
150 West Portal Avenue
San Francisco, CA 94127
(415) 665-0900
(415) 753-2480 fax
  American bistro cuisine

Gale Madyun
Gmadyun@aol.com
  Writer

Russell-McCloud and Associates
Patricia Russell-McCloud, J.D.,
  president
Professional orator and author
P.O. Box 31143
Atlanta, GA 31131
(404) 691-9841
(404) 691-1092 fax
www.prussellmccloud.com
prmlink@aol.com
  A professional motivational
speaking association.

Bibliography

John Hope Franklin and Alfred A. Moss, Jr. (1988), *From Slavery to Freedom*. New York: McGraw-Hill, Inc.

Charles Panati (1989) *Extraordinary Origins of Everyday Things*. New York: Harper & Row.

Michael P. Smith (1995), *Mardi Gras Indians*. Gretna, Louisiana: Pelican.

Susan Curtis (1996), *Essential Oils*. London: Regent Publishing Services, Ltd.

Gloria Nicol (1995), *Wreaths*. Menlo Park, California: Sunset Publishing Corporation.

Index